From One Root Many Flowers

From One Root Many Flowers

*A Century
of Family Life in
China and America*

Virginia C. Li

Prometheus Books

59 John Glenn Drive
Amherst, New York 14228-2197

Published 2003 by Prometheus Books

Inquiries should be addressed to
Prometheus Books
59 John Glenn Drive
Amherst, New York 14228–2197
VOICE: 716–691–0133, ext. 207
FAX: 716–564–2711
WWW.PROMETHEUSBOOKS.COM

07 06 05 04 03   5 4 3 2 1

Library of Congress Cataloging-in-Publication Data

Li, Virginia C.
     From one root many flowers : a century of family life in China and America /
Virginia C. Li.
          p. cm.
     Includes index.
     ISBN 1–59102–081–6 (alk. paper)
     1. Li family. 2. Li, Virginia C. 3. China—Biography. I. Title: Century of
family life in China and America. II. Title.

CS1169.L44 2003
929'.2'0951—dc21
                                                                              2003010834

Printed in the United States of America on acid-free paper

For the generations that follow

Contents

Part III. TWO WORLDS ENTWINE

Preface

The last time I saw my father, he was ninety-two years old sitting hunched and silent in a wheelchair in a hospital room. My father did not recognize me. "It's all right," I told him. "Go home to China, back to Nanhua Temple, where your heart and soul belong." I sat holding his hand, telling him to let go of this world.

When I was a little girl, my happiest moments were learning Tang poetry from my father. I used to stand before him, listening as he explained the poet's intent, the meaning of the words, and the rhythm of the poem. Sitting in his soldier's uniform, my father would select a page from the Book of Three Hundred Tang Poems, glance at the title, and recite the poem from memory. I would repeat each sentence after him, "Before my bed a pool of light. Is it frost on the ground? Eyes raised, I see the moon so bright; head bent, in homesickness I drown." My father would listen as I read the entire verse by myself. I liked being at my father's side, hearing the sound and rhythm of Tang poems and feeling the poet's sentiments in my heart. My father was a high government official in China's Nationalist party, a general, leader to tens of thousands of soldiers, and dedicated patriot and servant of the mainland. But on those occasions when he taught me poetry, all his attention was on me, and I wished he would continue forever.

I look out at the Pacific Ocean from my window. Seagulls circle over the water, sailboats dot the distant sea, surfers ride the waves, and cars speed along the Pacific Coast Highway. A helicopter hovers

9

overhead, filling the air with the sound of a loud vibrating motor. I am a creature of two worlds, one old and one new. I came across the Pacific fifty years ago and have been establishing my life in the United States ever since.

Intellectually, I regard myself as an American of Chinese descent. I have long since embraced the fact that my transplant is permanent, and I am glad that it is. But this does not mean that I have abandoned China; instead, I am now tied to two worlds. For four decades, my professional work has involved university teaching and research to promote health and prevent disease in the United States at the University of Maryland, Johns Hopkins University, and the University of California at Los Angeles, but also in China, the Pacific Rim countries, and beyond. Since the mid-1970s, I have traveled to China, sometimes several times a year, as a consultant in health programs at the invitation of the national government, universities, and international organizations.

I used to think that my father's world and my world were distinct. His was a world that was long past, one that was ingrained in the traditions and mores of the ancient sage Confucius. He never let go of this world of a time gone by and always felt the anguish of its loss. He never let go of the sentiments he had held as a loyal Chinese Nationalist.

My world, in contrast, was the New World in which I became American. Although the United States has given me opportunities and privileges, it has also presented me with challenges. I can never get beyond the vulnerability I feel because of my color and the country of my birth. Often I'm asked where I'm from. When I say the United States is my country and I am an American, I can predict the follow-up question: "What I mean is, what is your origin? Where are you *from*?"

As the years go by, I realize that many of the values I hold are those of my father—and my mother as well. While I may assert my own individuality, nevertheless their DNA and heritage are a part of me, and their words and values have had an enormous impact on the person I am.

My father spent much of his life torn between two conflicting sets of values. He was a gifted soldier with a born talent for leading men; he had a deeply rooted sense of loyalty and duty to his country and its government. At the same time, however, he also had the heart of a poet who abhorred killing and believed in the nonviolent teachings of Buddhism.

Since his death, I've gone through his private papers and correspondence, as well as diaries he kept for nearly sixty years. I had always known that during China's war of resistance against Japan, my father, known as the "Confucian general," had led a quarter of a million men into active combat. In the spring and summer of 1938, more than fifty thousand men, "brothers and sons," had perished. Reading through my father's papers, I have now come to believe that he accepted the position of governor of Guangdong Province under Chiang Kaishek's Nationalist government from 1938 to 1945, his best-known post, because it would free him from being forced to kill and ordering others to kill. During the final struggle with the Communists in 1949, when Mao Zedong's forces were making serious advances from the Northeast onward to the very heart of central China, my father tried to persuade Chiang to remain in China rather than retreating to Taiwan, urging him to stay and defend South China as loyal soldiers would. But Chiang regarded this as disloyalty.

This story is also about my mother, and her influence not only on my life, but on the lives of thousands of men and women who worked with her and the war-orphaned and refugee children who called her "Mama."

As a teenager in feudalistic China, her father kept her from going to school, insisting, instead, that she stay home and prepare his opium pipes. She vowed to gain a modern education and to work for a just society. With the support she received from my father, during the war years she went on to direct a rescue operation that saved the lives of thousands of war orphans who became her children. When my parents needed to earn a living in New York City in 1949, my mother became a restaurateur and breadwinner to support our family. My parents' fifty-five years of marriage was one of partnership, of love, and of struggle to fulfill the promise they made to each other.

My mother was proud of the fact that she voted in the first postwar presidential election in China, in 1948, even though her candidate lost. After she became a United States citizen, she never missed voting in the presidential election. In 1991, she reclaimed her dual citizenship and her right as member of the Chinese National Assembly and cast her vote in the democratic election in Taiwan.

The knowledge I've picked up from conversations, letters, their

diaries of some sixty years, and incidents I witnessed have helped me
piece together my parents' lives and times. It has enabled me to understand the values and the cultural inheritance they passed on to me.

Although I've been living in America for five decades, I continue
to feel proud when something is accomplished in China. Beginning
in the late 1970s, China's modernization has been rapid, its movement toward a more open society irreversible. I see this as I travel to
cities, towns, and villages in different parts of the country in con-
junction with my work. By the same token, I feel beaten when I see
mistakes China has made, or, because of ideological differences,
when she is undeservingly demonized.

Returning to China as an American, there is one incident that I
recall with singular clarity. It was 1973, during my first visit to
China. I went into the Friendship Store in the hotel where I was
staying in the city of Hangzhou, looking for souvenirs to bring
home. Except for some handicrafts, porcelains, art objects, and silks
that were available exclusively to visitors from abroad, I saw a
scarcity of consumer goods. I did manage to find a woodcarving of
two hummingbirds fluttering on peonies, all hand done, varnished
in golden brown, as delicate as a piece of embroidery.

The way luggage was thrown around in airports, I wanted to
make sure the woodcarving wouldn't get damaged. I asked the sales
clerk for a box so that I could give it protection inside the suitcase.
The clerk went into the back room for a good six or seven minutes,
then came back with an earth-colored paper box and set it down
onto the counter. It was the thinnest and flimsiest box I had ever
seen, virtually useless. "Don't you have anything better?" I was
tempted to ask. Instead, I ignored the box as I picked up my purchase
and headed toward the door. The clerk came running after me,
calling out, "Madam! This is for you!" he blurted out with an
urgency that conveyed his desire and effort to assist me with my
request. He handed me the box, and I took it from him politely.

I casually tossed the box into the wastebasket almost as soon as
I was back in my hotel room. Then, as if an invisible hand were
guiding me, I retrieved the box and put it on the table. I thought how
precious this box was to someone who could use it. A developing
and still poor country, China has five times our population on 60
percent as much arable land. Conservation is their key to survival.

The clerk might have even had to do some explanation to his supervisor as to why anyone would need a box for a piece of woodwork.

More than any other sight or sound from that trip, I've thought more about that flimsy box. It made me aware of the preciousness of material resources.

During that same trip, I saw notebooks no larger than the note pads we commonly see in Western hotel rooms, except that the pages were as thin as our airmail stationery. I was told that grain, oils, meats, and eggs were rationed because of scarcity and for reason of equitable distribution. I visited villages and saw systematic efforts applied to fermenting human and animal excreta to destroy parasites, turning it into "liquid gold," so that it could be safely used as fertilizer.

As a displaced person in the United Stated who became an American citizen, a wall has always separated me from the country of my birth. Even as a teenager, I was intimidated by the persecutions of the McCarthy era and repulsed by the cruel and wholesale liquidations which Communist China periodically conducted to cleanse its five "black elements," which meant landowners, rich peasants, rightists, people engaged in anti-Communist activities, and the "bad elements" such as those with overseas connections and criminals. During the Korean War, my anguish was made acute by the armed conflict between the United States and China.

This wall of separation began to break down for me during that first visit to China, as the country was edging toward a more open society. The United States had removed its blockade, and friendship was renewed between Chinese and Americans. These days when I say that I'm interested in China's well-being, I'm no longer afraid people might consider me to be a Red China sympathizer. The demarcation of "our world" and "their world" no longer comes in absolute terms as it had in the decades before. I embrace all of humanity as "my world" and "my people."

From historic roots deeply embedded in a land far away, to ones that have been uprooted and replanted again, I am fortunate to know firsthand how brave, new lives can blossom like beautiful flowers in another land. As the daughter of Chinese dignitaries, a transplanted refugee, mother, university professor, and international consultant, I have seen the human spirit of four generations of Chinese and then Americans attain triumph from despair and disappointment. This is a story of how two distinct worlds and proud cultures have come to work together, to offer a glimpse of hope and a future for humankind.

I am grateful to my family and friends who read drafts of this work. I thank my writing mentors Eric Wilson and Bruce Bauman for their comments and help in completing this memoir; Susan Emerling pored over my work with the touch of a Tang poet; Luisa Fels, Karl Harshbarger, Jane Atkins, and Joy Lorenzana for their sustained interest and encouragement in the course of my learning to write; and I am deeply indebted to Paul Kurtz and Steven L. Mitchell of Prometheus Books, and to my agent, Julie Popkin, for her counsel and unfailing support. Leonardo Chait, my husband, read every draft of this memoir with the insight of an immigrant from another country, and with love.

Part I
CHINA

Chapter One
China 1989

O n June 4, 1989, the morning of my daughter's wedding in
Bethesda, Maryland, I turned on the television and saw a
replay of the tanks rolling into the square toward the tents in the
dark night. Tiananmen Square, the Gate of Heavenly Peace, was an
old square under dynastic China. It is the largest square in the
world, covering a hundred acres in the capital of Beijing. Standing
on the terrace of the Monuments to the Heroes in the center of the
square were student leaders, bullhorns in their hands, shouting out
instructions. The television commentator's voice was urgent, rapidly recapping the students' demands for democracy, and the students were on a hunger strike. Workers were joining the demonstrations; supporters inside China and from abroad helped the students
to organize and put up their tents, some of which were still visible.

"Leave the square now!" "Stay and hold on!" The student
leaders were shouting contradictory orders. In the pandemonium, a
band of disheveled students was running for the exit. I saw an ambulance and a stretcher carrying away one of the wounded, with the
Great Hall of the People in the shadow. Elsewhere in the city, mobs
were overturning army trucks, buses, and police cars and setting
them afire.

China's tragedy was unfolding in full view of the world. Viewing
the passionate pleas of the young demonstrators, I remembered my
father's words describing thirteen young teachers and students he
had once released, who were alleged to be leftist sympathizers in

Shantou, back in 1937. "They're patriotic young people, regardless of their beliefs," he had told me. "They're the brightest of their generation. They deserve a chance for regeneration, regardless of their actions."

I had held the hope that nothing tragic would happen, that the students would leave Tienanmen Square, that the government would not use force, that no one would be killed. But in the confrontation, students, soldiers, and on-looking civilians were killed. The number initially reported by Western journalists was in the thousands, later acknowledged by the press as having been many fewer, and the Chinese government reported about three hundred. The exact number of lives lost may never be known.

After the tanks rolled into Tiananmen Square, Western tourists began canceling their visits to China. That summer, I had been invited by international agencies to do consulting work in China and Africa. I had to choose one and was inclined to Africa, because I had given up an opportunity to go there once before, when my children were young, and in all this time I had still never been to Africa. But I chose China instead. I wanted to see my friends, and to see what was happening to the country myself.

I left for China the first week of August. I wore my "China wardrobe" of plain blouses and dark skirts and pants. For years, I carried a large soft leather maroon bag that doubled as a briefcase, which my friends called my trademark. In my carry-on bag, I toted books, journal articles, a yellow pad and stationery, and enough yarn to knit a sweater. I have never slept on an airplane, even when it was a trans-Pacific flight. Not that I didn't want to, but I couldn't. Perhaps it was fear of flying. Thirty years ago, when I first started hopping to meetings around the country, I used to buy life insurance at the airport just before boarding. I carefully wrote down the names of my three children as beneficiaries and paid the premium. I don't remember exactly when I stopped buying insurance for flying, but it was many years ago. Now, I don't even notice the life insurance counter when I walk through the airport.

For these trans-Pacific flights, the first five or six hours were good for catching up on reading. I would write letters or outline a speech or lectures for the next two or three hours. After that, I would knit. I opened and closed my eyes again and again, envious of those in front, behind, and beside me, who slept like children at slumber parties after playing all night and finally falling asleep around daybreak. Ordinarily, half a glass of wine or a beer would be enough to make me drowsy. But not on an airplane, not a full glass of chardonnay, not cognac, nor sleeping pills. I had reconciled myself to the fact that I would always be flying wide awake, never mind how many hours. To make those hours bearable, I kept myself busy with knitting.

My first stop was Guangzhou, formerly known as Canton, which is the capital of Guangdong Province, a bustling special economic zone infused with money from overseas Chinese and foreign investments and once the hub of revolutionary activities that led to the overthrow of the Manchu dynasty in 1911. I had been invited to teach a two-week course on research methods at the Sun Yatsen Medical University School of Public Health, one of China's earliest and most established medical facilities, named after the father of the country. Immediately on arrival in Guangzhou, I was a guest at a dinner hosted by the United Front Bureau, an outreach arm of the Communist Party, the mission of which is to gain support for mainland China. I was shown a video of the students demonstrating in the streets of Beijing, burning dozens of buses and vehicles, while People's Liberation Army soldiers were wounded in the violence, including one who was hanged by the demonstrators. I was also presented with a copy of the video to take back to the United States, but I declined the offer. No doubt, my hosts would have liked me to help tell their side of the story, but I have always stayed within the parameters of my profession and science, then as now.

Many of the administrators and program managers who attended my workshop came from various provinces throughout China. I was pleased to be able to lecture in Mandarin Chinese. Although Chinese is my first language, I left the mainland for the United States at age thirteen. As a result, English has come to be my primary language. I had had the humiliating experience of needing a translator the first time I taught a course in China, back in 1981 at the Shanghai Medical University, because of my unfamiliarity with the technical terms in Chinese. But since then I'd acquired sufficient proficiency to lecture, and even read and write the simplified characters in China today. The atmosphere in the classroom was congenial but quiet. Unlike students in Western countries who ask questions, students in China are typically reticent. They are raised and taught from childhood to be obedient and to unflinchingly defer to the opinions and words of elders and authority. To change this mode of learning, I got them into group assignments to plan, and then to present and critique the programs from their own group work. They responded and became involved.

Guangzhou was nearing 43° Celsius, or 111° Fahrenheit. The classroom, without air-conditioning, was humid as well as hot. For the men who came from Inner Mongolia and the northern provinces, who were accustomed to a cold climate, the sticky hot weather was insufferable. Although I've prided myself on being flexible and able to adapt to whatever surroundings are presented to me, I was always given a higher degree of "creature comforts" by my Chinese hosts. Unlike the natives living at home, some without electric fans, or in the dormitory that had no air-conditioning, I had the luxury of staying in air-conditioned Western hotels that catered to outside visitors.

During breaks and the lunch hour, sometimes our conversations would turn to the student demonstrations that led to the "event" in Tienanmen. Several professors told me how, in Guangzhou, the faculty had organized themselves in relay, bringing water to the students at different points along the demonstration routes, urging them to keep calm and to return to the classroom. Knowing that students take their exams very seriously, some of the professors scheduled exams on announced demonstration dates to get the students off the streets. In contrast to the events that unfolded in Beijing, the demonstrations in Guangzhou had been orderly without incident.

Listening to the professors and the participants in the workshop, it was clear to me that their uppermost concern was peace and order, after having lived through ten years of turbulence in the Cultural Revolution (1966 to1976). They remembered the violent days when the raw energy of naïve young Red Guards had been turned loose, and manipulated by the extreme left led by Jiang Qing, Mao Zedong's wife, and her close allies, later known as the Gang of Four, ransacking cities and villages, and inflicting pain as well as bodily injuries on those who differed in outlook. The tyranny over people in every walk of life, on party cadres, the old and young, in schools and workplaces, and to homes was so horrific that chaos became the order of the day. School, offices, and factories were closed for ideological struggle. The country bled until all its veins collapsed.

"China cannot afford another upsurge like the Cultural Revolution," was a resounding theme that I heard that summer in Guangzhou and everywhere I went. I heard the lamentation, too, that students who stayed in Tiananmen Square up until the very end were hurt and some even paid with their lives, but their leaders were able to get out of China and went abroad.

From Guangzhou I then went to Beijing for a briefing at the office of the United Nations Development Program (UNDP) before undertaking a six-week mission for the agency. I would make an assessment of the UNDP-supported National Family Planning Education and Publicity Center in Beijing and its affiliated regional centers located in the provinces of Heilongjiang, Liaoning, Sichuan, and Shanghai and their media programs. I would visit the regional centers as well as clinics in cities and villages, and interview staffs and service recipients to get a sense of how family planning information and services were delivered.

One of my overriding interests when it came to public health in China was the subject of family planning. Few other topics seemed to be so urgent. Between 1945 and 1975, the Chinese population had more than doubled. In 1979, like braking a speeding car on the highway, China mounted a vigorous family planning campaign and framed its birth planning in terms of national survival. I have always thought the draconian measures instituted by the government for family planning in China was a case of "damned if you do, and damned if you don't."

China is physically slightly larger than the United States with a population that in 1980 was already hovering at 1 billion—five times greater than that of the United States. Today, China's population is nearing 1.3 billion. Two-thirds of China is mountainous, desert, or land unfit for cultivation. At the end of the 1970s, arable land per capita was only a third of an acre. Every year, the six million city-born young people who were reaching employment age were looking for jobs in their hometowns, and twenty million young people were entering into marriage in the country and as many babies were born.

The "One Child Policy" was actually a misnomer, because the National People's Congress, the country's policy-making body, did not pass the proposed one-child family law. Rural delegates had argued that a one-child policy would undermine old age security, because parents could not rely on a single child for support for late years. Daughters, after all, have less physical and earning power than sons for farm work, and when they marry they join the husband's family.

What followed was that regional and local levels varied in their family planning policies from a kind of guided "voluntarism" to doing nothing at all. The one-child policy was implemented in cities, but not in rural areas. "Mass voluntarism" meant the state paid for all contraceptive devices and services. Local support included a paid vacation for people who were planning a vasectomy, tubal ligation, IUD insertion, or an abortion, and the Pill was available to reproductive-age women at their workplace, or delivered to the home in many rural settings. People were given incentives, such as priorities for schooling for children and job assignments for parents. These measures, framed in terms of national survival and sacrifices, enabled China to reduce its birth rate by half within a decade.

A few years earlier, back in 1984, I had had a close look at Chinese family planning during a five-city tour when I was a guest of the State Family Planning Commission. In city after city, I heard cadres, "the core" staff, and officers of government agencies and organizations, including factories, speak of birth quotas. While this was foreign to my Western way of thinking, people in China were already accustomed to quotas for daily necessities such as clothes, grain, and oil, for the equitable distribution of resources, as well as for production. So it was not all that far-fetched to set quotas for births, as China did in many cities and areas. The birth quotas were meant to create equity, or fairness. It also created a "natural" surveillance system in which neighbors watched neighbors. It was inexpensive and involved the whole community.

Abortion was the last resort for contraceptive failure, not a method of choice. Unfortunately, incidents of coercive, late-term abortions occurred. Abuses have resulted from overzealous cadres, inadequate training, and the desire to take hold of the situation in a hurry. What I have observed was not the policymakers' indifference to the pain the quota system caused, but rather poor management in some cases, and human error in others. Education and persuasion, together with incentives and disincentives, had enabled China to achieve a high degree of voluntariness in its family planning program.

My brother Victor, an avid China observer, had once said to me, "Imagine the logistics of moving one billion people from one chair to the next. Family planning is logistically difficult to begin with. It includes supplies and technical know-how in a most private matter. Without the voluntary cooperation of the great majority, it would have been impossible to move the people from one chair to another, let alone to have halved the birth rate within a decade—as China actually managed to do." I myself am aware, from the standpoint of both public health and medical care, how painstaking it is to get patients to follow any medical regimens and self-help, whether this is with medication, quitting cigarette smoking, or dieting. What China was able to accomplish was nothing short of a miracle. By the year 2000, China achieved some four hundred million fewer births, more than the combined populations of the United States, Australia, and New Zealand plus another one hundred million.

In the summer of 1989, at the National Family Planning Education and Publicity Center in Beijing, I reviewed films and videotapes the center produced, randomly selecting them from the shelves and asking the center director and the producers for the ones they deemed the best. I also went through the pamphlets, posters, and slides on adolescence, marriage and family, safe motherhood and children's health, as well as family planning and an array of educational materials, scanning them for readability and comprehension. The films that I reviewed all depicted urban living that has modern conveniences, something that is very remote from rural living, which means 80 percent of the population. The producers explained that the media program wanted to push a forward look for modernization and that rural people emulate urban people, "So that it is a way of educating them about what China will become."

Judging from all the educational materials, it was clear that the burden of family planning was on women. This burden reflected the fact that, with the exception of vasectomy and condom, all contraceptive methods were designed for women; men were reluctant to undergo vasectomies because of the prevalent belief that they would lose their virility as well as their muscle strength, and condoms were less reliable.

My visit to the Beijing center gave me some insights on the urban bias that kept surfacing in the information presented: it was due to the concern that producers and directors had for artistic quality and their preference for focusing on the more affluent urban scenes. On top of that was the tiered system, where each level is responsible for providing training and assistance to the level below it. The national center staff interacted with the regional and city-level staff and was totally out of touch with staff serving towns and villages.

A friend had invited me to dinner at her home the night before I was to leave for Harbin, famed for its annual ice sculpture and lantern festival and capital of Heilongjiang Province. When she heard that I would be in the northernmost province that borders Siberia, she insisted that I borrow her navy blue poplin raincoat to wear on top of my knitted thick mohair coat. "The weather is freezing cold in the Northeast even in early September. You need more warm clothes than you've brought," she told me. I accepted her thoughtful offer.

My escort on the mission, a Mr. Lu, was the liaison officer in the UNDP Beijing office. He was of medium build, dressed in a dark Western suit, low-key, and spoke fluent English. We flew to Harbin and were met by the director of the Harbin center, a woman in her forties, and a retinue of cadres.

Harbin's wide streets, European-style architecture, churches, and onion domes are the legacy of Russian influence. At the turn of the nineteenth century, a humiliated China had conceded ports to foreign powers with extraterritorial rights after the defeat of the Boxer Rebellion.

The Harbin regional center was housed in a multistory building. The director gave an interesting briefing on the annual competitions held for the poster theme, radio talk show, songs, and skits. The competitions were open to professionals and amateurs alike. The reward was public recognition rather than any monetary prize. Winners of song and skit competitions were invited to participate in a show production, which was recorded for television airing and videotaping.

Afterward, I reviewed the educational materials using the same procedure as I had used in the Beijing center. This assessment, too, as with the subsequent assessments in the other three subcenters, reflected a strong urban bias.

From Harbin we boarded the train at midnight and traveled to a medium-sized county several hundred miles away with a population of half a million, where I would also visit nearby towns and villages. My visit to the county, arranged through the Harbin center, turned out to be most memorable.

Miss Ling, a petite young cadre of the Harbin center, was assigned to accompany us on this tour. We boarded the train before midnight. Miss Ling and I shared a private compartment. She suggested that I take the lower berth and proceeded to make up the bed for me, turning the sheets inside out. "They don't change the sheets as they are supposed to," Miss Ling told me. She then put a brand-new washcloth, which she had brought along, on top of the pillow for me. When she had taken care of me, she got up to the upper berth and did the same for herself.

At dawn the director of the local host agency met us at the platform. Director Tan was a clean-shaven man in a smart trench coat, no different from the fashion that one would see in New York or London. The temperature was near zero. Thank goodness I had my friend's raincoat for an extra layer!

Miss Ling introduced Mr. Lu and me to Director Tan. I must have looked like a native to Director Tan in my bulging, borrowed navy poplin raincoat. He nodded his head, but did not say a word to me. Before I had a chance to extend a greeting, he had turned to Mr. Lu saying, "We have two cars waiting outside."

When we came out of the station to the square, Director Tan signaled me with his hand to take the front seat of the black sedan, while he and Mr. Lu got into the back seat. Ms. Ling got into the second car, a van. Director Tan said nothing to me during the ride to the hotel or at the hotel lobby. My itinerary for the week was relayed to me through Mr. Lu. The relay went on even when we visited his agency.

I saw in Director Tan a vintage colonial mentality. He would have preferred to meet a white man a head taller to look up to, instead of a woman of the same ethnicity engaging him at eye level. I felt my anger come to a boil inside me. But I did not let it come to the surface for others to see, instead maintaining a pleasant and somewhat casual demeanor about what was going on. I had also seen this colonial mentality on many occasions in my work around the Pacific Rim countries. Now the show of obsequiousness and deference to Westerners was self-imposed. In China, some government agencies and universities refused to invite consultants who were ethnic Chinese, in preference for a white Westerner, believing that they could offer more. International agencies understood this. An officer of a large international agency in Beijing once explained to me why he was hiring consultants who had little or no knowledge of China: "We frankly prefer Westerners who don't understand Chinese ways or who can pretend they don't know Chinese ways. Their very ignorance allows them to say things the Chinese don't want to hear. If a Westerner makes a mistake or is offensive, it is okay. It was ignorance. That is not so with you. They expect you to understand better." This was unfortunate, because it was a perpetuation of the foreign imperial past and the colonial mentality, deliberate or otherwise. More critically, it restrained many willing and capable overseas Chinese resources who could help deliver advanced know-how and expertise for the country's development, as well as bridge understanding between China and the rest of the world.

For the next four days, I listened to briefings, visited clinics and hospitals and peasants' homes, asked questions, and mingled with the cadres and the locals in towns and villages; all this had been arranged through the local family planning agency, headed by Director Tan.

In China, family planning is everybody's business, involving all community organizations and government agencies. Among its promoters were the Women's Federation and the Family Planning Association. The latter had a membership that numbered in the tens of millions, who were retired professionals from all walks of life. In town halls, village cooperatives, clinics, factories, and schools I saw the ingenuity of working with severely limited resources, such as using bulletin boards to spread the word. They would display pictorial illustrations showing the diminishing acreage per capita in the last five decades and explain the necessity of family planning to the villagers. Peasants could relate to this manner of communication readily, and it helped make the promotion of a small family and contraception understandable and easier to accept by people who farmed and were accustomed to having many children.

In all these visits, Director Tan and I traveled in the same car and sat at the same tables. Still, he and I had not spoken a word to each other.

Directing his remarks in Mandarin to Mr. Lu, Director Tan told us, "This is one of the towns where we have just implemented a pilot 'key household' approach. It has been very successful in broadening family planning to address the quality of life for rural women. Selected households are identified as centers of activities for daily living. Women who are neighbors meet regularly to socialize and talk about family planning and about things that interest them, such as child rearing and farming, and making handicrafts. We expect to implement the 'key household' approach to the entire region."

Now, I'm a native Mandarin speaker, but dutifully, Mr. Lu turned and relayed to me what Director Tan had just said—as if he were a translator. I couldn't help take note of the absurdity of the situation. Just imagine a conversation among three native English speakers, sitting side by side with each other.

Person one to person two in the middle: "Hi, my name is John."

Person two turning to person three: "He says, "hello, please call him John.""

Person three to person two: "It's nice to meet you. How are you doing today?"

Person two turning back to person one: "He's happy to meet you and wants to know how you're doing today."

Person one: "I'm fine, thanks."

Person two to person three: "He says, he's fine, thanks."

This was the exact nature of our dialogue for the entire week.

"How are these households selected?" I asked.

Mr. Lu turned to Director Tan to repeat to him the question I just posed.

"Generally speaking, the key households are somewhat better off economically. These families have larger homes with courtyards and space for gatherings." Director Tan went on to explain that the women in the key households work with the town cadres in organizing the meetings, but that the meetings are informal, more like a social club where women talk, exchange information, or share their skills. The women receive no compensation, but they are recognized as progressive members in the community. In Communist China, this has the implicit meaning of being a good citizen and is highly valued.

Again, Mr. Lu relayed the information. Whenever Director Tan wanted to tell me something, it was through Mr. Lu. If I had a question that the local cadres could not answer, I would turn to Mr. Lu, who would then get the answer from Director Tan and pass it on to me.

In my numerous trips to China as an international consultant, or even as an interested visitor, I was always shown the best and more prosperous parts of China. Over time, I came to detect a rehearsed response in my interviews with the locals. Here as elsewhere, it was apparent to me that elaborate preparations had been made for my visit. I saw fresh coats of paint on walls and colorful new posters with small families and nursing mothers in peasant homes, where articulate women enthusiastically endorsed family planning.

I wanted to get the real picture, and so I came up with ways to interact with families that had not been prearranged and coached. On the way by car to visit the villages, I would request to make unannounced visits to homes that I picked at random. My requests were never turned down. Usually I ended up visiting both the homes they had selected as well as those I had picked myself. More often than not, I found women in the homes I had picked to be just as knowledgeable about family planning. In the rural areas, when the first child was a daughter, then a second child was allowed. The couple would be out of luck if they had two daughters and had wanted a son to carry on the family name and support them in their old age.

An odd game reflecting the extreme graciousness of my Chinese hosts came to be played with my oversized handbag in my visit to every agency, every town and city, here and elsewhere. Actually, I refer to it as a handbag, but most people would likely mistake it for a small piece of luggage. In customary Chinese courtesy, as soon as I stepped out of the car, someone would immediately reach for my bag, with the intent of relieving me of such a burden. "Please, I prefer to keep my handbag," I would tell them, clutching it to my body with both arms. "Oh, let me carry it for you," they would insist, as they attempted to wrest the bag from me with their own viselike grip. And then he or she would hold onto my bag and not let it go. In opposition, I would try to loosen the bag from his or her grip. As someone who is only five feet two inches tall, more often than not, I would eventually succumb to their persistence, and finally relinquish it to the holder. This tug-of-war with my handbag would repeat itself at almost every stop, resulting in a surreal kind of ballet, with two or three people fighting for my bag and my fighting to keep it for myself, each of us pulling and tugging with determination and clenched teeth below our polite and smiling faces. I liked keeping my bag by my side so that I could reach for my note pad, pen, name card, or a tissue at ease. But even when I succeeded in keeping the bag by my side after the initial tussle, it would still disappear the moment I took my attention off of it, even for just an instant. The person who took it would watch it, carry it, and then hand it back to me when it was time for me to leave.

On the third day of my visit, we traveled to a remote village near the Siberian border. Silvery icicles decorated the tree branches and sparkled under the clear sky and cold sun, and ice cracked under the wheels on the country road. Coming to a fork in the road, the county magistrate, who was my host for the day, informed me that the destination was only a mile down the road to the left and we would visit a home there. I asked if we could turn right and visit a different village instead. Hesitating for a moment, Magistrate Zhang asked the driver to pull the car over to the side of the road, and the car behind us slowed down to a stop. Magistrate Zhang, tall and balding, bundled in a thick dark cotton quilted jacket, got out of the car to speak with the party secretary, who was in the other car. In Communist China, the party secretary was always the one who set the guidelines and had the final say. The magistrate returned triumphantly and directed the driver to turn right.

We came to a village in twenty minutes. The driver parked the car by the side of the road about a hundred yards from a complex of several small, weather-beaten, mud-brick houses with slanting tile roofs. Three women were shucking corn in the courtyard in front of a ton of golden kernels heaped high. The women were dressed in heavy, padded dark gray winter jackets, their heads wrapped with knitted scarves. I asked Magistrate Zhang if we could visit a home in this complex. Magistrate Zhang said he first had to ask for permission. He got out of the car and walked toward the women, spoke with them, and then went inside the house in the center of the complex.

In a moment, the magistrate came back out and signaled us to join him. I greeted the women sitting on the straw hassocks shucking corn. The women smiled at me but said nothing. They knew I was a visitor by the fact that I came in a vehicle with government officials. Our party went inside the house, stepping over nearly a foot high barrier at the front door onto the cleanly swept dirt floor of the home. The only light shone through a window no larger than one and a half feet by two feet on the front end of the house. A *kang*, a hollowed-out brick bed that allowed for burning coals underneath, was attached to one side of the wall, a small rectangular table was in the center of the room, and two wood benches were against the wall. Two vases of plastic flowers graced each side, with a single light bulb dangling from the ceiling. And although the household did not even have running water, in the center back of the room, a nineteen-inch television sat on top of a high table. Such is the dualistic existence of rural Chinese people, who toil daily to maintain even a most basic livelihood, while at the same time are curious and hungry for a taste of modernization.

Magistrate Zhang introduced me to the master of the house, then he introduced Mr. Lu and Director Tan. The old man had on a dark blue padded jacket and pants, not unlike the ones worn by the women shucking corn, and a fur hat on his head. Deep ridges lined his angular face. He looked uninterested, but politely he told me to sit on the *kang* bed that had a thick red quilt on top. I felt the warm heat generated from the smoldering fire underneath.

"Lao Bo, old uncle," I said to the host. "I hope you don't mind our intrusion. I'd like to talk with you and ask a few things about family planning. Is that all right?"

The youngest of the women we had seen outside brought tea to us in porcelain cups. The old man said she was his eldest grandson's wife and asked us to drink the tea to warm up.

"You have a nice home," I told him. "How long have you lived here?"

"This is my ancestral home. I grew up here. Except for the six years in the People's Liberation Army, I have lived here all my life."

"How many children do you have?" I continued.

"I had nine children, four died in their childhood. My two daughters are married and live with their husbands' families. My two sons, their wives, and my old wife live with me. My youngest son works in Harbin. He is not married."

The old man had loosened up somewhat, holding a cup of tea with both hands. In response to my asking what features were available on television, he said that twice a week the family planning program was carried on one of its two channels in the early evening. He liked the science and technology program on agriculture and animal husbandry, which was aired every night of the week.

"How has family planning affected you?" I probed quietly.

"My children all have small families. Altogether I have three inside-grandchildren and three outside-grandchildren." "Inside," referred to sons' children and "outside" to daughters' children.

"What do you think of small families?"

The old man launched into a discourse about the government's strict family planning policy, a result of the scarcity of land and too many people. His grandchildren will have only one or maybe two children each. Sipping his tea, the old man said he had one great-granddaughter. He was not disappointed that it was a girl, because China had done away with the feudal society. In the new society, there is no difference between the sexes. But he would like the next great-grandchild to be a boy. The family needed muscles for farming and income. If he was unhappy about the government's call for small families, he didn't show it.

When the visit was over, I held the old man's hand as I said goodbye and thanked him for his hospitality. "Lao Bo," I said, "I am so pleased that I met you today. You take care of yourself." I took an Eisenhower dollar from my purse and presented it to him as a souvenir, explaining that the man on the face of the coin was the great American general who had directed the African and European theaters in World War II, and who went on to become president of the United States. The old man was delighted and surprised with the gift. "Ah." His mouth opened wide, showing his missing molars. "You keep well," I said in parting. The three women were working on the corn just as they were when we came. They looked and smiled at us. I waved at them.

The driver had already turned on the engine when I saw the old man running toward us, waving his hand. I rolled down the window and waved.

"You come back again. You come back to see us soon!" he shouted.

"You take care of yourself and keep well," I shouted back.

The car jerked forward on the dirt road. I turned my head around until the old man and the three women merged into a single speck with the landscape under the big sky.

On our ride back to our hotel in the city, Mr. Lu, Magistrate Zhang, and I had a discussion on the icy landscape of the Northeast and Siberia and farming in extreme cold climates. That led to my asking about the reparations China had made to the Soviet Union more than two decades earlier when Nikita Krushchev pulled the Soviet technicians out of China, taking the blueprints of the engineering projects they were working on with the Chinese. Krushchev demanded payment for the work the Soviets had contributed, which

China paid in minerals and food. This payment unfortunately coincided with the great famine caused by three years of devastating drought coupled with mismanagement. It was reported that over a quarter of a million Chinese died in this famine.

"When I was in my teens," said Magistrate Zhang, "my family and the people in my village boiled young leaves and roots to fill our empty stomachs. Death was everywhere."

"What about you, Mr. Lu?" I asked.

"My family lived in Shanghai, so it wasn't as bad. Food was rationed. A lot of people had edema because of malnutrition. We had more grain than the communes since cities got their grain from the state, which got its quotas from the communes."

Director Tan sat stoically in the front seat, speaking an occasional word or two to the driver only. We still had not spoken to each other. I think that by now we both regretted the standoff. Having spent several days in close proximity, I had a better view of Director Tan. He was a bureaucrat who took himself just a bit too seriously. Tan was proud of the accomplishments in family planning under his direction, steering its services to improve the activities of daily life concerns. I believed he cared, and I tried not to think further why he behaved in the manner he did, or what his opinion was about me.

When we assembled the next morning for a final round, Director Tan reached for my bag as soon as we met at the hotel, his expression soft. I believed that was his way to end the standoff. I thanked him for his gesture and did not fight to keep the bag.

At the banquet Director Tan hosted that evening, I was seated on his right side.

"Thank you for hosting my visit." I told Director Tan. "I'm impressed with the vitality of the family planning work in the towns and villages, especially the key household approach. The cadres are dedicated workers. My five days here have been very worthwhile, very informative."

"We are happy you came." Director Tan told me. "You are very thorough in your questioning and we want you to see as much as possible. The work is a lot easier now than when we first began. We are paying more attention to quality-of-life concerns. The key household approach is a step in that direction."

I picked up my glass and toasted him and the party around the table. Director Tan and I shook hands.

Over the course of my thirty years of traveling to China and working on all kinds of public health projects there, I have come across numerous Director Tans, at many different levels of county, municipal, and national government. They are part of a generation that has grown up in strict and rigid thinking. For many, their best years and efforts have been buried in bureaucracy and, at times, misguided policies. Proud and patriotic, each day they must come to terms with and find themselves facing forces and encountering changes that are extreme as well as dogmatic, and sometimes even threatening to them. At the same time, their evident dedication and undying belief in a better and greater China is an inspiration.

Chapter Two
Chrysanthemum That Grew in Winter

My mother was eighty-five years old before she could bring herself to tell me the full story of her mother's suicide. When I was growing up, I knew that our "Waipuo," the Chinese term for maternal grandmother, had taken her own life when my mother was only fourteen months old. Mother talked about it, but not in any detail. She told us only that Waipuo had been unhappy and that Waigong, our maternal grandfather, had been neglectful and unloving even before she had disgraced herself by giving birth to a girl.

My mother never saw a picture of her mother and never knew what she looked like. In fact, she never even knew her real name, for, in keeping with the feudal Chinese tradition of treating women almost as nonpersons, she was never referred to as anything but "Wang Shie" ("a Wang person") known only by her surname.

My mother, Wu Chufang, was born into the wealthy Mandarin House of Wu in September 1911, just weeks before the founding of the republic. The revolution, galvanized by Sun Yatsen, overthrew the Qing dynasty, which had ruled China for nearly three hundred years.

In the early days, the family made and sold tofu, for their livelihood. The House of Wu came to prominence in the middle of the nineteenth century after the Taiping (Great Peace) Rebellion, the most serious challenge to the Manchu dynasty before the 1911 revolution. The leader of the Taiping Rebellion was Hung Hsiuchuan, who belonged to the underprivileged Hakka minority in southern China's Guangdong region. He had been converted to Christianity, and founded the Society of God Worshippers. He believed himself to be the younger brother of Jesus, calling himself the "Second Son of Heaven." He attempted to depose the Manchus and regain the empire for the dominant Han Chinese. The Taiping "Heavenly Kingdom" dynasty and ideology of reform decreed that all land belonged to the state, and every household was to receive sufficient land for its cultivation in proportion to its size. Women were declared equal to men. Seen not only as a threat to the Manchu rulers, but also as a desecration of traditional values, the rebellion was rejected by the Han Chinese themselves. Dissent and power struggles within soon destroyed the kingdom.

My mother's great-grandfather, Wu Tinghua, and his younger brother, Wu Tingbin, served in the Manchu military and helped put down the rebellion. Emperor Xianfeng then rewarded Wu Tinghua by making him Tsu Fu—governor—of Yichang prefecture in Hubei Province, where he settled. Some years later, he was appointed governor of the entire province, but he died before he was to assume the post.

Later, during the Boxer Rebellion of 1898 to 1901, the dowager empress Cixi and the imperial family fled to Shandong Province from Beijing, then known as Peiping. Wu Tingbin, the province's military leader, became their protector. After Cixi returned to Beijing, she appointed him governor of the two northern provinces of Shandong and Shanxi. His name and deeds were chiseled into the face of Grand Mountain, Taishan, where they can still be seen today.

The governor's estate, built by Wu Tinghua, was a vast, sumptuous compound made up of many individual residences both linked and separated by elaborate gardens and courtyards. Just beyond the front gate stood a magnificent semicircular garden planted with magnolia trees. The two-story first mansion contained fine ebony-furnished sitting rooms on the first floor and studies upstairs. Open, roofed walkways linked this mansion to a dozen smaller, single-story buildings on each side of a large central courtyard in front and individual smaller courtyards in the back. These smaller buildings housed the immediate family. The entire estate was resplendent with trees and flowers and small ponds.

The family estate truly exemplified the Chinese proverb,

houmensiehai ("The nobleman's compound is as large as the ocean"). Each branch of the family had its own courtyard and complex of rooms. When my mother was growing up, three generations of extended families lived at the estate. She and her cousins would play around the two huge white stone lions that stood outside the front gate. The lions had bulging eyes, and each held in its mouth a rolling stone bead as large as a human head. They pulled and turned the beads to make the lions "talk."

I once visited the Wu family estate with my mother when I was one year old, but I have no memory of it. During the Sino-Japan War (1937–1945), the Japanese leveled all the houses inside the estate and built a road through it to provide direct access to the city.

Wu Hongjin, known to me as Waigong, the common name for maternal grandfather, was the fourth of eight sons. His biological father was Wu Chaochang, but when he was one year old, he was adopted by his father's younger brother Wu Chaowang, who had no sons of his own. In Chinese culture, siblings share a middle name, as do cousins of the same generation so that they can be easily identified in the family genealogy.

Waigong was an intelligent, even precocious, child. When he was only four years old, his tutor gave him the opening line of a couplet, which are parallel sentences of themed or rhymed Chinese characters, "Flowers cast their shadows beneath the moon." Instantly he responded with, "Bamboo sways silently in the wind."

For many generations, men of Wu distinguished themselves by winning high honors in the imperial examinations, and it became a family tradition to erect a marble column bearing the examination date and the scholarly title awarded to each. More than thirty columns, among them ones honoring Waigong and his seven brothers, stood in the memorial grounds on the family estate.

The men of the House of Wu were also gentlemen of leisure, accustomed to luxury and extravagance. Their success in the imperial examinations garnered them bureaucratic positions, and they delegated much of their work to subordinates. Meanwhile, they lived like other upper-class men of their time—frequenting courtesans, gambling at mahjong, composing poems, singing opera, entertaining lavishly, and even smoking opium. Waigong held a succession of minor bureaucratic positions in various towns and counties and seldom returned to the family estate.

His marriage in 1910 to Wang Shie, our Waipuo, was his second. His first wife had come from a wealthy Yichang merchant family. She suffered from physical disabilities and perhaps mental instability as well, so when her family asked for her to be sent home, he allowed her to leave.

Waipuo was the daughter of a tailor who had a shop in a town near Yichang. My mother never learned how the match had come about, but she was told that Waigong had married her in the proper manner. A sedan chair draped in bridal red carried her to the Wu estate, but the bearers did not carry her in through the front gate, though it would ordinarily have been used for such an important event as a wedding. Because the Wus viewed Waipuo as their social inferior, they ordered her brought to the side gate, and because her family was not with her, she had no one to protest on her behalf.

When she was growing up, my mother heard whispers that, starting with the day Waipuo arrived, the family treated her badly. She soon found herself totally alone, defenseless, and terrorized by her mother-in-law, who was known as San Nainai ("Third Mistress"). As Chinese society is hierarchical, siblings are addressed by their birth order, and the younger would defer to the older for matters related to the family, meaning the extended family.

The following year, Sun Yatsen's revolution and the founding of the Republic left China's prominent families who had served the Manchu dynasty anxious about what the future might hold. The head of the family decided to seek the protection of the Wu forebears by taking refuge at the ancestral hall, about thirty-five kilometers from Yichang.

It was during this passage that Waipuo, then only nineteen, gave birth to my mother in a tent by the roadside. Her husband was out of town. Because of the superstitious belief that the blood of postpartum women was unclean and would bring bad luck, the villagers nearby refused to give her lodgings. The only shelter available was a shed that had been used as a pigpen, so the family servants made up a rough frame bed, and there Waipuo spent her month of lying-in.

My mother often told me that she was haunted by thoughts of how her mother must have felt lying alone in that pigpen with her infant daughter in her arms.

"Sometimes I think I can hear her weeping over my father's neglect, and because she had failed to bear a son," she said. "To this day, I believe that if I'd been a boy, she wouldn't have killed herself."

I grew up in a household where my parents made no distinction between daughters and sons. But I knew only too well that she was referring to the fact that in China a woman had no standing in her husband's family until she had given birth to a son. Because they were only burdens to their family, girls were as disposable as "water in a bucket." After years of being fed and clothed, they would marry "out" to their husband's family, who would reap the benefit of the extra pair of hands. Sons, on the other hand, would carry on the family name; they also had a filial duty to honor, defend, and protect their mother for her entire life.

While Waipuo was recovering, the republican government decreed that the imperial family and its court officials would be allowed to keep most of their privileges and properties. The Wus therefore returned to the family estate, and life went on much as before.

My mother's grandfather, whom she called San Yeh Yeh (Third Grandfather), was the head of his household, but it was his wife, San Nainai, who actually ruled. A nasty and mean-spirited woman, she was so detested by everyone that even her sisters-in-law refused to address her by a kin term, calling her instead only by her formal position name, San Nainai (Third Grandmother).

Her cruelty was legendary. If the maidservants did the slightest thing to displease her, she would lash them with a bamboo whip until their skin was raw. Whenever a child cried or misbehaved, the threat "San Nainai is coming" was all that was needed for the child to quiet down immediately.

"I didn't like my grandmother," my mother said, "especially when I had to sit at meals with her. She would pick up a chicken or duck wing or a drumstick with her chopsticks and bite into it, and if she couldn't chew it, she would take it out of her mouth and place it in my bowl. I hated that." But my mother dared not protest. She would take one bite and leave the rest in her bowl, hoping that her grandmother would not notice.

San Nainai did not allow San Yeh Yeh to take an official position, to freely come and go and to attend to the family business, or to have some social life outside the family. She was afraid that he would go to brothels and meet other women. The Wus had enough income from their land, rental properties, and other business to support a life of leisure for all, and San Nainai saw no reason why her husband should pursue anything outside the home.

San Yeh Yeh was a devout Buddhist, a man without pretensions who lived a simple life. He ate separately from the women, as was the custom of the time, most often alone in his study. For his midday and evening meals he would have soup and four vegetarian dishes. Occasionally he would dine in one of the reception halls with friends or male relatives. But for the most part he spent his days at home reading, feeding his birds, and planting flowers in his big garden.

My mother knew that some scandal had driven her mother to kill herself. Female relatives and servants whispered about it, but it was only years later that she managed to force the truth out of her nanny, Naima.

Late one morning, San Nainai had come into Waipuo's bedchamber and found the bedding rumpled, although the servants had made it up earlier. Because of this, she accused her daughter-in-law of having gone to bed with San Yeh Yeh.

"I don't think that anyone believed this terrible, vicious slander," my mother said, "but San Nainai's word simply could not be challenged."

The House of Wu was feudal in the extreme, and tradition demanded that elders be obeyed without question and without exception. To defy or contradict an elder was unthinkable. In whispers, word of San Nainai's attack on her daughter-in-law spread scandal throughout the female population of the family compound.

Waipuo was devastated by the vicious smear. Alone and with no way to defend herself, she took the only honorable course open to her. She carried my mother, then only fourteen months old, to Second Uncle's quarters, knelt down before him, kowtowed, and asked him to look after her infant daughter. Because Waigong was out of town as usual, Second Uncle did not find her request unusual. He never suspected her real intention. Waipuo then returned to her bedchamber and killed herself by swallowing poison.

A few days later, the truth emerged. A family cousin and her eight-year-old daughter, Pingping, had been visiting at the time. Pingping confessed that she had gone into Waipuo's bedchamber to play with her baby cousin, my mother. Finding no one there, she climbed up onto the big, canopied bed and, for the fun of it, bounced up and down on the thick, soft quilts. When she heard someone come into the outer room, she scrambled down and hid behind the canopy. San Nainai came into the bedroom, saw the untidy bedding, and accused Waipuo of having committed the vilest of crimes. She never saw Pingping hiding in the room.

After Waipuo's burial, Pingping began having nightmares. She saw Waipuo's ghost standing next to her bed at night, looking at her mournfully. By the third night Pingping could no longer keep the secret to herself, and she confessed to her mother.

More than six decades later, I had been puzzled when, during her first visit to China, Mother refused to meet with one elderly relative. Only at my begging did my mother reluctantly agree to see her for ten minutes. It was more than fifteen years later that my mother told me that the old woman was Pingping. "I couldn't bear to look at her because she made me think about what had happened to my mother," my mother explained.

No one ever dared tell San Yeh Yeh the truth about Waipuo's suicide—everyone was too afraid of San Nainai. San Yeh Yeh was sorrowful about his daughter-in-law's suicide but did not appear to know any more than that it was an unfortunate happening.

After seven decades of silence, in halting, painful fragments, Mother revealed Waipuo's tragedy to me. "Waigong was summoned home," she told me. "When he got there, he looked at Waipuo's coffin without expression nor an ouce of remorse, and said, 'So, what's there to get excited about?'"

Hearing that, I felt outrage. What a despicable human being. But I couldn't say that to my mother. Her whole life long, the worst thing she ever said about her father was, "He was a spoiled, selfish man who had eaten out of a jade bowl since childhood."

"Did you hate him?" I asked.

"No. I couldn't let myself feel hatred for him. The way I was raised made it impossible. In those days in China, it was not even thinkable to feel anger or resentment for your parents."

She told me that Waipuo was not laid to rest in the family burial grounds, nor did the Wus enshrine a memorial tablet to her in the ancestral hall as was custom for deceased family members. The family denied her the respect traditionally shown to the dead because she had committed suicide and because she had failed to bear a son.

"After your father and I were married," Mother went on, "I went back to Yichang and had her remains moved to the family burial grounds. I also erected a tablet for her in the ancestral hall. You were with me, but you probably don't remember. You were only a little over a year old."

"Did Papa go with you?"

"No. He was on duty with his troops, so he had an aide accompany us to take care of us and make sure that everything was done right."

"Did anyone in the family object to your moving her remains and erecting a tablet for her?"

"No." My mother's voice was soft and slightly shaking. "Your papa was well known by then, and the family treated me differently, not like before. This time, they obeyed my wishes."

She then opened her desk drawer and took out a letter from Waigong, dictated years later just before he died, asking her for money and requesting that she continue to support her stepmother and a son, by adoption, who was his nephew.

Mother pointed to the postscript of this particular letter and said, "You see, here he apologizes for having treated me and Waipuo so badly."

I read the postscript, which said, "I regret the wrongs done in the past, there is no time left to make it up to you." It was only two lines, but they comforted my mother for all the wrongs he had committed and for his neglect of her. After my mother's death in 1999, I went through the letters Waigong had written to my mother and father, dating back to 1928. In every letter he asked for money. I felt so sorry for my mother for the burden and humiliation she must have felt. I also felt the deepest respect for my father because all the years of my life I never heard him say one unkind word about Waigong and he maintained his filial commitment to him as he had promised Mother at the time of their courtship.

Despite her mother's death and her father's prolonged absences, Mother's second-class status and indifferent fate in the Wu household was softened by San Yeh Yeh's love. He never made her feel that she was unwanted because she was a girl. She often kept him company in his garden, where they would play with the birds and trim the flowers together. He used his collection of calligraphy to teach her to read, write, and recite poetry. And each night he read to her at bedtime.

My mother loved dogs and cats. San Yeh Yeh disliked cats because they sometimes caught and killed his birds, but because he loved my mother he allowed her to have them.

"He used to tell me, 'They're good at catching rats, and I hate rats because they kill birds too,'" she said. "He was also a master of *kung fu* and *wushu*. Several times I saw him throw a knife at a scurrying rat from yards away and kill it instantly. Many times, I saw him jump up and kick leaves on the trees in our garden, which were hanging at least a foot or more above his head." But San Yeh Yeh and his brothers were the last in their family to undergo the intense training that mastering *kung fu* and *wushu* demanded, and these skills were lost to my grandfather and his brothers.

My mother had no early memories of her father, although Naima, her nanny, told her that despite his dismissive comments at Waipuo's funeral, he had held my mother in his arms and wept. He spent all the years of her early childhood away from Yichang in a series of bureaucratic positions and eventually became head of the salt bureau in Zhuozhou, located south of Beijing. When she was nine, he returned to the family's estate to celebrate San Yeh Yeh's sixtieth birthday.

"They took me to the pier to greet him," my mother recalled. "But to me he was just a tall, round-faced stranger. I remember that with his thick glasses and long, dark-blue silk gown, he looked very much like a scholar."

Behind him came his new wife—a beautiful young Manchurian woman in pink, who minced along tossing her head and making overly exaggerated and affected gestures with her hands in a manner that did not strike my mother as that of a well-born lady.

"Her name was Shao Dezie. She was sixteen," Mother said. "I knew that there was something not quite right about her because no one ever said anything about her family or her origins." I later learned from a cousin in Beijing that she was a courtesan, or what most people today would refer to as a high-class escort.

At the pier, Waigong looked at my mother but he neither smiled nor spoke to her. When they arrived home, he ordered her to kneel and kowtow to her stepmother.

"Waigong expected me to show her the same respect that I would have shown my own mother and I didn't dare to oppose him. I called her *niang*, which is another term for 'mother.'"

When Waigong returned to Zhuozhou after the birthday celebration, he took my mother with them. They lived in a rented mansion, one of a pair in a large walled-in garden behind a four-paneled gate. The owner was a spinster whose father and forefathers had served in the Manchu court but whose family fortunes had since declined.

"My stepmother sent her twelve-year-old sister to school, but refused to send me," my mother told me. "I longed to go, but when I asked Waigong to send me, he said it was improper for girls to go about in public. That was just an excuse, because he believed that it was pointless to teach girls anything beyond reading and writing."

Eventually, Waigong agreed to hire a tutor for her. On her first day of class, my mother donned a ceremonial red gown and burned incense to honor her ancestors. She then bowed to her elderly teacher and presented him with a large red envelope that contained his fee. That night Waigong held a banquet to celebrate the occasion and perhaps to display that he was an enlightened, progressive father.

"Every day the tutor made me memorize pages and pages from the *Si Su Wujing*, the Four Books and Five Classics," Mother said. "I had no idea what I was memorizing, and he never bothered to explain anything or to find out whether I understood."

She tried her best to comprehend the texts, but her only help came from the dictionary. Day after day, her tutor would merely sit at his desk smoking his long bamboo water pipe and burying his nose in a book. After several months of this, my mother lost all interest in studying.

A year later, Waigong was appointed *jinshaoyi*, mayor of Beijing. The move to Beijing gave my mother a firsthand view of both the old China and the China that was taking its first steps toward modernization.

For the first eight months, the family lived with Waigong's oldest brother, an eminent lawyer and member of the high court in Tianjin and later in Beijing. Waigong then took grander quarters near the edge of the city, across from a palace belonging to a Manchu prince.

The palace was still the home of several *wangfeis*—imperial concubines—of a grand-uncle of China's last emperor, Hsuantung, who abdicated in 1912. Mother was fascinated by the comings and goings of the eunuchs who were the *wangfeis'* personal attendants. One day she saw the incredibly opulent funeral procession of a *wangfei.* Dozens of horse-drawn carriages draped with yellow silk and satin appeared, laden with priceless gifts that would be buried with her. Glazed clay figurines of courtiers to serve the dead royal concubine, silk robes, carved stone animals, urns and bowls made of gold, silver, and jade, miniature cooking utensils—everything the *wangfei* would have used in life—were all displayed like a bride's dowry. Troupes of musicians playing flutes, cymbals, and gongs accompanied the cortege.

"The procession stretched for kilometers," my mother told me. "It was several hours after the first carriage had left the palace grounds that the last one departed."

A Wu cousin once told me that Waigong and his Manchu wife had something resembling an "open marriage," but my mother never called it that. She said only that Waigong often went to courtesans and prostitutes. He would leave the house each morning and not return until late in the evening. During the day, her stepmother would entertain male friends at home with mahjong . . . and whatever else. Waigong appeared not to care, my mother said, as long as her guests were gone when he came home and she tended to him.

Although Waigong believed it improper for my mother to go about in public, her stepmother got her out of the way by sending her off to performances of *pingju,* Peking opera. Women and girls were expected to remain within the confines of their family compound, but the opera was considered an acceptable entertainment.

My mother lost herself in the lyrics, elaborate costumes, and mythical characters that were dramatized in story. She loved seeing the heroes and heroines of Chinese history and legendary characters such as the Monkey King, the mischievous hero of the classic tale *Journey to the West,* come alive on stage to the raucous accompaniment of the clappers and cymbals and the soft melody of the violinlike *huchin.* She was enthralled by the formal, ritualized movements—walking in a circle represented a long journey, pointing to the temple symbolized embarrassment, and gesturing with a whip indicated riding a horse. Female impersonators known as *huadan* performed the women's roles, gliding across the stage as gracefully as swans and singing in high-pitched, keening voices. The actors' elaborate face paint and fabulous costumes, and the troupes of acrobats who performed hair-raising stunts, only heightened the spectacle. Many Chinese provinces had their own distinctive schools of

opera, but *pingju*, Peking opera, was the essence of Chinese oral culture and an important channel through which traditional values
were passed on from one generation to the next.

"Complimentary tickets to the best seats in the house could
always be found for the mayor's household, so for two years I spent
four or five afternoons or evenings a week at the opera in the company of female relatives, family friends, or servants. For a few hours
I daydreamed and it was a good escape. That's how I got addicted to
Peking opera," my mother revealed to me.

A year or so after Waigong moved his household to their new
residence, he gave in and finally allowed my mother to attend classes
at a one-room schoolhouse nearby. The teacher was a young woman
who wore long Western-style skirts and had bobbed her hair to just
below her ears, a style that would have been unthinkable a generation earlier.

My mother was older than most of the other students, whom the
teacher could not keep in order. She would have the girls bring their
books and stand in front of her for reading lessons. Whenever they
poked their classmates or got into mischief, which happened often,
she would jump up from her seat and admonish the students. The
disturbance made serious study almost impossible.

In late 1923, a flood devastated the city of Yichang and damaged San
Yeh Yeh's home. While it was being restored, he came to Beijing.

"He took me aside and told me that he had really come to see me
because he missed me so much," my mother told me. "So he asked
my father if I could go back with him. Waigong agreed, but I know
that it was my stepmother who was happiest to see me leave."

As soon as they arrived back in Yichang, San Yeh Yeh enrolled
my mother in a primary school, the first real school she ever
attended. She spent the next two years happily studying composi-
tion, arithmetic, history, geography, and domestic science. For the
first time in her life, she experienced the support to pursue the
things she wanted to do.

This period of reprive turned out to be all too short-lived. Two
years later, in 1925, rival warlords began fighting for control of
Peiping. In the siege that followed, Waigong and his entire house-

hold joined the thousands of refugees fleeing the city, and returned to the family estate in Yichang.

The following year, San Yeh Yeh died of tuberculosis, as had his own father, one uncle, one of his brothers, and a number of cousins. He was sixty-seven.

Waigong had never had a son, but he allowed my mother to don a boy's white hemp mourning garments for the funeral, which was a rare act indeed. The two then stood together to greet the mourners. As guests would arrive and pay their respects by kneeling and touching their foreheads to the ground in front of San Yeh Yeh's memorial tablet, Waigong and my mother would kowtow as well.

"I cried for days," my mother said. "But being there next to my father meant so much to me. I felt comforted believing that I was being treated as the young heir mourning my grandfather. It was one of the few occasions that I can ever remember feeling any type of kinship and acknowledgment from my father."

At the family estate, Waigong had plenty of free time and not much to do except to entertain himself and his social friends. During his years as a ranking official, he had grown used to having his ego stroked. He would often invite his cronies to the estate for food, drink, and the purest opium that money could buy, and would glow with pleasure and dissipation while his cronies ate, drank, smoked their fill, and flattered him nonstop. In Chinese the term is *pai ma pi* ("patting the horse's rear"). Waigong was so spoiled that if a meal was not to his liking, he would simply overturn the table, shattering dishes and spilling food everywhere. My mother would watch in silent outrage while the servants cleaned up the mess; the rest of the household would just go about as if nothing happened.

After she finished primary school, my mother asked her father to enroll her in Iona Middle School, a Protestant missionary school in Yichang. He reluctantly agreed. But each semester, she had to brace herself to beg her father for her tuition money.

Waigong saw no reason for her to continue her schooling, especially in a foreign-run school. He would keep her standing in front of him for an hour at a time without saying one word to her. Eventually, he would reach into his pocket to take out a handful of silver coins.

Throwing them onto the floor he would shout, "Take them!"

My mother, fighting to hold back her tears and withholding both her shame and anger, had to get down on her hands and knees and crawl around picking up the coins.

Even after managing to enroll, she often missed school because Waigong kept her home to prepare his pipe on the days when he smoked opium, which was every day he was in town. She would have to spoon the sticky black paste out of the jar, knead it into a ball, put it into a cup, light a lamp, and then heat the cup over it until the opium began to bubble. Then, holding her breath to avoid inhaling the fumes, she had to scrape out the paste and knead it again, repeating the procedure until the opium was viscous enough to be smoked.

She hated the sticky black opium, and she hated missing school. She hated serving the drug to her father and seeing him lying on the couch in a stupor, oblivious to the world and to how he was treating her. But no Chinese daughter of that period would ever have dared show displeasure, let alone anger, toward her parents. Nor would any son, for that matter. Children had to obey, revere, and honor their parents, and pay reverence to their ancestors. Rebellion was simply not tolerated, either in the family or in the larger society. During all the centuries of dynastic China, unfilial behavior toward one's parents had been a capital offense. In fact, the enemies of government ministers sometimes resorted to accusations of unfilial behavior because those accused could be put to death or exiled by imperial decree.

Waigong smoked two ounces of pure opium each day, the cost of which could have bought enough rice to feed a family of five or six for a month. When he entertained his friends, the cost multiplied many times over. During the war against Japan, when the Nationalist government enforced strict prohibitions against opium smoking, Waigong secretly fed his habit with opium tablets instead. Only after 1949, when the Communists made all the addicts quit, did he give it up. He had smoked away all his wealth. Ironically, this actually helped him after the Communists took power in China, since as a member of the "propertyless class" he was spared the fate of those who, like his older brother, were labeled as landlords and imprisoned because they owned property.

One day, after her teachers chose her to act in a stage play, Waigong pulled my mother out of school entirely, saying such behavior was indecent.

Next to San Yeh Yeh my mother most loved her nanny, Naima. Naima had cared for the children of the House of Wu for some years, and after Waipuo killed herself my mother was placed in her care. Naima became her surrogate mother, caring for her as if she had come from her womb. When Waigong took my mother to Zhuozhou and Beijing, Naima gathered up her savings and returned to her home village to farm with her husband and children, as she had always hoped to do.

Naima was plagued by misfortune. When robbers broke into her house and stole all her money, the poor woman returned to the Wu estate to become the family cook. Every morning she would go with a young maidservant to the market near the center of town to shop for fresh meat, fish, and vegetables.

One morning on her way to market a rabid dog with saliva dripping from its jaws lunged at her, sinking its teeth into her wrist. Terrified, Naima wiped the blood away with her apron and went straight home. The housekeeper put a black medicinal patch on the wound and concocted an herbal drink for her.

When my mother, who was then about sixteen, learned of the attack, she, too, was terrified, for she knew what an agonizing death lay in store for anyone who had been bitten by a rabid animal. She begged her stepmother to send for a doctor. Naima had served the Wu family for more than twenty years, but her stepmother merely sent word to Naima's son, telling him that he should come and take her back to her home village. My mother pleaded with her not to send Naima away, but in vain. That was the last time my mother ever saw Naima. She died a few days later in her son's home.

Waigong was furious when he saw my mother crying over Naima's death. "You should weep only for your parents, not for a servant," he scolded her.

"Of all the possessions we lost in the fall of Guangzhou to Japanese occupation," my mother told me, "the one I still miss most is a photo of Naima holding me when I was two years old. I used to keep it in the safe, and I'd often take it out and look at it when I felt alone or when I wanted to recall her goodness and kindness to me. But it was lost, along with everything else . . . even today, I miss that photo."

Naima's death taught my mother that the lot of the poor was a miserable and too often tragic one. The poor had no choice but to endure, to submit to the fate meted out by their masters. Many a night my mother would picture Naima lying there dying, delirious and thirsting for a sip of water but unable to drink. She thought, too, of her mother's suicide. And she decided that she had to break free from her family. On her way to and from school, she had caught glimpses of teenage girls wearing blue school uniforms, who were being identified as "the new breed" of young women. She wanted to be one of them.

"I swore to my mother's spirit that I would be worthy of the life she had given me," she told me. "I swore to honor her every day of my life. I was determined to become a voice for her generation—for all women who had endured so much. I would become a voice for my own generation."

In June 1929 my father was stationed in Yichang City in Hubei Province that was also the ancestral home of the wealthy and prominent House of Wu. He was then the Nationalist Army's Fourth Division's acting commander as well as acting pacification commissioner of the district who oversaw both security and civil administration of the area. At an elaborate dinner that Waigong held for the division officers, my father lost his heart to an exquisite young girl in a black silk jacket and long skirt, sitting quietly with the other ladies of the Wu household at one end of the huge living room. He couldn't stop looking at her porcelain smooth oval face, alluring lips, and large, luminous eyes. She radiated intelligence and an innocent sensuality. She was eighteen; he was thirty-four.

"This is the girl I want to marry," he excitedly told his friend and military counselor, Han Hanyin, the next morning. Without a moment wasted, Han along with his wife took it upon themselves to become his matchmakers. At the time, the Hans were renting lodgings at the Wu family's Tsu Fu estate. Mrs. Han, who had studied music in Japan, was ten years older than my mother and had befriended her. She told her that Li Han Hun, the Fourth Division's commander, was interested in her.

"I told her I had no idea who he was," my mother would always say with a laugh. "To me, all the officers looked alike in their crew-cuts and mustard-green uniforms. I also said I didn't find any of them attractive because they all smoked cigarettes, and I detested any form of smoking."

But Mrs. Han quickly pointed out to my mother that the commander she was referring to was not a smoker. "You'll be able to spot him easily," she said. "He's slender, of medium height, with bright eyes, finely drawn eyebrows, and an assured, but modest coutenance. His teeth are white and not yellow like the ones who smoke."

At Waigong's next dinner party, my mother sat next to Mrs. Han. "I saw her looking in my direction across the room," my father recorded in his diaries. "She left after a short time. The fact she was looking in my direction gave me the courage to pursue her."

The next day, he wrote her a letter expressing his admiration and his desire for a future together. Mrs. Han delivered the letter to my mother immediately, but he had to wait three weeks before she brought him a reply.

I asked my mother why she left early that evening and why she waited so long to respond to my father's letter. "Decorum demanded it," said my mother. "Otherwise I would have been regarded as being ill-bred for a young woman of my social standing. But your father's letter won my heart from the moment I finished reading it. In his words, I could tell that he was a man of honor and dedication, but also someone who could appreciate and even wish for a romantic and simple life. Rather than driving ambition, he was driven by his duty to country. And he possessed his own deep beliefs of what made one's life good and worthwhile, like love, family, and friends."

Although they went through the formalities of matchmaking, theirs was a true affair of the heart. They exchanged letters and had several meetings in the estate gardens with the Hans as chaperons. They even shared an outing or two with a large circle of friends hosted by Waigong. "Papa always tried to edge close to me," my mother once told me, pointing at a photo that showed my grandfather and the officers in an outing, my father squatting next to my mother.

My father spent almost as much time courting Waigong as he did courting my mother. He had to prove to Waigong, who prided himself on his family's prestige and lineage, that he was worthy of his daughter, that he was not just a soldier but also a man of culture. To earn Waigon's approval, my father had to overcome the image captured in the proverb, *Hao tie bu da ding, hao nan er bu dang bing* ("Good iron is not wasted on nails; nor do good men become soldiers").

So my father began exchanging with his future father-in-law poems he had written. This was a traditional game played by learned scholars in which the gift of a poem would obligate another poem in reply. It could go on indefinitely.

Waigong had already made one earlier attempt to marry my mother off to a merchant's son, but she had threatened to enter a Buddhist nunnery if he tried to force her into marriage. In her schooling, my mother got the modern ideas of freedom and romantic love, and she was determined she would be a modern woman. Furthermore, she did not want to be the daughter-in-law of a family that had succumbed to opium smoking.

A month after their first meeting, my father asked my mother to marry him. She instantly agreed, knowing that he loved her and would open a new life for her. They became formally engaged on the evening before the Chinese mid-August festival, which celebrates the mythical romance of two separated lovers—the Cowherd and Weaver Maid. The following day, my father was ordered to move his troops south to Hankou, many days of travel away.

"What do you most hope for after we marry?" he asked her the night of their engagement.

"A university education," my mother said, after a brief pause. "I hope to be able to someday help others to become more self-reliant. An education is what I would need to do that."

My father looked deep into my mother's eyes. Touched by her pure heart and courageous spirit, he made a vow to her right there, "I promise to support you in every way I possibly can."

This exchange expressed the essence of their relationship: a close bond between two people who had grown up in traditional China but who hoped to create a life together in a modernized homeland.

As an engagement gift, he selected two matching gold coins and gave one to my mother. From that day on, she wore hers on a simple, braided-ribbon cord around her neck and he wore his on a silk rope around his waist. They promised each other that they would be together, in war and in peace, on every August Moon festival to come. He promised to write her at least once a week, warning her that if she failed to hear from him for three months, it would probably mean that he had been killed in battle. He urged her to follow the movement of the troops, which would inform her of his where-abouts, and to read the daily newspapers.

He then gave my mother one other parting gift, a poem that he had written for her father to read but dedicated to her. In 1991, for her eightieth birthday, I had a seal carver engrave the characters of the poem on Chinese polished stone "chops" and gave one to each of my brothers and sisters and to every one of our children as well. The sentiments expressed in the poem is captured below:

> Battle cries resounded night and day
> Three months my precious horses trotted on dusty grounds
> By the streams I saw grasses growing freely
> I wanted to sing to you though my tears would flow
> The mountainside was frozen under the shining moon
> Remember your warrior, my beloved!
> Soft words flowed, fond hearts beat
> We sealed our future together beneath the August moon.
> Singing my song to you, my betrothed
> I heard drums beating calling me to the battlefield
> Our dreams suspended in parting
> Our souls longing from distant shores

In 1997, two years before her death, my mother gave me two volumes of love letters, pasted onto almost transparent rice paper, that my father had written to her between 1928 and 1932. She had brought all his letters with her to the United States. Unfortunately, about half of them were lost when the basement of our house in White Plains was flooded after a heavy rainstorm.

My father wrote to my mother often, sometimes daily. He wrote more than three hundred letters to her, which he numbered in sequence. Because of wartime conditions, some went astray.

Although she kept his letters, none of hers survived. Because he was on combat duty and constantly on the move with his men, often in harsh and unpredictable conditions, he destroyed her letters each time he received new marching orders. Perhaps he also felt they were too private.

To preserve his letters, I detached the brittle, dried-out letters from the pages and stored them in plastic sleeves.

As I read Father's letters, I was surprised to discover that he had a sense of humor and even a playfulness that I had never witnessed or knew he possessed. I was also deeply moved by his devotion to his betrothed. He would refer to himself as the mythical "Monkey King" because he was so skinny. He often addressed her as Kuanyin, after the Buddhist incarnation of compassion who put off entering into nirvana and chose to remain on earth to relieve the sufferings of all living beings.

"Ah, how I wish to be the Monkey King incarnate," he wrote on one occasion. "I would somersault a thousand kilometers to be by your side." In another letter he told her that he wished he could just be a dog crouching by her side and what a happy life that would be. "So you want to study law and become a lawyer. It makes me tremble to think that I could be brought before you and tried for a misdemeanor," he teased her in yet another of his letters.

My father sent most of his letters to my mother via Mrs. Han. In those days, it was considered improper for even engaged couples to correspond too frequently, and parents routinely opened their children's mail. He also continued attempting to win over Waigong and his wife by writing to them. But he let my mother know that those letters were meant for her as well, and Waigong shared them with her.

I also discovered that at one point my mother was contemplating suicide because Waigong had smoked away his entire fortune, and he and her stepmother were pressuring her to break off the engagement with my father, and instead, marry a richer man. Mother defied them, saying, "I will marry Bohao—Father's alternate name—or no one." She again threatened to enter a Buddhist nunnery if they pushed her too hard. Her will on this matter was immovable.

My mother wrote to my father of her troubles and he urged her to escape her difficult home situation by going to Japan to study. On January 1, 1930, he wrote: "Should your father be unwilling to support the cost of your study in Japan, I will gladly take care of the expense, so you must not worry about how to support yourself. . . . In the event that your study in Japan is delayed, you should concentrate on learning English. Someday we will visit Europe and America together to broaden our horizons. Your best course is to study in Japan, and I will do everything to help you to realize your desire for higher education."

Even as Waigong had second thoughts about him as a son-in-law, my father never waivered from his devotion to my mother and his filial duty to his prospective in-laws.

"We should respect the traditional morality that it is the duty of children to honor and provide for their parents," he wrote to her four months later. "As I said to you before, I will honor your father and stepmother as my own. You are their only child, and I fully intend to take care of them on your behalf. . . . Your [step]mother is cruel to insist that you break off your engagement with me, and I am surprised that your father has also changed his mind [about us]. . . . I've thought about leaving the military for other pursuits, as you suggested, and going with you to Japan to study. But for the time being, this is not a realistic option. . . . Our love for each other is free and sacred unto death, and neither heaven nor earth nor the pressure of parents can pull us apart."

The plan for my mother to study in Japan came so very close to being realized. At one point, my father even sent five hundred Yen to his old friend Mrs. Han to pay for my mother's passage there. But as tensions grew between China and Japan, my mother had to give up her dream of studying in Japan. I used to wonder why she knew Japanese, and it was only after reading my father's letters that I learned of that failed plan. Meanwhile, for the next three years, the growing Japanese threat, as well as the ever-present specter of marauding bandits that plagued the country, kept my father's forces on the alert, on the move, and apart from my mother.

Although my parents were *so* deeply in love, my father was still a man of his era, and it turned out that he had not been totally honest with my mother during their courtship and engagement. He did not reveal to her until much later that he had actually been married twice before.

When my father was eighteen, his mother, Ahnai, had contracted a traditional arranged marriage for him with a young woman named Chen Jin from a neighboring village, who bore him a son before dying in a plague epidemic two years later. My father told my mother about this first marriage soon after he began courting her, explaining that his mother was bringing up the boy; but it was only near the end of their three-year engagement that he revealed the existence of a second wife and of the four children she had borne him.

This second marriage was again arranged by his mother. It took place in 1924. The second wife, Pong Chihing, was from my grand-mother's village. Because Father was constantly on the move with his troops, she and the children lived mostly in Guangzhou or in Guangzhou Bay with Ahnai, as did my father's son from his first marriage.

The taking of multiple wives was completely acceptable for Chinese men of that era, but my mother was devastated.

"I was too afraid of losing you to tell you earlier," my father explained, trying to justify his conspiracy of silence with the Hans, who had known about his marriages when they had begun matchmaking.

My mother was deeply hurt, and it took some little while to forgive him. But she knew how much he loved her, and so she agreed to go ahead with their marriage. Her anguish was mitigated as my grandmother Ahnai mediated and my mother was married as my father's *pinqi*—wife of equal standing. Pong Chihing was so traumatized that she laid ill for many months. This concealment haunted my father for the remainder of his life for having "wronged two good women."

The men of my father's generation were caught between the conflicting tides of old and new that were occurring in China at the time. In traditional Chinese culture, parents arranged marriages for children when they were teenagers or even younger. The arrangement was seen as dutiful and an assurance for the perpetuation of the family lineage. But in the new culture, the modern wife stood by her husband's side and offered the support he needed socially and even intellectually. Many important men, and even not-so-important men, who left their villages to seek their future in China's burgeoning cities left their village wives behind. They then went on to take new wives who were better educated, more cultured, and much younger than themselves and the wives they had married when they were immature teens. The new wife was considered the lawful *pinqi*.

In the male-dominated China of that period, husbands could dissolve marriages with a simple public announcement or by putting aside the unwanted spouse and ignoring her. Both Sun Yatsen and Chiang Kaishek followed this pattern. When Chiang married his third wife, the beautiful young American-educated Soong Meiling, he merely announced the dissolution of his earlier unions in the daily newspapers. Sun never bothered with such an announcement in separating himself from his previous wife. Inevitably, men like Sun and Chiang became role models for the men of their generation.

My parents were finally married in Shaoguan City in July 1932. Instead of the traditional red gown, my mother chose to wear a Western-style wedding dress of gleaming white satin and a waist-length white veil. They celebrated afterward with a simple banquet attended by their parents and my father's closest officer friends. "I had no dowry except for the two cats I had brought with me from Yichang, " said Mother, referring to them as her "bridesmaids."

They set up their first home together in Shaoguan, where my father had just been appointed pacification commissioner of Guangdong's Northwest District and commander of the Third Independent Division. In this position, he was responsible for both military operations and civil administration in twenty-four counties with a combined population of more than fifteen million people.

During this period, he ordered the construction of the Tsujiang Bridge, a magnificent and modern structure, and encouraged the counties to develop hydroelectric power for farming and forestry. His commitment to Buddhism also led him to raise funds for the renovation of Shaoguan's fifth-century Nanhua Temple, originally built in 502 C.E. and located east of Shaoguan. It is the largest Buddhist temple in South China.

My parents' first home was a rented house with a gated wall that enclosed an expansive garden inside large walled-in grounds.

Ten months after their marriage, I was born. They named me Li Cheng, for the Cheng River that flows through northwestern Guangdong. In today's *pinyin* system for translating Chinese into English, my Chinese name is spelled Li Zhen, and the river is now called the "Zhenjiang." My brother Shao was born thirteen months later. Shao was named for Shaoguan.

Although civil war had ceased, banditry was everywhere. In addition, traitors spied for the Japanese, whose aggression in the spring and summer of 1932 had precipitated fierce fighting in Shanghai. My father taught my mother how to shoot with a revolver for self-protection. When I was growing up, I heard my mother teasing my father about a shooting contest that was held in the garden grounds around the house. Because her shots were even more accurate than his, Father left the grounds for his study and stayed there for the remainder of the game. My mother told me that after that contest, she never shot in contests again, because it wounded my father's pride in front of people.

Once, while my father was away on an inspection tour, my mother actually pointed a gun at an intruder and ordered him to leave the house, her finger ready to pull the trigger. The frightened intruder quickly ran out of the house.

Life in Shaoguan was lonely for my mother, who spoke Mandarin and Hubei dialect but was unable to communicate in the local Cantonese dialect. Only a few of the officers' wives spoke Mandarin. My mother wanted to learn Cantonese in order to get to know the officers' wives, and so she asked the ladies to teach her Cantonese. The ladies agreed on the condition of her willingness to play mahjong with them.

The condition the ladies imposed created a predicament for my mother, because my father had decreed gambling illegal. Although not everyone who played mahjong gambled, many did, and the mahjong game was a gray area. The fact that the ladies played mahjong at all could be construed as gambling. My mother knew it would be terribly embarrassing to my father if it became known that his wife indulged in mahjong against the order he had issued to the public. But if she refused to play, she would remain isolated with no one to teach her Cantonese.

She decided that learning Cantonese was of sufficient importance to her and so she agreed to the ladies' demand. Every morning, after my father left for work, several ladies came to the house with a mahjong set hidden inside a basket. They put a quilt on the table to muffle the sound of the clattering mahjong tiles hitting the table. My mother took the added precaution of posting a servant at the gate to look out for visitors and for my father, in the event my father came home for lunch unexpectedly. While playing mahjong with the other ladies, my mother practiced her Cantonese by reading from a book she had bought on how to speak Cantonese. Most of her learning was simply trial and error. During one playing session, she eagerly told everyone of her recent trip. In her heavily Mandarin-accented Cantonese, she said, "I flew on the airplane to Kowloon and stayed in a hotel." Suddenly, the whole table broke out laughing in such hysterics that tears streamed from everyone's eyes. Everyone, that is, except for my mother's. Clearly, she was missing out on the joke. It's no wonder. What had actually come out of my mother's mouth was, "I sat on the flying chicken going to the dog cage and lived in the dog house." After regaining their composure, the other ladies just shook their heads and said to each other, "*Beinu*, Northern girl," the nickname they had given her.

Many Cantonese words were homonyms of Mandarin words, but the dialects differed in sound and tone. Anyone who has ever heard them both spoken can easily recognize that Cantonese has a much harsher sound than Mandarin. And many words that have the same sound in Mandarin have a different sound and meaning in Cantonese.

The officer's wives spent as much time talking and laughing at my mother's attempts to speak Cantonese as they did playing mahjong. After three months' time, my mother was able to speak the language fluently and was able to discontinue her risky mahjong games with the ladies.

My mother dressed my brother and me in Western-style outfits, white leather shoes in summer and brown ones in winter. We were always at the door to greet Papa when he came home.

Like all upper-class women of the time, my mother had servants to do the cooking, housecleaning, and gardening while nannies looked after my brother and me. With a great deal of time on her hands, my father suggested that Mother organize a home economics club for the wives of the officers in the Pacification Commission. He offered the club the use of the grounds around their house, which also had an animal pen and a guest house.

The home economics club gave my mother a mission to work with the other women. Some fifty officers' wives joined the club and planned their activities of adult education for self-improvement. The majority of the wives were in their twenties, and some of them, having never gone to school, were illiterate. To address this, several members who were graduates of teacher-training schools taught literacy classes in the guest house. The club bought a loom and sewing machines, seeds and fertilizer for planting, and ten little pigs. The women learned weaving and tailoring; they planted vegetables on the garden's spacious grounds and initiated a pig-raising project.

The ladies cooked the fresh green leafy vegetables in a big cauldron for the pig feed and they added extra nutrients to speed the growth of the pigs. The club harvested enough melons, squash, strawberries, peas, lettuce, tomatoes, and *bok choy* for all the families, with food left over. The mature pigs were sold at the market, but the money from the sale was barely enough to cover the cost of their feed and the firewood. "We learned a lesson in planning and balancing costs and profits," my mother told me.

This was my mother's first, real hands-on experience in managing resources. It was her first experience in education and improving self-sufficiency that would eventually result in helping thousands of war refugee children and widows in China over the coming years.

The club came to an end in 1935, when my father was appointed Pacification Commissioner for the Eastern District of Guangdong and our family left Shaoguan.

Chapter Three

The Soldier-Poet's Path

"*I* am a soldier." I've never forgotten the pride in my father's voice whenever he said this. My father, Li Hanhun, was born on November 23, 1895, in Lingtou, a village in Wuchuan County in southern Guangdong Province. He was the second child and the first son born to Li Tseyan and his wife Pong Baomu, a daughter from a well-to-do family in a neighboring village. Their marriage had been arranged when my grandfather was sixteen and his future wife was two years older. Their first child was a daughter. Then came my father, two more sons, and finally a second daughter. My grandmother was known simply as Ahnai, which in my father's village was the general Chinese term for "grandmother." I met her as a child, when she came to visit my parents in Shaoguan, but I was only two, too young to remember her.

Li family legend had it that my grandfather's branch of the family, which included nearly twenty of the families living in Lingtou, traced its origins back to a prince of the tenth-century Tang court in Xian who had been exiled to the coastal Guangdong region. In centuries past, when China's capital was located far inland, Guangdong was where convicts and ministers who had displeased the emperor were banished. Exile included not only the culprits but also their entire family clan, which could number in the hundreds.

My father's generation was the twenty-second of the line, and I find it quite amazing to think that my brothers and sisters and I, living here in America, are the twenty-third generation from the village of Lingtou on the other side of the Pacific Ocean.

Like three generations of Li ancestors before him, my father's father was a salt merchant. The Lis had created a prosperous business, but by the end of the nineteenth century, as a result of the restrictive treaties that China had been forced to sign with foreign powers starting in the mid-1800s, the trade had come under tight state control. My grandfather grew disenchanted with the foreign domination of the customs bureau that controlled the salt trade. He gave up the family business, bought some land, and set himself up to become a rice farmer. My father used to tell stories of waking up in the morning as a very small boy and seeing his father come into the house with his legs caked with mud, after having already spent several hours out in the rice paddies.

Although the Lis were merchants, they placed the greatest value on learning. It was, therefore, my grandfather's longtime wish to be a scholar. He dreamed of following the centuries-old tradition in which Chinese scholars strove to pass the nationwide imperial examinations to become a scholar and to receive government appointments that would bring honor to their families. As a young man, he made two attempts at taking the provincial-level imperial examinations. He failed both times, but his love of learning was so great that although he was not wealthy he used his life savings to build and support a school in the village. Its name, Yuying, means "nurturing the heroic young." It has been rebuilt and still exists today.

My grandfather hoped to see his elder son succeed where he had failed, so when my father was only four, he gave him a second name, as was traditional when children began their schooling. The name was "Bohao" meaning "first among the accomplished." My grandfather hired two brothers who were renowned both for their learning and their moral character to tutor his two sons as well as two young nephews. The tutors were given room and board as well as a salary. Such a tradition was an honored practice through the centuries, and pupils would revere their teachers in the manner in which they revered their parents.

Under their tutelage, my father studied the classics. His teachers would assign a theme having to do with nature, history, spirituality, or some other topic, and my father would have to write a poem or a prose work on that theme within an allotted time. The tutors would judge his work for its linguistic clarity, depth of reflection, mood and rhythm. Sometimes they would compose the first line of a couplet and my father would then compose a second line that would complete its meaning, rhythm, and every other element. He also spent much time studying Confucian ethics and philosophy, which would shape his values throughout his life.

"When the tutors went back to their own homes during lunar New Year and holidays, your father traveled with them so that he would not miss his lessons," a cousin in Hong Kong once told me. My cousin's father was one of the young nephews who studied with my father. "He was the only one who did this, and your grandparents would give him permission go. It was well known in our village that your father's oil lamp would burn long after the household turned dark. His lamp would be lit early in the morning, and he would be at his desk reading."

My father would admire those tutors his entire life. Even four decades later, when he was governor of Guangdong, he wrote a poem to one of them to honor his birthday; he always sent the teachers gifts at the start of the new year.

When his father died of throat cancer, my father, as the eldest male heir, received title to the family farm. He was sixteen. A few days after the funeral, Third Uncle, who was a second-degree relative living next door, invited my father into his house and then tried to force him to sign over the land. When my father refused, Third Uncle began beating him with his long bamboo water pipe. It happened that my father's older sister, who had been outside feeding the chickens, had seen him go into the house. Well aware of the uncle's greed, she stationed herself near the fence and kept watch, and when he didn't come out after a while, she ran to the front door and pounded on it, shouting that my father was needed at once because Ahnai was sick and vomiting blood. Third Uncle had to let him go.

When they got home, Ahnai's face was ashen with terror. "You must flee immediately, as soon as it gets dark. If you stay here, he will harm you or even kill you." She handed him a purse that contained sixty silver yuan of her savings. "Go to Guangzhou Bay," she told him. "I've already sent your cousin to tell your second uncle"—her younger brother—"that you're coming. He'll go with you on the boat to Guangzhou. Your kin Pong Yuhua is there. He will look after you."

"But how can I leave you all alone and unprotected?" my father protested.

"No harm will come to us," Ahnai assured him, "but you must

leave immediately. Go now, and study and learn all you can. Some-day you'll come back and bring honor to your ancestors. And remember—never do anything that would bring shame to the family."

My father knew he must go. He knelt before her and touched his forehead to the ground in the three traditional kowtows of respect and promised that he wouldn't fail her.

Ahnai stood up straight and held her head high despite tears streaming from her eyes. My father's brother and sisters clung to him. "Don't go!" they wept.

"You must obey our mother," he told them. "Take care of her always."

Then he swung the cloth sack of food and clothing that Ahnai had packed for him over his shoulder and slipped out the back door into the darkness.

He avoided the main road and instead picked his way along the raised earthen walkways that crisscrossed the village's rice paddies. Each time he saw a flickering lantern coming toward him he dropped to the ground, his heart pounding like a drum, and dared not move until long after the light had disappeared. He desperately wanted to turn back, but he walked on as Ahnai had told him to do, carefully skirting village after village. His only guide was the light of the stars.

The March night was chilly, and his tears were cold on his cheeks. "I'm the oldest son," he thought bitterly, "but I'm still too young to take my father's place as the man of the household. And I'm too weak to protect my mother and brother and sisters." With anger and frustration in his heart, he promised himself angrily that someday he would return and right the wrongs that his family had suffered.

Only the croaking of the frogs and the occasional barking of a dog broke the night's stillness. At daybreak, he began passing small groups of peasants with hoes on their shoulders, driving their water buffaloes to the fields. There, they would spend the long day cracking their whips over their beasts' backs and pushing the iron plows to turn the soil. The sun rose and the morning grew warm, but my father kept walking south toward Guangzhou Bay. He stopped only to eat and catch some sleep under the trees. As soon as he felt rested, he started off again, walking as fast as he could.

By noon he reached the harbor at Guangzhou Bay, he found where his uncle waiting, boat tickets in hand. They boarded the barge for the two-day voyage to the city of Guangzhou and were herded into the passenger hold, where the only way to sleep was sitting up—and there was barely room to do that on the crowded benches. The floor was littered with tangerine and orange peels, olive pits, cracked melon seeds, peanut shells, and other debris. As the boat rocked to the provincial capital, which foreigners referred to as "Canton," the passengers puffed their water pipes and told stories. From time to time a passenger would make his way behind the wooden panels at the rear of the hold and relieve himself or rush out on deck to vomit over the side.

My father watched the barges loaded with crates, sacks, and barrels, and worried about his family back home and about the future that lay ahead of him in the strange city that he could glimpse in the distance. "Aiya . . . a . . . aiya . . . a . . . aiya . . . a . . ." the coolies, men of bitter strength, cried, as they drove their long, heavy bamboo poles to the bottom of the river to propel the barges forward. Their singing rose and fell with the steady movement of their straining arms and bodies, and the water and sky came together in harmony with their cries, which they disguised as songs.

The city of Guangzhou in 1912 was a dazzling sight. Everywhere my father looked, he beheld broad, paved streets crowded with horse-drawn carriages, sedan chairs carried by uniformed bearers, and rickshaws being pulled by barefoot coolies. He noticed that many people wore silk brocade, which in his hometown was worn only by the well-to-do and only on holidays. The streets were lined with buildings three and four stories high, some with balconies.

He followed his uncle to the army barracks on the south side of the city where his maternal kin, Captain Pong Yuhua, was living. He was thirteen years my father's senior.

Pong was a thin, intense man who wore his hair cropped close to his skull. He taught political science to the new officers, and he wore his uniform with pride. His small room contained only a desk, a chest of drawers, and a bed covered with a neatly folded mustard-yellow blanket. A mosquito net hung from the ceiling over the bed.

For several moments he studied my father's high forehead, bright eyes, finely drawn eyebrows, and slender build. "You look so much like your father," he said at last.

That night my father slept on a folding canvas cot in Pong's room. He stayed there for a month, and during that time Pong became his friend, confidant, and mentor.

Pong Yuhua had been barely out of his teens when, like thousands of other educated young Chinese, he had answered Sun Yatsen's call to overthrow the Manchus who had ruled China during the three centuries of the Qing dynasty.

Sun Yatsen, who was to become the Father of the Republic of China, was born in 1866 in Hsiangshan, one hundred and ten kilometers from Guangzhou. He was trained as a doctor but gave up his career after spending time in Hawaii and England, where he was exposed to Western ideas about democracy and political reform.

In 1895 he returned to China and began agitating for change. Soon there gathered around him a multitude of idealistic young revolutionaries, many of whom had also studied abroad. The first ten uprisings they led, between 1907 and 1911, were badly equipped, ill-organized, poorly coordinated and easily put down. The Manchu government ferreted out revolutionary activities relentlessly. Thousands of these young patriots were executed for treason.

Among those who lost their lives was Pong Hong, one of Pong Yuhua's own cousins. Pong Hong had been among the young revolutionaries captured during the tenth revolutionary uprising, the March 1911 storming of Guangzhou's imperial government grounds. When Pong Hong and his comrades refused to inform on the movement, they were beheaded. These young men were dreamers and revolutionaries filled with love for China and a cause larger than themselves. Similar to so many thousands of others of their generation who wanted a free and democratic China, Pong Hong was only twenty-five years old when he met his fate.

In all, eighty-six martyrs either died during the uprising or were executed. Huanghuagong—Yellow Flower Monument—in Guangzhou, where seventy-two of them are buried, became the most famous revolutionary monument in pre-Communist China.

Every March 8, when I was in grade school, we used to sing, "Yellow flowers bloom, yellow flowers fall, they who are gone are never to return. . . ." Even as a young child, the martyrdom of these young lives touched me deeply. To this day, I find myself humming that memorial hymn every March, and I still feel the intensity of their patriotism.

In October 1911, just eight months later, Sun's allies overthrew the provincial government of Wuchang and the republic was born. Sun's *Sanmin Ju I* ("Three Principles of the People") advocated the Chinese people's right to ethnic dignity and sovereignty; to a government that would serve them and be responsible to them; and to the economic development necessary to their welfare. Sun, convinced that the lot of the peasants must be improved, further advocated that those who tilled the soil should own it. The ultimate goals of his revolution were freedom, justice, and equality within China and among the world of nations. It was the start of a new era of change for China.

Each night my father and Pong Yuhua talked about the revolution and the birth of the republic. Pong would pound his fist on his desk as he described the hundred and fifty years of humiliation China had suffered since the Manchus had allowed France, Great Britain, Russia, Germany, Portugal, and Japan to open treaty ports and concession territories in many coastal cities. The foreign powers carved the concession territories to their own liking and interests, like slicing a melon up into pieces for their taking.

My father knew about the arrogance and evil of foreign oppression because the west side of Guangzhou Bay and its harbor, totaling 2,130 kilometers and located only fifty kilometers from his home county, was a French concession territory. The French regulated trade, imported their own laws and religion, and paid and protected many of the native criminal elements to enforce their will. These gangsters bullied the citizenry and murdered those who refused to comply, hiding their crimes behind their foreign masters.

Pong also railed against the opium trade, which had been poisoning China since the mid-nineteenth century, when Britain forced China to accept large shipments of Indian opium to balance its own imports of Chinese tea and silk. My father, who as a boy had seen the wives and children of addicts weeping outside the opium dens and begging their husbands and fathers to come home, knew firsthand about the scourge of opium. Many addicts pawned or sold their houses, land, and all their other property to buy opium. Some even sold their daughters.

The scourge had struck even closer to home, for even my grandfather, learned man though he was, had become an addict during his salt-trade years. Determined to kick his addiction, he asked my grandmother to stand by him and then shut himself up in the family's ancestral hall, where the tablets of the dead were kept, with only his bedding and twenty pots of flowers. My grandmother brought him food morning, noon and night, but for many days he left it untouched. Sometimes she took my father along, and he had to watch helplessly as his father writhed and groaned on the cement floor like a terrified hog brought to slaughter.

After two weeks my grandfather's body finally rid itself of the narcotic and his hellish struggle ended. For the rest of his life, he was happiest working in the fields alongside his hired hands. The event had a profound influence on my father. He never touched cigarettes and scowled whenever opium was mentioned.

"It's our generation's responsibility to eliminate the foreign treaties and to transform the new republic into a strong nation," Pong told my father during those evenings in his room. "China must rise up. The revolution has given China a new destiny."

One night while they were speaking, Pong took his scissors and cut off my father's queue. The traditional long, braided "pigtail" was imposed by the Manchus. But during the early, burgeoning years of the revolution, it had become a reminder of China's humiliation under the Manchus. Men who continued to wear the queue were seen as feudal and behind the times. Some of the more zealous revolutionaries used to carry scissors and cut off the queues of the men they came across on the street.

My father picked up his queue that now lay at his feet. He held it up and stared at it for several seconds. "I'm for the Republic all the way," he said, and without pause for sentiment, dumped it into the trash basket.

Pong also believed that education was crucial to the survival of the new republic. For thousands of years learning had meant the classics, the purpose of which was to make a man a better man in the context of dynastic China. The neglect of the sciences and technology in classical Confucian education had left China backward, making it vulnerable to both aggressive foreign powers and its own corrupt, despotic rulers.

My father heeded Pong's words and decided to take the examinations for admission to Guangzhou University. He rented a room near the barracks, searched through the bookstores, bought the books he needed, and spent the next four months studying. He was admitted to the special law class, but within a month the money Ahnai had given him was gone, and he had to withdraw.

Then he learned that Huangpu Junior Cadet Academy—founded during the final years of the Manchu reign as part of a belated program of reform and modernization—was recruiting students. This class would be the first to be admitted since the founding of the republic. The cadets would receive a free education, free board, and free uniforms.

Thousands of young men from all over Guangdong and beyond signed up to take the examination, but only 120 were admitted. My father was among them, and in time his class was to become a "Who's Who" of that era of China.

His success in that examination sealed his future. He would become a soldier.

At the Huangpu cadet school, he learned that obedience was the essence of military discipline. He also learned that discipline, patience, and the ability to endure hardship were the core of a good soldier. Because of his slender build, he lacked his classmates' physical prowess, and for a while he doubted that he had the stamina for the drills and exercises demanded of cadets. Nevertheless, his earnestness and effort gained him support from his teachers, who encouraged him to persist. He graduated second in his class in 1914. His next goal was to further continue his education.

In the fall of 1914 he began attending the Number Two Wuchang Military Preparatory School in Hubei Province, a training program that readied young men to compete for a place at the nation's top military academy, the Baoding Army Officers School in Hebei Province. At the Wuchang school his strongest subjects were mathematics and the classics. In fact, his outstanding achievements were to change the school's grading system. When his classics instructor found one of his compositions far superior to two others to which he had already given the top grade of 100, he scored my father's work 120. From then on, the school adopted 120 as its highest standard of literary excellence.

At about this time, my father and many of his classmates became embroiled in a growing movement against Yuan Shikai. Yuan, a premier and the most powerful general in the Manchu court, had been instrumental in forcing the boy Emperor Hsuantung to abdicate. To entice Yuan to execute the plot, Sun Yatsen had consented to give up his provisional presidency so that Yuan could become the first president of the republic. But it soon became clear that Yuan wanted to become emperor.

My father had joined Sun's Alliance for the Chinese Revolution, the forerunner to what would become the Guomindang, China's Nationalist Party, swearing his allegiance to the alliance and to the republic. In 1915, my father joined the Nationalist Party. He and more than a hundred of his classmates crossed over from Wuchang to the city of Hankou. There, they were sworn in at a secret meeting in Hankou's Japanese concession, which housed the headquarters of the anti-Yuan movement for the area. The area was technically outside Chinese jurisdiction because of the imperialist principle of extraterritoriality, which dictated that foreign settlements were under the control of their home government.

By then the Nationalist Party had been driven underground by Yuan and turned to clandestine activities, including recruiting the Wuchang cadets, in the hope that they would spread the revolutionary movement to the regular troops.

In March 1916, Yuan staged a coup and proclaimed himself emperor.

During the subsequent crackdown in the Wuchang school, a number of cadets suspected of participating in the anti-Yuan movement were arrested. My father escaped along with many of his classmates. He managed to do so by slashing his thigh with a knife and soaking his handkerchief with the blood. Pretending to have coughed up the blood, he got a pass to go to the city hospital. Once in the city, he made it across the Yangtze River over to Hankou.

There he met up with six of his classmates and the Reverend Robert E. Wood, minister of St. Michael's Church in Wuchang. Wood, a supporter of Sun's revolution, gave the young men Bibles, disguised them as seminarians, and led them onto the train to Shanghai, more than a day's journey away. Once they reached Shanghai, my father and a number of other cadets hid out in the French concession with relative safety.

My father remained in Shanghai for six months. During his time there, he received word that his beloved mentor Pong Yuhua had been killed while taking part in an anti-Yuan skirmish in Guangdong. His death affected my father as deeply as had Pong Hong's martyrdom.

Back during his studies at Huangpu and Wuchang, my father had earned pocket money by selling short stories to newspapers and magazines. He had published these under several pen names because the school authorities frowned on activities that took the cadets away from their studies. Now, to support himself while in Shanghai, my father sold a novel, *Shaumeiyin* (Shadows of Plum Blossoms on the Snow), that ran in a daily newspaper as a serial. He had written the martial arts novel at the Wuchang military school. As each chapter was finished, his classmates would copy the pages and circulate them to the other cadets, who read them enthusiastically. The novel was never published in book form, and the manuscript, which was kept in a safe in our house in Guangzhou, was lost after the city fell to the Japanese in October 1938. All that remained were a couple of poems, which were recorded in Father's diaries.

Yuan Shikai's imperial dream collapsed when he fell ill and died eighty-one days into his reign. The authorities reopened the Wuchang military school, and the cadets who had escaped and were expelled were now exonerated and reinstated. My father and his comrades returned to their studies. The following year, my father was admitted to Baoding Military Academy, located in southern Hebei Province. He concentrated in studies on the infantry, and in the summer of 1919 he graduated with honors at the age of twenty-four.

My father always spoke of his eight years in cadet school as the most carefree time of his life. His only unpleasant memory was the stink of the cadets' goatskin winter coats at the Baoding school. The school lacked heat, so the cadets wore their coats everywhere, indoors as well as out. But because the doors and windows in the classrooms and mess hall were kept closed to keep out drafts and seal in any heat, the stench of poorly processed goatskin was hard to bear.

Immediately after he graduated, my father was recruited by Yan Xishan, the military governor of Shanxi Province in the north, and named an editor of the army's military magazine. Three months later, my father asked for medical leave and went to Beijing to seek treatment for his hearing problem, which was growing worse. Unfortunately, the treatment failed.

My father had lost his hearing while he was a cadet at Huangpu, when he went to a street-corner practitioner to have his ears cleaned—a practice that was customary in that era. Unfortunately, the man punctured both eardrums with his seven-inch-long iron pick. My father felt some pain, and blood oozed from his ears, but he was young and didn't think much about it. In later years his hearing problem was exacerbated by bomb explosions in battlefields. He admitted that he had come to dread meetings and military briefings. "Imagine a commander who can't hear and has to rely on an aide or colleague to tell him what's being discussed," he told me.

When I read his diaries after his death, I found several entries in which he wrote that his hearing loss was so traumatic and frustrating to him that he had contemplated suicide at times.

Before returning to the army, he went back home to visit his family. Although he had returned home several times on earlier occasions, while studying at the Baoding Military Academy, the school was far away from his family's home in Wuchuan County and he had not been back in some time.

He found his mother and his siblings subsisting on a diet of rice mixed with taro and yams, like the poor peasants. During all his time away, his mother's letters had been reassuring if not cheerful. He later learned that when he wrote to her and told her he was entering cadet school, she had been both pleased and worried. But she had kept her misgivings to herself and always wrote back encouraging letters, telling him to study hard and to always remember that service to their country was his supreme duty as a soldier. Never once had she mentioned that the family was destitute.

Consumed with guilt, my father resigned his service for Governor Yan and took a job teaching geography and physical education in the Wuchuan county high school for six months. He used his earnings to buy seed and fertilizer for the family rice farm. The next crop brought in enough money that his mother could hire a few more farm hands to work in the fields.

By the mid-1920s, Chiang Kaishek was a rising star in Sun Yatsen's revolutionary coalition. Sun valued him and depended upon him because, despite Sun's prestige, he lacked an army; he had no real influence over the warlords, and his revolutionary comrades were divided. Sun realized that he alone could not unify the country and, in 1923, recognizing Chiang's talent and commitment as a revolutionary military leader, sent him to the Soviet Union to study the organization and training of the Red Army. The following year when Chiang returned, Sun appointed him superintendent of the newly established Whampoa Military Academy in Guangzhou. This appointment enabled Chiang to build a strong following among the student officers. The so-called Whampoa clique would become the core of his power base and a powerful political asset in the years to come.

Between 1917 and 1927, often referred to as the warlord era, civil war raged throughout China. Today, more than seventy years later, it is difficult to conceive of the almost complete chaos that prevailed in China during that time. Lines of allegiance were not always clear. The schisms and shifts within the Nationalist Party and among the warlords changed kaleidoscopically. Allies became foes and then allies again almost overnight, and many warlords doubled as revolutionaries at the same time. The most powerful warlords, most of them provincial governors and military leaders who had held absolute power within their territories under the Manchus, occupied whole provinces. The constant change in alliances would bring about new configurations, and with each new configuration came new animosities and often bloodshed.

The warlords controlled much of China's northern territories from Manchuria to Beijing. Sun, along with his allies in the revolutionary government and their many competing factions, held the southwest stretching from Guangdong to Yunnan Province. The revolutionaries were just as divided. They battled the warlords, battled among themselves, and battled the Communists. The chaos was such that time and again there would be two simultaneous governments in China—one in Guangzhou, identified with the southern revolutionaries, and the other, in Beijing, a reconfiguration of some of the northern warlords after Yuan's demise. The rest of China was divided among the remaining warlords who conquered each other and annexed each other's holdings. The partitioning of China begun by the foreign powers in the 1860s was now complete.

My father experienced his first battle in July 1924—with civil war raging throughout much of China—in the vicinity of Lian County north of Xijiang. The foe was the warlord Chen Tientai, who was a former commander of the Seventh Army based west of

Guangdong in the northern coastal province of Guangxi and who was bent on extending his power east into the coastal province.

By this time, my father was twenty-nine and a battalion commander in the Third Division's Sixth Brigade. He and his battalion of about a thousand men were ordered out into battle along with several regiments of three to four thousand men each.

He was excited to be facing battle at last, but, when the time finally came, he found the carnage of warfare horrifying. Fireballs thundered from the cannons, sending thick columns of black smoke rising to the sky as my father led his men against the enemy. Pistols cracked like firecrackers. Soldiers wielded swords and machetes, crying "*Sha! Sha! Sha!* Kill! Kill! Kill!" During the course of that day, the world around him became one vast, bloody mess.

A passing soldier, seeing that my father had lost his helmet, took off his own and put it on his head, then ran ahead through the smoke into the melee. A moment later the soldier lurched and fell to the ground. My father, dodging a hail of whining bullets, ran past the soldier's motionless body. He later discovered that his own red neckerchief, a color identification worn by officers and men, bore two clean bullet holes. Miraculously he had not been hit.

When at last the guns fell silent, broken bodies and torn limbs lay scattered across the hilly plain; the stench of decayed flesh filled the air. As the life ebbed out of them, the wounded moaned and writhed on the shattered field. Those who could move tried to crawl to safety.

My father never forgot the heavy loss of life on both sides. For the rest of his life, he spoke of this initiation into warfare as "flesh, blood and ashes." He mourned the hundreds of young men who had forfeited their lives. Most of them had never chosen to go to war, but rather had been thrown into battle by fate.

"Those whom we killed were nameless and faceless," he would say. "We knew them only as enemies. We fought the warlords, fought our rivals, fought the bandits, fought our friends who had become our foes. I killed and I ordered my soldiers to kill. It was either us or the enemy."

In this and other battles that followed, the number of bodies left on the field equaled or outnumbered the survivors, and often those who did survive were left utterly broken. Over the years, my father often thought about the unknown man who had given up his helmet to save his life. He kept the red neckerchief with its two bullet holes as a reminder of that first battle and of the valiant soldier's gift. Many a night his dreams echoed with the cries of the dead soldiers and the wailing of their grieving parents, wives and children.

In the summer of 1925, on the grounds of having failed to follow Nationalist Party policy, Chiang ordered the Third Division to disarm. Many of the officers were dismissed; my father was among those retained. This power struggle only deepened my father's increasing misgivings about the army.

He was becoming aware of and disillusioned by the rampant graft, corruption, and injustice. One common form of graft was procuring provisions and salaries for nonexistent troops. Officers who lacked an independent income found it difficult to support their families, and, of course, simple human avarice was very much at work.

Nepotism was also rampant. China's traditional principle of filial loyalty—the supreme obligation to protect and take care of one's family in all matters—had made nepotism a way of life for centuries. In the military, it only deepened the great rift between "the elite army"—which received better equipment and better supplies of food, clothes, medicine, and desirable goods, and which belonged to the supreme commander—and "the others." Commanders appointed their relatives and cronies to posts in their command, and through them they exerted as much control as they could over all available resources.

He saw that the process of conscription was rife with injustice. Most soldiers were conscripts who were poor peasants chosen by lottery. By paying off corrupt officials or paying poor families to send their own sons instead, wealthy families could keep their sons out of the army. New inductees with their hands tied behind their backs were marched to the army at gunpoint by the local militia and then forced to stand at attention while the commanding army officers "welcomed" them.

"Down with the warlords!" the officers would shout. "Support the Central Government!"

The inductees wept as they mouthed the slogans. They were needed at home to till the soil and care for their parents. They could not understand why they were being sent to fight their countrymen. Recruits received only minimal training, subsistence rations, and a rifle. Most looked upon conscription as a death sentence.

My father soon realized that, in war, victory and defeat meant not only blood, guts, and hatred for the enemy, but also intrigue and struggles for power and the spoils of war. Sickened by the slaughter he had witnessed in battle and by the greed and corruption he saw everywhere in the army, he grew more and more uncertain about the army officer's path he had taken.

So in late summer 1925 he took a leave from the army and retreated to the Baiyun Monastery in the Xichiao Mountains southwest of Guangdong.

At the Baiyun monastery, my father shaved his head. He donned gray robes he had borrowed and joined the monks in their chanting. Three times a day for the next two months he sat in the lotus position, folded his hands, and meditated, emptying his mind of worldly thoughts so that he might gain enlightenment.

The monastery was a spiritual haven where flickering incense lent its fragrance to the tranquil air. There, all forms of life were sacred. The monks strove not to kill any living creature, not even the mosquitoes that sucked the blood from their bodies or killed them with malaria, for Buddha taught the oneness of life in all beings. Chirping birds and buzzing cicadas punctuated the resonant chants of the gray-robed Buddhist monks and offered a counterpoint to the chiming bells that marked the times for prayer and offerings.

When he was not meditating, my father studied the Buddhist path by reading sutras and Buddhist scriptures. The serenity of the monastery and the hours of prayer and contemplation comforted him. He began to wonder whether he should embrace Buddhism in its fullness and contemplated living the solitary life of a monk. He went to the abbot for guidance.

"What do you seek in Buddha?" asked the abbot in a soft voice. His face was peaceful, and he held a string of prayer beads between his palms. His shaved head was dotted with the pea-sized scars of the ritual incense burns he had received when he had taken his vows and renounced the world.

"I seek nothingness," answered my father, "for all things are dust."

"What do you seek in life?"

"I seek goodness in man, and to be just and compassionate to all men."

"There is a conflict between what you seek in Buddha and what you seek in life," the abbot replied. "In embracing Buddha, you must have everything and desire nothing. Go and do good in this life. Walk in Buddha's footsteps so that in the next life you too may become a buddha."

Buddhist studies taught my father that each of us must act and live by what we discover to be true, because our life remains a matter of personal choice. "Be a lamp unto yourself," Buddha said, meaning that we must remain true to ourselves rather than to organizational dictates, for it is our actions as individuals that matter. As my father studied, pondered, and prayed, he kept remembering Sun Yatsen's deathbed admonition that "the revolution had yet to succeed; all comrades must strive onward."

My father's soul yearned for Buddha, but his heart beat for his country. He wanted to see China become strong and free, to throw off the shame she had suffered under a century of imperialism. He wanted his countrymen to have food to eat, protection from oppression, and safety for their families. His two kinsmen Pong Hong and Pong Yuhua had loved their country, had fought for it, and had given their young lives so that China might be free of feudal bondage and foreign oppression. My father felt he could do no less.

He knew that in Buddhism he could seek truth and goodness, not by withdrawing from the world, but rather by living compassion for all in the course of his daily life, whatever it might be.

If my father never fully reconciled his spiritual convictions with his patriotic, political, and revolutionary ones, it was nevertheless those beliefs that allowed him to be both a Buddhist and a soldier for his entire life.

Buddha also said, "The man who talks much of his teaching but does not live it himself is like a herder counting someone else's cattle." So in December my father renewed his pledge to the revolution and to the Nationalist Party, and returned to the army in Guangzhou.

Soon after his return, he joined the Fourth Army's Twelfth Division at the invitation of Zhang Fakui, a deputy commander and one of his old Huangpu classmates. My father became chief of staff of the Fourth Army's Thirty-sixth Regiment.

In the summer of 1926, the Fourth Army was one of five armies totaling about 50,000 men mobilized by Chiang Kaishek in what would become the first Northern Expedition against the warlords. Chiang had recently been appointed supreme commander of all Nationalist armed forces, and he now boasted the rank of "Generalissimo." The expedition's goal mission was to unify the country and specifically to eliminate the warlord Wu Peifu, who was based in Wuchang. With a force of 50,000 troops, Wu controlled large areas of the central Chinese provinces of Southern Hubei and Hebei.

For two months my father's regiment fought fiercely against Wu's forces, first in Dingxiqiao and then later in Hoshinqiao, in Hebei. When my father entered Hoshinqiao, he saw two bloody heads dangling from the branches of a willow tree outside the city's main gate. Before Wu retreated in his armored tank, he had ordered two of his commanders executed for cowardice, as a warning to others.

The Fourth Army then moved on to Wuchang and reached its outskirts in mid-August. There the troops joined 30,000 others that had massed for the assault on the city.

Located in Hubei Province at the confluence of the Yangtze and Han rivers, Wuchang was an industrial center still protected behind ancient walls many feet thick. My father's regiment was one of two that were ordered to scale the walls, but Wu's troops kept up such heavy fire from their protected positions that the attempts failed. The losses were so heavy that the command quarter ordered them to abandon a frontal attack and institute a blockade. As food supplies dwindled, many of Wu's troops tried to escape, only to be captured and killed or forced back behind the walls.

Four weeks into the siege, just as Wuchang seemed on the verge of surrender, comradeship turned into treachery. On October 1, the Twelfth Division, including my father's regiment, was suddenly ordered to Jinniu by the commander-in-chief at the front, also in Hubei Province, ostensibly to reinforce the Nationalist revolutionary forces in Jiangxi. But no sooner had the division arrived than it was ordered back to Wuchang.

It was then learned that Generalissimo Chiang Kaishek had forbidden any unit of the Fourth Army to leave Wuchang without his personal approval. By the time the division got back to Wuchang, the commander in chief at the front had negotiated Wu Peifu's surrender and taken credit for the capture of Wuchang, which was to become the first major victory in the Northern Expedition.

A few months later, Chiang ordered the Fourth Army to be stationed in Wuchang. When the news reached the city, the cheering citizens sounded gongs and set off firecrackers. At the welcoming ceremony, the city elders presented the commanders with a plaque that lauded it as *Tieh Chun*—the "iron" Army—for its bravery, discipline, and integrity.

During this era, some armies were notorious for pillaging and stealing from the peasants, often with the tacit or open encouragement of their commanding officers. Wherever they were, the soldiers of the Fourth Army treated the people with respect and did their best to help them, protect them, and win them over to the Nationalist revolution. My father and his fellow officers made it their job to meet with the city elders to explain the goals of Sun's revolution and try to persuade them to support the cause.

By this time, the Communist Party, founded in 1920 by Li Dazhao and Chen Dujui, had become an important presence in national politics. The party had gained strength and legitimacy because of Sun Yatsen's policy of cooperation, which had been adopted in 1924. Sun's death the following year brought out into the open the deep mistrust that many of his followers felt regarding the Communists and the possibilities of Nationalist-Communist cooperation. Chief among these antagonists was Chiang Kaishek. Between 1927 and 1937, while Japan was launching its aggression in China, Chiang mounted five campaigns to eliminate the Communists as a political force. Thousands of captured Communist Party members and suspected sympathizers were killed, and still more were jailed or driven to remote areas of the country. Among those executed was Yang Kaihui, the first wife of Hunan-born Communist Mao Zedong, who barely escaped with his life. Because Mao believed that support from China's vast feudal peasantry would be the key to the success of Communism, he focused on organizing in the countryside. Over time, in no small part because its soldiers helped them instead of stealing from them, and because of its propaganda slogan, "land for the peasants," the Red Army gained support from the peasants.

At the time of the First Northern Expedition, the Communists were actively pushing for the abolition of the holdings of the landlords and the expulsion of foreign imperialists from Nanjing, Shanghai, and Wuhan, through instigating demonstrations and fomenting strikes.

In January 1927 my father and a number of other Fourth Army

officers and troops stationed in Wuchang were on hand in nearby Wuhan, when the Nationalist government negotiated the return of the city's British concessions to Chinese control. My father always treasured his memory of the widespread street celebrations as the people rejoiced over this symbol of newborn national integrity.

In April 1927 Communists in Shanghai were organizing strikes and demonstrations to take over the city. Chiang ordered his troops to seize the city and liquidate the Communists. Several hundred men were captured and shot. As the Communists continued agitating in many cities, Wang Jinwei, who was the number two man under Sun Yatsen, and who had previously sided with Nationalist-Communist cooperation, joined forces with Chiang and called a top-level conference at Lushan, a mountain resort 118 kilometers southwest of Wuhan. The conference was to devise a strategy to purge the Communists, thus rejecting Sun's policy of cooperation, because both factions saw the Communists as a serious threat.

My father, who by then had been named commander of the Fourth Army's Twenty-fifth Division, was among the divisional commanders summoned to the conference. Two weeks before the conference was to begin, he had met with Ye Ting, a divisional commander in the Eleventh Army. Ye Ting was one of his closest comrades-at-arms, for they had fought side by side in Dingxiqiao, Hoshinqiao, and Wuchang. Ye Ting said he believed that cooperation between the Nationalists and the Communists was essential if the warlords were to be defeated; he then asked my father which side he would take, should the increasingly fragile alliance collapse.

"In principle, I agree with the policy of cooperation," my father replied. "But if there's a rift, I'll remain loyal to the Nationalist Party, and follow orders. . . . And you?"

My father found it odd when Ye Ting merely laughed and changed the subject, but he gave it little thought. The following evening Ye invited my father to a dinner for a group of commanders from various branches of the army. Among them were He Long, commander in chief of the Twentieth Army, Ye Jianying, another Fourth Army commander, and Zhu De, who would later lead the Long March with Mao.

The evening was one of high-spirited banter, and no one mentioned politics. My father later said that he hadn't known it at the time, but he was the only army officer present who was not secretly a Communist.

The night before the conference was to begin, on July 31, 1927, all the other commanders had reported except Ye Ting and He Long. It turned out that He and Ye, having managed for years to conceal their true loyalties, had summoned their troops to take part in the uprising that the Communists had long planned in the city of Nanchang.

That December, a second Communist uprising took place in Guangzhou. While the troops were ordered to Guangxi, Ye Jianying, who had been left in charge of the Fourth Army's Guangzhou command post, joined with the Communists in an attempt to take over the city. The rebels attacked the municipal government buildings and the Bureau of Public Security—the police headquarters. Government forces quickly put down the uprising, but the killing that followed plunged the city into turmoil and terror. "It was horrific that so many innocent people died in the massacre," my father noted in his diary. "Shops were closed and the people retreated to their homes, not daring to go out into the streets. For days the slaughter went on. Thousands of Communists, suspected Communists and innocent bystanders were gunned down virtually at random. The government forces had orders to shoot on sight anyone seen wearing a red armband or red scarf—in fact, anyone wearing even a trace of red."

The direct involvement of Fourth Army commanders with the Communists left the army on shaky ground. Chiang branded the Fourth Army a Communist nest; he fired its commander in chief, Zhang Fakui, and replaced him with Liao Peinan, one of Zhang's division commanders. To escape the very real possibility of reprisals, Zhang and his deputy Huang Chichiang fled first to Hong Kong and then to Japan.

Because they felt shamed and betrayed, the animosity against the Fourth Army was strongest among the commanders of the other armies based in Guangdong. So, by volunteering to take part in the Third Northern Expedition, which began in January 1928, the Fourth's commanders tried to salvage its reputation and prove its loyalty. My father was with the troops who had left Guangzhou when they were attacked by the forces of the powerful General Chen Zitang. Chen, known as the "Southern Emperor," was the leader of a powerful Guangdong faction and regarded the Fourth Army as being a troublemaker inside his domain.

"We had to fight bitterly to defend ourselves against many of our former classmates and allies," my father was to recall decades later, his sadness still evident. "The hatred we had for each other made our fighting more ferocious than when we had gone against the war-lords. We were mercilessly pursued. We survived only because our endurance was greater than the enemy's."

For the next three months my father led his exhausted, shivering men thousands of kilometers northward across the provinces of Gansu, Anhui, and Jiangsu. The winter cold was bitter. Rain or shine, the mustard-green line of troops plodded through the hills and the valleys, each man carrying his own bedroll, rice, and ammuni-tion. Two-man teams hauled machine guns, boxes of cartridges, medical supplies, and cooking cauldrons on shoulder poles.

As the days dragged on, food grew scarcer. The soldiers added water in cooking the rice to make a thin porridge, and they added sweet potatoes or whatever other food was available. Weak from mal-nutrition, lacking warm clothes, shod only in straw sandals, they struggled forward on frostbitten feet with the flesh on their heels and toes hardening into the painful sores that the Chinese call "radishes."

Although army regulations stated that combat troops were to receive provisions and supplies from the central government, the troops of the Fourth Army had none. For more than a month they went without winter jackets and blankets. The northward trek would have been grueling at any time, but for the men of the Fourth Army, natives of the warm climate of the south, the hardships were especially severe.

It took five months, until April, for the Fourth Army to reach Pukou near Nanjing. As the troops arrived at the Pukou station by train, my father heard gunfire close by and realized that his men were to be sent into combat immediately. But they were in no con-dition to fight; they had already suffered so much in the battles with Chen's troops as well as from cold and malnutrition.

When my father asked his superior Liao Peinan for a week of rest and recuperation for his troops, Liao, a new commander who might have felt that he needed to prove himself a tough leader, denied the request.

My father had long suspected that the Nationalist central gov-ernment's high military command was engaged in a deliberate attempt to annihilate the Fourth Army. Now he was convinced. According to an ancient and much-respected Chinese tradition, any official or general who found his conscience to be in direct opposition to the will of his emperor or superior could honorably resign his post and return to his native soil to farm.

After Liao's refusal, my father chose this as his only recourse. When he learned that Chiang Kaishek was arriving to address the troops the next day, he wrote a letter stating that the high command's treatment of his troops was both cruel to the men and detrimental to the welfare of the country. He then tendered his resignation on the grounds that he refused to sacrifice thousands of men in such an inhumane manner.

He instructed his deputy to deliver the letter to Chiang and placed his deputy in command of the division. Then he put his belongings into a backpack, left the camp on foot and accompanied by only one aide, and got on a train to Shanghai; from there he boarded a ship to Japan and joined Zhang Fakui and his other Fourth Army comrades who were already in exile.

My father was to remain in Japan for the next seven months. During that time he came to believe that this country was far more disciplined than China, its people better educated, and its military science and technology far more advanced. In addition, the Japanese enjoyed more freedom of speech than did the Chinese.

Mount Fuji was as glorious and enchanting as he had imagined. The sight of its snowy peak caressing the sky brought peace to his soul. When he visited a temple close by, he felt as if he were back at the Baiyun Monastery. He lit incense for all dead soldiers—his own as well as the enemy's—and bowed to the ground amidst the ringing of the bells and the sonorous chanting.

While in Tokyo, he also sought treatment for his hearing loss from the two best-known ear specialists in the city, but to no avail. He was preparing to go to Germany to seek treatment when he began receiving letters from his comrades in China urging him to return. It was time to come back, they told him, as the Nationalist revolution was still to be won. So in December 1928, he returned.

By the time he resumed his position as chief of staff, the Fourth Army had been scaled down by two-thirds to become the Fourth Division, with little more than three thousand men. It was now stationed in the northeastern province of Shandong.

The cuts had resulted both from the loss of soldiers who had died in battle and from the Nationalist high command's refusal to provide new recruits. Clearly, Chiang would never forget the complicity of the Fourth Army commanders in the Nanchang and Guangzhou uprisings the previous year.

When Chiang ordered the division cut by one more regiment, the commanders realized that further reductions lay ahead. In protest, the division and regimental commanders sent a telegram to Chiang requesting that the Fourth Division be disbanded entirely. Chiang denied the request and then proceeded to order cut after cut until the division was reduced to a single training regiment of about one thousand men.

In February 1929 my father took sick leave and went to Hong Kong to be treated for a mild lung ailment. After barely a month in Hong Kong, his leave was canceled and he was ordered back to duty; another civil war had broken out. This time the enemy was Li Zongren, an ally of the Northern Expedition and a dominant member of the Guangxi faction. Li had used his position as head of the Wuhan Political Commission in dismissing the governor of Hunan Province without authorization from the central government. It plunged the country into yet another round of conflict.

Chiang's forces, the newly reconstituted Fourth Division included, went on to win what was referred to as the "Chiang-Li War." As the kaleidoscope turned, twenty years later, after Chiang lost the battle of Waihai and was retreating to Taiwan just before the 1949 Communist Revolution, Li, who was then Chiang's vice president, was to become acting president of the Republic of China.

Japan's goal of conquering China had already manifested itself in early 1915 with Japan's Twenty-one Demands. When World War I broke out, Japan took advantage of the situation by attacking Germany's leasehold Jiaozhou in Shandong. In 1919, the Versailles Treaty awarded Shandong, Germany's concession in China, to Japan. This was over China's protest and the fact that China had sent 175,000 laborers overseas, mostly to France, to help the Allies in fighting the war, digging trenches, and burying the dead. On September 18, 1931, known as 918 in Chinese history, Japanese forces seized Mukden in northwest Manchuria. Japan then occupied all large cities in Manchuria and continued to expand its operations, now occupying Jehol Province.

Early in 1932, the Japanese attacked Shanghai. The Nineteenth Army—a Guangdong faction over which Chiang Kaishek had no control—fought the Japanese for two months. There were no reinforcements from Chiang. Losing many men and having no more ammunition, the Nineteenth Army retreated to Fujian on China's southern coast. There its commanders proclaimed the establishment of an independent republic, which was quickly liquidated by Chiang.

In the meantime, Japan had created the puppet regime Manchukuo, which consisted of Manchuria and Jehol Province. The last Manchu emperor, Hsuantung, was installed under the name of Pu Yi. In 1935, Japan, having occupied most of the area, tried to create a North China autonomous region of five provinces that included Chahar, Suiyuan, Shandong, Shanxi and Hebei. It was then that China decided that it would no longer put up with Japan's aggression—and would fight. Still, Chiang Kaishek persisted in looking at Japan's aggression as a disease of the skin, with Communism being a disease of the heart.

Because of Chiang's hesitation in declaring war against Japanese aggression, he was kidnapped, on December 12, 1936, by the young marshall Zhang Xueliang in what was known as the Xian Incident. The incident forced Chiang to unite his Nationalist forces with the Communists in the fight for national survival in the resistance war against Japan's invasion.

When my father became Pacification Commissioner, whose job was to maintain peace and order, first of Guangdong's Northwest District, in 1932, and then the Eastern District, in 1935, he was under the command of General Chen Jitang, the "Southern Emperor." The Eastern District encompassed twenty-six counties and the seaport Shantou, which was a troublesome spot. For years Japanese merchants had been smuggling goods by ship through the eastern tip of Shantou port. Just as my father became Pacification Commissioner of the Eastern District, the magistrate of Chiehyang confiscated a large quantity of rice, beans, and oil that had been smuggled in by Japanese profiteers.

Japan immediately sent its Fifth Torpedo Fleet to Shantou. Commander Shimomuro led seven torpedo boats into the harbor and demanded that my father account for the confiscation.

My father, who was the area's chief military commander and who also oversaw civil administration, boarded the Japanese warship with a company of guards, grenades strapped to their waists; a battalion of soldiers stood watching from the pier. Like two wrestlers trying to feel each other out, Shimomuro and my father faced each other on the deck of the Japanese gunboat.

"You must know that Japanese merchants who smuggle goods into Chinese territory are violating Chinese law. Without exception, Shantou is entitled to a customs duty on all imports. Japanese smuggling must stop." My father spoke through his interpreter.

Shimomuro—short, lean and taut, his men behind him, bayonets shimmering in the sun—surveyed the men who had come on board before he spoke through his translator. "I come by the order of the Emperor of the Japanese Empire to protect the rights of Japanese merchants."

Firm but courteous, my father told Shimomuro that reasonable men ought to resolve what had led to the confrontation between the two sides, respecting the rights and sovereignty of both China and Japan. He then invited Shimomuro to discuss the matter at his headquarters.

Shimomuro met with my father at the Pacification Commission's headquarters several times. "We exchanged our views as individuals rather than representative authorities," my father was to record in his diary. "We agreed that the case would be handled by the Shantou Municipal Government and Chaozhou-Meixian Bureau of Customs and the Japanese Consulate."

The Bureau of Customs and the Japanese Consulate reached an agreement: the confiscated goods would be returned to the Japanese owners; the owners would pay customs duties; Japanese merchants would pay customs on all future imports to Shantou municipality. After that, Japanese import taxes paid to Shantou increased almost twenty-fold. Before the Japanese torpedo fleet left the harbor, Shimomuro presented my father with a large Japanese vase as an expression of his esteem.

Elated over the settlement, the commission staff and my father celebrated in a local restaurant, drinking and blowing off steam and the tension of the previous weeks. A waiter brought out a tray with a plate of a dozen little silky pink mice squirming feebly and held it out to my father.

"I dare you all to wash down these tiny live mice with this Shaoxin wine," said my father's deputy commander, his face already flush with alcohol. "This is a local specialty of Chaozhou. No different than eating raw oysters."

"Good stuff, good stuff. Good for your health," cheered the jolly waiter in a spotted apron, a portly man with a moon face, whose eyes disappeared into a thin line as he grinned.

"Come on, come on, chief, you are the bravest," bellowed the deputy commander, ordinarily a man of few words, but a bit tipsy and boisterous this night. At the moment he was extremely loose and relieved, since he would have had to take control of the situation had there been an explosion on the boat. "Watch me!" He picked up a tiny pink mouse with his fingers, dropped it into his wine cup, and with one big swallow he emptied the contents and then poured himself another cup of wine.

The rest of the officers, my father included, looked at each other. Then suddenly, everyone picked up a mouse and tossed it down with a gulp of wine. For the rest of the evening, it was all challenges and acts of machismo and unabashed laughter. When my father got home that night, he giddily told my mother what he had eaten. Instead of joining him in a good laugh though, he was met with a penetrating glare of shock and disapproval. But how could she really be upset at him after such a close call. They looked back on the drama of the past few days, just happy to have gotten through it. Still, my mother made him promise never to eat live mice again.

A year later, in 1936, my father had a second confrontation with the Japanese with regard to the "Tsunoda Incident," where a Japanese Consulate guard was found dead on the street. The Japanese Consulate claimed that the guard had been killed by a pistol shot—this in spite of the fact that no gunshot wound had been found on the guard's body.

This time, the Third Japanese Fleet stationed in the Shantou harbor immediately fired several hundred rounds in the harbor. Within days, three Japanese admirals arrived with their warships and torpedo boats demanding compensation.

The admirals came to my father's headquarters, warning that the guard's death was a serious matter between Japan and China. Alternating enticement and threats, they spoke of dire consequences should China refuse to pay damages and deliver an apology.

Vice Admiral Oikawa Koshiro, commander of the Third Fleet, handed my father his name card. On the back of the card was a poem by the Chinese poet Shao Xiaofu written in the Song Period nearly one thousand years earlier:

> Why is the path of the road so narrow?
> A narrow path attracts no passerby
> Without passersby, the path becomes more narrow still,
> Thorns spring forth wherever man walks.

Of this meeting, my father wrote in his diary, "Koshiro used the poem to suggest that in the course of one's life, a path should always be open for oneself as well as for others. He was hinting to me that I must open a new path for myself—without saying that there would be war, and that Japan would defeat China."

After my father's death, I came across an envelope among my father's records marked "Important document on the Tsunoda Incident in Shantou" in my father's handwriting. In it I found Koshiro's name card with the poem written in pencil; there was also an officially stamped letter accusing my father of mishandling the matter regarding the guard's death—with the pronouncement that he be held responsible for the consequences.

While the Japanese Consulate pressed its demands for reparation and an apology, my father received no directions from his superior General Chen Zitang, or from the central government. My father saw Japan's demand for an apology as an insult and under no circumstance would he yield to shaming the national honor. He believed unshakably that a soldier's duty was to defend his country. Not wanting to second guess what was in the larger scheme of things and urgently in need of clear directions, on July 2 he sent a telegram to Chen, requesting instructions. The next day he received a single-sentence reply from Chen saying, "You may proceed as you see fit and as the situation permits."

The one-sentence reply revealed a power struggle and an emerging national crisis. While the Generalissimo was delaying the decision both for an all-out fight against Japanese aggression and for annihilating the Communists, Chen was forming an alliance with Li Zongren, a military chieftain of the Guanxi faction, calling their joint forces China's Revolutionary Army of Resistance Against the Japanese Aggression for National Salvation. It was a declaration of separation from Chiang Kaishek's supreme command and the central government, which would draw the country into the imminent danger of civil war on the eve of Japanese invasion.

In Shantou, with the pressure from the presence of the Japanese fleets and Japan's persistent demand for apology and reparations, tension mounted. My father was caught in an untenable situation, and his only recourse was to leave Chen's service. He had already tendered his resignation once before, but Chen had refused to accept it. Instead, Chen, suspecting my father's loyalty, promoted him to Deputy Commander of the Second Army. Since power and the control of troop movements rested with the commander and not the deputy, the promotion effectively removed Father as commander of the Sixth Division.

Unwilling to follow Chen's declaration of independence from the central government, my father acted, putting Shantou on alert with all the forces at his disposal, including the militia. On July 4, he wrote his letter of resignation to Chen, stating that he could not support the position he was taking in risking national security, and urging him to safeguard the honor and integrity of the nation. My father made it clear that he had no other motive than serving his country honorably.

Then he deposited all the funds of the commission in his headquarters' safety box and instructed his aide to telegram his letter to Chen as soon as the boat he was on had left Shantou harbor for Hong Kong.

Secretly, my father instructed my mother to take my brother Shao and me to Hong Kong within forty-eight hours. During the years he was commissioner of the Northeast District, while my father resided in Shantou, my mother lived in Guangzhou with Shao and me. Keeping his engagement promise to my mother, my father had agreed to this arrangement and commuted monthly, so that my mother would be able to study at the Sun Yatsen University. The ladies home economics club had kindled my mother's interest in agriculture. My father persuaded the president of the university Mr. Zhou Lu to open its door to women and the college changed its policy the following year. To help my mother pass the entrance examination, my father hired two teachers to tutor my mother in science and mathematics. My mother was one of the eight female students admitted to the agricultural college in 1935. His telegram instructing my mother to take the family to Hong Kong immediately was transmitted to my mother through Madame Zhou Lu. The Zhous and my parents were trusted friends. To relay the message, Madame Zhou invited my mother to lunch at a restaurant and delivered the telegram to her inside a magazine along with five boat tickets to Hong Kong.

Pregnant with a third child on the way, my mother boarded the boat at the Guangzhou Pier, with my brother and me. Immediately, she took to her bunk and pretended to be sick, pulling the bed sheet and blanket over her head. Soldiers, being alerted that my mother might be planning to leave Guangzhou, came on board the boat to make a cabin-to-cabin search for her. When they came into her cabin, they demanded to know who was lying on the bunk. Our nannies scolded the soldiers and told them not to disturb the woman who was lying in bed, sick with influenza. Deterred, the soldiers turned their attention to the suitcases, poking around at their contents. Not finding anything, they then left. Agents also searched the maternity hospitals in Guangzhou.

A few days later, on July 6, my father sailed for Hong Kong, arriving at noon the next day. Immediately he dispatched a kinsman to Guangzhou to let his sworn-brother Deng Longguang know that he must leave for Hong Kong for his own safety. My father and Deng were from the same home district and had been classmates in cadet schools. They had jointly owned a business property in Guangzhou Bay and once used it as a hotel. Army salaries were miserly, and so those without independent wealth had to find other means to help support their families.

In Guangzhou, Chen ordered the arrest of Deng, whose close friendship with my father made him a suspect. Deng dressed himself in a plain shirt and pants to be inconspicuous, hid in a movie theater, and then escaped for Hong Kong by train.

It was another three days before we joined our father in a hideaway, an apartment on the Peak in Hong Kong that belonged to a friend. Until then, my mother and we children had been hiding in a friend's home overlooking the colonial governor's residence. Three weeks later, my mother gave birth to my sister Chi at the hideaway.

From his hideaway my father dispatched a telegram disclosing his resignation to Chairman Lin Shen and to Generalissimo Chiang Kaishek, pledging his support to the central government and the commander in chief. He released to the press his letter of resignation to Chen. The daily newspapers around the country—which had reported the Tsunoda Incident and the actions of the municipal government, the commission, and my father—immediately picked up the story, hailing it as a *fengginguayin*, after a well-known historical event in the Three Kingdoms in Later Han dynasty about 220 C.E. This was a tumultuous period in China's history that lasted many decades in which military governors and warlords who owed nominal allegiance to the emperor fought for dominance and independence and where treacheries and heroism abounded. Guang Yu, a most able general known for his right conducts and loyalty to neighbors, acted on his conscience and loyalty to his allies. Refusing to be bribed by his adversary, he returned a gift of gold and gave up his seal of authority. Guan's deeds were venerated and immortalized in the *Romance of the Three Kingdoms*, and he continues to be worshipped as a cultural hero.

In Guangzhou, Chen's trusted longtime aide and right-hand man, General Yu Hanmou, broke with Chen. Yu and the commander of Guangdong's air force took off to Nanjing with nine planes, pledging their support to Chiang. At one point, Yu and a group of commanders under Chen, my father included, had held several secret meetings to deliberate the possibility of staging an uprising against their superior Chen. They concluded that their combined forces would not be able to withstand the forces held by Chen.

The crisis of civil war abated when Li Zongren reversed his course, swearing his allegiance to the central government and to the commander in chief Chiang Kaishek. To his credit, Chen gave up his army and power base and left for Hong Kong in voluntary exile, thus sparing the country an internal split. Elsewhere in the country, generals, warlords, Communists and even bandits pledged their support to Chiang as the national leader fighting against Japanese aggression.

After the incident of my father's resignation passed, the central government offered him the mayorship of Guangzhou, which had previously been held by Chen. Declining the offer, my father reiterated what he had said in his letter of resignation: the action he took had not been motivated by personal gain. He would like nothing better than to have his former posts back. His wish was granted.

Back in Shantou, my father had yet another confrontation with the Japanese fleets.

In April 1937, the pretext of the death of a Taiwanese in

Shantou became Japan's excuse for once more demanding compensation and an apology from the Shantou municipal government. When the municipal police arrested a member of the Japanese Consulate staff for failing to procure a residence permit, Japan escalated its demand to now include punishment of the police officers responsible for the arrest and the elimination of the requirement for residence permits. Eight Japanese warships sailed into Shantou harbor, among them an aircraft carrier.

The municipal government refused the demands and so did my father. Anticipating an all-out armed conflict, my father drew up his will and prepared for Shantou to be his burial ground.

The Japanese Consulate took its demands to the provincial governor in Guangzhou, and the governor acquiesced to all the demands. "For the shame China suffered, I could only breathe a long sigh of regret," my father wrote of his anguish over this loss of honor.

Late in the night of July 7, 1937, on the pretext that one of their soldiers was missing, the Japanese demanded permission to enter and search the town of Yuenpin, fifteen kilometers southwest of Beijing.

When the Chinese soldiers refused permission for the search, Japanese soldiers opened fire at Lukuochiao (Marco Polo Bridge) south of Beijing, and Chinese soldiers exchanged fire with them throughout the night. By morning, the Japanese had overtaken the train station. The occupation of the town gave the Japanese control of all the southern rail entries to Beijing.

Ten days after the Lukuochiao Incident, Chiang Kaishek declared, "The final moment had arrived; Chinese must save the nation with no alternative but victory."

Chapter Four

On the Front Line

*I*n the reorganization preparing for war, my father became commander in chief of the Sixy-fourth Army, made up of several divisions, directly under the command of the central government. In August 1937, Father requested active duty for the defense of Nanjing. His request was denied.

Nanjing, the nation's capital, fell in December, and the central government was relocated to Wuhan. In early spring, the Sixty-fourth Army was ordered northward to report to the military headquarters of the First War Zone in Wuhan. My father, after a meeting with the president of the Military Council and supreme commander Chiang Kaishek, moved his troops to Kaifeng in Henan Province in the central plains. The Japanese were targeting the province to gain control of two of China's major railways.

Father reported to General Xue Yue, commander in chief of the First Group Army on the central plains. On May 19, Xue ordered him to take charge of the first front line to retake the occupied town of Luohuang in southern interior of Henan. The town had a medium-sized train station and was prized for controlling the movement of troops and supplies.

Xue had ordered three army divisions to join forces for the assault. One of the Sixty-fourth Army's divisions, the 155th, stormed Luohuang immediately, breaking through the front gate. The infantrymen held the train station for three hours before the enemy pushed them back. The other two divisions from the Twenty-seventh

Army and the Seventy-first Army had not taken up their positions for the assault. On the rumor that Lanfeng County, which was to the south of Luohuang, was lost, they had retreated seventy kilometers instead. Since one million troops were left stranded without transport, this calamity put the entire central plains in danger.

For a second assault to retake Luohuang, Xue placed all three divisions under Father's command, with the authority to execute on the spot any officer up to the rank of division commander who disobeyed an order.

To shield the entrance to Luohuangzai station, the Japanese had lined up the trains to reinforce their defense and placed tanks and armored vehicles behind the train cars. For three days and three nights, Chinese artillery and hand grenades bombarded the enemy. On the morning of May 27, Chinese forces overtook Luohuang station.

Inside the town, fighting continued throughout the day. Each explosion erupted in black smoke and fire; bayonets, rocks and naked hands hacked, chopped and stabbed in hand-to-hand combat. With no anti-aircraft artillery at his disposal, my father watched helplessly as the enemy aircraft—with Japan's head commander of the China theater Doihara on board—ascended to the sky and disappeared into the clouds. In his escape, Doihara left his sword with his personal insignia behind.

The battle of Luohuang marked the first Chinese victory over Japanese occupying forces that reclaimed lost territory. In postbattle euphoria, one of my father's officers stacked ten old coins on a block to test the sharpness of Doihara's sword, which was rumored to cut through steel. With one swing of the sword, the coins split in half.

"The sky was serenely blue," my father was to recall of the Luohuang battle years later. "Dead and broken bodies were all over the streets. Blood caked the cobblestones. For all three divisions and for the enemy, the casualties were heavy. But the heaviest casualties were dealt to the 155th Division. We lost two-thirds of its men." He was ever mindful of the ancient proverb, *Yijiangongchen wangugu*, "A victorious battle rests on ten thousand dried bones." He would later recite this line whenever he reminisced about the battles he fought.

For his leadership in the battle of Luohuang, my father was promoted to commander in chief of the Twenty-ninth Army Corps. But before he had time for a briefing on his new post, he received a telephone call from Xue ordering him to move his troops to Gui-de, which was under siege. Gui-de was a command quarter and a key county to the security of Hankou and the tri-city complex, which included Wuhan, Wuchang, and Hanyang. Unfortunately, Gui-de fell before my father's troops reached the area. With the collapse of a number of fronts, the whole central plain was in crisis.

The supreme command headquarters ordered all troops closer to Hankou and to prepare to retreat to Sichuan Province in the southwest in order to fortify Chungking, the nation's wartime capital. Sitting on a wedge of cliffs, Chungking was a natural fortress protected by thick fog, below which flowed the Jialing and Yangtze rivers serving as transport routes. Its protective location also benefited from Sichuan's fifty million peasants who tilled the fertile fields, keeping the granaries filled and providing rice for soldiers and civilians, including a surplus for needy inland areas.

On May 31, the supreme command headquarters directed my father to reroute within one week to Meixian in Mei County, Henan, west of the Peining-Hankou rail line. Then the central plains command headquarters ordered all forces to pull out of the plains for strategic retreat. Behind the order was the acknowledgment that Chinese ground troops could not match the superior Japanese air and naval power. The strategy was to hold on to southwest China, where the mountainous terrain offered natural protection, and to wear down the enemy by prolonging the war.

My father thought the strategic retreat was the wrong decision, but he was duty-bound to obey orders. Over a million Chinese troops were in the central plains, and victory had been reported on several fronts. At Taierzhuang, under General Li Zongren, several Japanese divisions had been annihilated, and the country rallied. On this retreat, my father bared his anguish in his journal:

> The news of the troops leaving got out to the civilians in no time. Local residents came in delegations and in small groups with their old and young, begging that they not be abandoned. Some threw themselves at my feet, pleading for mercy and protection. Peasants feared that the Japanese would return and kill them all. Frightened, illiterate and defenseless, the peasants asked why the troops were leaving when they had pushed the enemy back and won. The people knew the enemy would burn everything, loot everything and kill everyone. The Nanjing massacre had shown that the peasants

would be gathered up, shot, and thrown into holes they themselves would have to dig. Women would be raped and then mutilated for sport, men and children bayoneted and decapitated for sword practice. They would be left to a merciless enemy. . . . What am I to say? How am I to explain to the people that this is a strategic retreat? How are peasants to understand what a strategic retreat is all about when we commanders do not understand it ourselves?

A day later my father agonized further:

My soul cried out in shame as I watched the peasants plead and wail at their fate. For every town and village we defended, we befriended local residents, enlisted and mobilized their support against the enemy. The townspeople and village peasants collaborated and volunteered as our intelligence agents, fed us information on the movements of the enemy. Mourning for the soldiers who died for their defense, grateful peasants sacrificed their precious chickens and pigs; they burned incense for our dead soldiers in prayer—so that the dead would leave the living world in peace with a full stomach, as their souls made their way into the underworld of the dead.

The Sixty-fourth Army left Henan and retreated southward. On June 8, the dikes of the Yellow River were broken, and the levees, built by the best Chinese engineers, crumbled. The government had ordered the dikes broken to deter the enemy's advance.

The angry river roared, rumbling like trains speeding on dozens of rails all at once. The ground vibrated as houses, trees and tombstones were pushed away in the current. The sky was as bright as the most glorious summer day, but the earth was a muddy sea for as far as the eye could see. Fields and houses were submerged in water, countless animal carcasses stayed afloat, and people fled. The 3,395-mile (5,464 km) Yellow River stretched over six provinces and cut deep into the deposits of sand and loess. The muddiest river in the world, it carries more than two pounds of silt per cubic foot of water and has no mercy when it floods.

The flood uprooted millions of people and brought untold suffering to Henan and four other provinces. Its effects were to linger for decades. Birds had no nests, and fish floated dead in the churning brown water. The raging river made no distinction among species or between rich and poor in its terrible destruction. Mixed in the floating debris were dead snakes, fowl, pigs, goats, and oxen—animals so precious that normally they were slaughtered only for special festivals. Then the sky cracked open, pouring out torrential rain as if crying for the dead.

My father and his troops were under orders to reach Mahueling in Jiangxi Province without delay. They climbed up the hills to avoid the water, carrying grain sacks on their shoulders; they were rationed to one meal a day. Their movements were as slow and hesitant as those of earthworms. Caked with mud, unwashed, stomachs empty, they clung to their weapons and ammunition. For days they walked and waded in the plains and alleys, through the water, seeing countless bloated animal carcasses and human corpses, nauseated by the stench of the decomposing flesh. There was no telling how many people died of drowning, how many died of starvation. Thousands of men in the march were lost to disease and malnutrition. There was no relief, no help given! Life was cheap! Meanwhile the flood and all the suffering temporarily stopped the Japanese army's advancement.

Decades later, my father wrote about his battlefield encounters in an article he entitled "I Am a Passerby on the Battlefield." It was painful for him to remember the flood that resulted from the government's destruction of the dike and the devastation this caused to the people and the land. To him, this was an eternal crime that had no redemption.

The Sixty-fourth Army came to Luoyang, the old capital of the Tang dynasty. For a day the troops rested there, and Father and several of his comrades climbed the scenic mountain. Amidst the tall trees, the rocks and the waterfall, the birds chirped and tranquillity prevailed. They quietly and mournfully talked about the battles they had fought, about the wounded, the dying and the dead, and the villagers who had pleaded with them and those who fled. Hell was lodged in their memories.

Writing for solace as much as to reflect on life and feeling couched between heaven and earth, my father, even under the dire conditions of the battlefield, often wrote poems to allow his emotions to escape. When they descended from the mountain and returned to the camp base, my father wrote the "Toll of Luohuang":

Bloody battle brought demise to the enemy in Luohuang;
Roaring Yellow River flooded central Henan.
Hanging by a hair was the fate of my Motherland;
Dust flown, veiling the eyes.
Righteous mournful combatants should be blessed;
Truth holding fairness shunning prejudice.
Tidings spread throughout the land, joy to my faithful
    countrymen;
Through thorns and blades, the nation's honor saved.

In times of war and in the midst of the most horrible things they have just seen, soldiers seek solace and escape in any way they can. In the aftermath of fresh carnage, my father offered his companions the challenge of composing a poem to match the one with which he commemorated the Luohuang blood bath. On the condition that someone could come forth with a poem within ten minutes, the prize would be a dinner for all the officers when they arrived at their destination. His chief secretary gallantly accomplished the feat.

During a debriefing, the commander in chief of the Fourth War Zone commended my father on his well-fought battles, noting that his tactics were works of art. Father said that the carnage was such that there was no artistry he could speak of, for they'd fought until they were *lauhua liushui*, "like fallen flower petals in a flowing stream." The commander noted that fallen flower petals in flowing streams were indeed art to behold. Then he presented Father with a red banner embroidered with the characters *gang-chun*, "steel army."

In Guangzhou and Hong Kong, my mother was active in raising funds for medicine and supplies for the troops on the front line. Many of the war-relief volunteers were officers' wives and students, as well as movie stars, actors, and society matrons. Donation boxes were placed in bus and train stations, theaters, restaurants and stores, and volunteers solicited contributions from the rich and famous, as well as from ordinary people.

In the summer of 1938 Mother joined a group of eighteen women—officers' wives and society matrons—visiting field hospitals and troop stations. The women wore khaki shirts and jodhpurs, and for two weeks—courtesy of the army—they went by train and by truck through the fighting zones along the Longhai Railway Line. They visited the sick and wounded with gifts of towels, powdered milk, and blankets; they greeted troops and presented each soldier with a cash gift of two yuan. At one stop, they presented five ambulances and medical supplies—purchased with donated money—to field hospitals.

At all hours of the day and night, the wounded were brought in trucks and on stretchers to the temples and ancestral halls that had been converted to temporary military hospitals. The field hospitals lacked supplies and proper facilities. My mother saw the wounded lying groaning on straw on the ground, some with limbs missing, some with burned and ulcerated bodies and feverish faces, their cracked lips dry and puffy. A putrid smell of dried blood, body stench, gangrene, and vomit permeated every room and corridor. Flies stuck on blood-soaked bandages and soiled blankets that had turned brown and crusty. Bandages were simply washed and reused. Bleary-eyed and exhausted doctors and nurses did their best with few supplies and little medicine. At times the hospitals had neither morphine nor so much as a single aspirin for the mortal pain of those who went under the knives wielded by the surgeons.

During a visit to a field hospital, my mother tried to calm a soldier lying on the floor mat crying inconsolably, his face pale, lips cracked, a soiled blanket covering his lower body. She was to remember their painful encounter even decades later: "I squatted beside him, asking if he would like to have some water. He shook his head to say no; I asked if he would like to send a letter home and offered to write one for him. He shook his head and choked as if he were having an asthma attack. 'Do you know what fighting the war did to me?' he said, sobbing. 'I can never be like a normal man. . . . Never will I have a child. I am the end of my family line.' The shrapnel of a grenade had struck his groin area. I said to him, 'China's four hundred fifty million people are your children. Every one of us is indebted to your sacrifice.'" But in my heart I knew that what I said gave him no comfort. For this soldier, his personal loss and the eternal loss to his family were irreparable.

Only on one occasion and for only two hours, my parents' paths crossed in the outskirts of Wuhan, long enough for them to share a meal in the mess hall. My father warned that Guangzhou might become a target for occupation and urged my mother to move the family to Hong Kong for safety as soon as possible. Even then Japanese air raids were dropping bombs on Guangzhou. Hong Kong was safe, at least for the present, since the crown colony was under British rule and Britain was not a party to the Sino-Japan War. In September, Mother packed some suitcases and moved the family to Hong Kong.

Meanwhile my father was fighting in the county of Jiujiang as part of the defense of Wuhan, under the direction of Zhang Fakui, commander in chief of the Eighth Route Army. The Japanese fleet had sailed from Shanghai to Jiujiang, and bombers were raiding the area daily from the air.

My father's artillery unit sank several Japanese warships, but that only served to intensify the bombing from the Japanese planes. On the 23rd of July, part of the Eighth Route Army collapsed, followed by the collapse of the Seventieth Army in the same vicinity. Shortly after that, the Japanese broke the blockade line for the Yangtze Defense in Jiangxi Province.

During the ensuing emergency, the supreme command appointed my father deputy commander of the Eighth Army Group. "Addressing the troops for the first time as their deputy commander, I asked for three minutes of silence to remember the sons and brothers who had fallen. I choked as I spoke," I read in my father's diary. He told the men they were duty-bound to fight to save the Motherland from enslavement, to protect their parents and children from bombs and gunfire, their wives and sisters from ravage. The sacrifices asked of them were nothing less than their flesh and blood.

"Battlefield appeals made to the fighting men, telling them to honor the love they had for their family and homeland—this was the hardest thing for a commander to do, knowing full well what was being asked of them," Father told me. "In war, a strategy backed by weapons and a determined spirit for combat are critical to winning the battle. Strategy had to do with logistics and support, but the motivation of the soldiers and their willingness to fight and to die were just as important. In that first strike, anger and hatred toward the enemy, along with the men's patriotism, was absolutely essential in order for the fighting men to annihilate or resist the enemy. Once the men were aroused and they saw comrades and friends fallen or wounded, their instinct for revenge became their driving force to fight with everything they had. Without the will to fight, all the numbers and sophisticated weapons would come to naught." The faces he saw were men so young, men who might be dead tomorrow, men who should be tilling the fields and serving their parents in their villages.

The assembled men and officers raised their voices singing the Brave Soldiers Marching Song:

Rise up, people who will not be enslaved,
Let our flesh and blood form the new Great Wall of China . . .

In the letters my mother kept, my father told of the terrible losses he witnessed in his troops:

We fought one bloody combat after another in fields and alleys. The topography of the central plains gave the advantage to the enemies with their airplanes and tanks. Our arsenals were like those of the Napoleonic era. Whenever the Japanese columns were in motion, their airplanes swung into action to protect the movements of the troops, dropping their bombs on us. Silvery wings circled the sky. The enemy planes flew so low that we could see the pilots inside with their goggles on. Columns of black smoke rose with each explosion of bombs dropped from the air. When the enemy planes droned above us, we dove into trenches. But as soon as the planes left, we emerged and returned fire to the enemy with artillery fire and hand grenades. What we lacked in modern machine power, we compensated for in numbers and columns of fighting men. Every inch of territory defended and every battle won was with flesh, blood, and a will that had been set afire in fury and hatred for the enemies who had invaded our land, burned our homes, and raped our women. While we did not succeed in annihilating the enemy, we did succeed in protecting the Longhai Rail Line and in allowing forty-two freight trains to move both ammunition and over one million troops across four provinces to the hinterland.

Although he had been granted the authority to put to death any officer up to the rank of brigadier general for disobeying a military order, my father did not savor this authority and was grateful that he never had to use it. While his troops were stationed in Shantou at the start of the war, in 1937, the military court ordered the execution of five soldiers who had murdered their platoon sergeant. The crime took place on a hillside away from the camp. In an act of anger and vengeance, the five men smashed the sergeant's head with rocks and mutilated his body. Subsequent investigation found that the sergeant was much hated by his men because he meted out cruel punishment to the soldiers that included the withholding of food, beatings, standing under the hot sun for hours, and other physical assaults.

My father had the power to commute the sentences but did not. "Murder is a crime," he noted in his diary. "Military discipline has to be strictly maintained, especially at a time when war is imminent." The night before the execution, he paced the floor until dawn. At daybreak five shots rang out, five men were dead—five sons and brothers. "I felt more horror in those five shots than any other I had ever known. Who was at fault? The soldiers who had committed the crime, or the sergeant who had been cruel to his men? Or was it the battalion captain, the regiment commander, or myself the commander in chief—who was blind to the explosive situation and who could have intervened?"

The resigned and frightened faces of the five men and the ringing out of the shots were to remain with my father for the rest of his life.

On July 25th, the Japanese fleets reached the harbor of Jiujiang and planes began to drop incendiary bombs down onto the city. For several days Father's troops fought the Japanese who had landed in Jiujiang. Moving southward, his troops joined in the defense of the rail line north of Mahueling and its train station. The enemy bombarded Mahueling heavily and used poison gas against the Chinese troops.

By early September, Japanese troops were closing in on Mahueling. My father was ordered to the town of De-an and was given the responsibility of directing a number of forces in areas adjoining Mahueling.

Among the many tragedies in China's War of Resistance was that most of the troops were poorly equipped, poorly fed, poorly clothed, and poorly attended to when wounded. Without overlooking a single resource available to him, my father wrote to my mother for help: "If money is available [from donations], do purchase 6,000 winter vests for the troops. What we need most is masks to protect the soldiers from poison gas. Do your best to get us at least 500 masks. They need not be expensive ones. We can surely use them and soon. . . ."

During one of the few moments of levity that he was able to share with my mother, he teasingly wrote: "The general, yours truly, is said to ride a handsome horse. Let me tell you that his so-called handsome horse is not much larger than a dog. Do try to find a horse for me. It does not have to be a big and handsome horse, only one that can climb mountain and gallops."

With their meager machine guns and grenades, the Chinese infantry were no match for Japanese tanks, armored vehicles and air bombers. Japanese planes bombed the shelters and tunnels, then they flew low to spot troop movements and supply lines. For every inch defended or recovered, the lives of thousands of young Chinese men were sacrificed.

The summer and fall of 1938 was one of the darkest times in China's War of Resistance. On October 21, Guangzhou fell and Wuhan followed on October 25. The supreme headquarters ordered a final strategic retreat.

My father's headquarters at the De-an front line was located in a vacated landlord's house with a large courtyard, hidden among the trees on the hillside. His command desk was an old wooden table on which there was a single telephone. Behind the desk was his bed—a wooden door with some straw matting. All the doors in the house were taken down for beds, and officers and staff shared the rooms. The soldiers wore puttees on their bare legs and the officers wore slacks. Many of the officers wore straw sandals just like the soldiers.

Day after day, the Japanese bombed the front line, sometimes several times a day. My father directed the fighting during the raids, sometimes eating only one meal a day. Fewer than five kilometers away, soldiers were engaged in hand-to-hand combat. Half of the townspeople and villagers had fled to safer ground. What Father feared most was poison gas, which the Japanese had used on other fronts. The soldiers had no protection against this and would not be able to fight back; they would choke while the gas seeped its way through their lungs.

But despite the constant dangers being faced, troop morale remained high, for on their front the fighting had gone well. My father's soldiers were able to capture Japanese ammunition and equipment that included rifles, machine guns, gas masks, field glasses, and swords that had belonged to officers. They took protective charms such as the "thousand-stitch belts" and diaries from the bodies of dead Japanese soldiers.

My father ordered the diaries translated into Chinese and examined for secret codes and army intelligence. One of the Japanese officers who was killed on August 5 was Captain Nakajima of the Third Column of the Thirteenth Division. The following entries were found in his pocket:

> July 7–10. Landed in Shanghai feeling the cruelty of war. Even though we must win victory regardless of the means, why and for whom am I perpetrating this cruelty? I know in my heart, but I dare not speak with my lips.
>
> July 20. This year at the Cherry Blossom Festival, I took a picture of my whole family. They will not be able to look at this photo when the cherry blossoms open again. Gazing at the photo, I wept without end. Next year when the cherry blossoms bloom, will my son be an orphan, my wife a widow, and my white-haired mother not know where to search for her son?
>
> August 1. A fierce battle was fought and the cannons shook the entire mountain. One shell fell dangerously close to me. My commander and an officer of the Eighth Unit and all together over a hundred men were killed. Many more are sick. On average ten out of fifteen men in each unit are ill.
>
> August 4. I am tired to death and my body, so thin of skin and bones, commits these cruel acts. In my conscience, I dare not face my parents. The Chinese soldiers have the sacrificial spirit and modern armament, as well as the geographical advantage over us. They watch us carefully and are not as tired as the Imperial Army. We have great hardship transporting supplies. There seems little hope of winning the war. We were attacked and shelled several times in the night. I was often in grave danger today under the shell-fire of the enemy. Only four other officers and I are left. Today, we sent for reinforcements.

"What Captain Nakajima referred to as modern armament was no more than hand grenades," my father wrote. He was so touched by the Japanese captain's diary and a family photograph taken from his pocket that he made note in his own diary: "In my heart, I bear no hatred for this Japanese captain. War is war. I am a Chinese general and he an enemy captain. We had to kill him and all the enemies to win the war. But I do not feel that he was my enemy, and my conscience is unquiet about him. I feel the pain of his soul and the loss of his family as I look at his family photo of his elderly parents, the young captain himself, his wife, and an infant in the wife's arms."

Among the journalists who visited the De-an front were Freda Utley from Great Britain and Leslie Smith of the Reuters news agency. Utley was the author of *Japan's Feet of Clay*, a widely read book at the time. She maintained that because of the lack of natural resources, and because of its dependence on outside supplies of raw materials, Japan's military strength was much less than generally assumed, because of its own decrepit economy.

Utley and Smith spent four days at my father's headquarters at the farmhouse and were eager to observe combat action. Smith repeatedly requested permission to follow the soldiers to the front. For his safety, Father turned down his request, but he did allow him to observe from the hilltop. Utley was authorized to talk with anyone in the compound quarters. They, too, slept in doorless rooms with wooden doors as beds.

Between commanding and observing on the battleground, my father, with the help of a translator, spent many hours talking with the visitors. He was most appreciative of the foreign journalists' interest in China and that they had braved the dangers of the battlefront to visit De-an. This was when countries in Europe were observing Japan's invasion of China neutrally, and the United States was selling steel and raw materials to Japan. Before Utley and Smith departed De-an, Father presented Smith with a pair of Japanese field glasses and Utley with a sword that had three gold chrysanthemums imprinted on the hilt—it had belonged to a dead officer of the Doihara Division in the Luohuang battle. He also gave Miss Utley several pages of the diary from the Japanese captain.

By mid-August, as many as thirty enemy airplanes were dropping bombs all around De-an daily. Positions changed several times between the two sides in the constant "seesaw" of battles lost and won over the plains and hills of De-an. Both sides—the Chinese defending and Japanese attacking—attempted to occupy the territory.

On September 1, Chinese soldiers met the enemy head-on in hand-to-hand combat, and both sides lost heavily. Over the month-long fighting, the casualties were such that not one of the nine divisions (of 3,000 men each) under my father's command had 1,000 men left.

Finally, for seven days Chinese soldiers fought the Japanese in hand-to-hand combat in the outskirts and the streets of De-an. Father knew that he couldn't hold on, but continued to fight until October 30. Speaking by phone with the supreme commander Chiang Kaishek who was in Nanchang, he received instructions to move to the south bank of the Hsin River southwest of De-an. Only then did the fighting in De-an end. My father had requested reinforcements, but the collapse on the other fronts had made that impossible. During one battle my father went without sleep for three days and three nights, going back and forth between working at his command desk and observing the troops at the battle line. On October 16, he fell ill from exhaustion and dysentery in the retreat northward and had to be carried off in a canvas stretcher.

Nearly five decades later, my niece Cathy, a brown-eyed, brunette Princeton student who has the features of her German father, called up her mother, my sister Chi, and asked if Grandpa's name was Li Han-Yuan. For her class assignment, Cathy was reading Freda Utley's *China at War*, published in London by Faber and Faber in 1939. Her mother told her "yes," explaining that Grandpa used the spelling Li Han-Hun and that there might be still other spellings such as Lee Hon Won, depending upon whether it was Mandarin or Cantonese and who was doing the translation. Excited, Cathy told her mother that Utley wrote about her visit to the shelter of the farmhouse which was the headquarters of General Li Han-Yuan, who commanded three Cantonese divisions in the De-an front—adding "There are photos of Grandpa in the book."

Utley wrote that General Li "was the most attractive personality among the generals I met in China. Small, thin, with an intellectual brow and a friendly smile, he conveyed an impression of humanness and good temper, and had the most philosophical outlook. You could talk with him about European affairs, the agrarian problem in China, and the fundamental problems of human society. He neither smoked nor drank and could not have slept more than three or four hours in twenty-four hours." Utley observed that the headquarters had a pleasing informality and there was an atmosphere of democracy and caring, which was reciprocated in the soldiers' affection toward him;

she noted that the soldiers were unusually smart and well groomed. In *China at War*, I found that the translation of the Japanese captain's diaries that my father had given to Utley during her visit to Dean was identical to what was recorded in my father's diaries.

I found Freda Utley's vivid description of my father under enemy fire utterly fascinating as well as gratifying. I had always known my father as a man without pretense who went about doing his job, even in anguish, exhaustion, and under pressure.

Two months after Guangzhou fell, on December 23, 1938, my father was summoned to a special meeting with Generalissimo Chiang Kaishek. Chiang told my father that corruption had run rampant in Guangdong Province, and he feared that unless the situation was brought under control with a new initiative in civil administration to support the war effort, the entire province would fall. Chiang said he needed help and offered my father the governorship. My father would share the responsibilities for Guangdong Province with General Yu Hanmou—Yu would be the military commander and my father the chief civilian administrator.

"I know you are incorruptible, and I believe you can eliminate the evil and salvage the province," Chiang told him encouragingly.

Chiang spoke of the difficult job ahead. The problems in Guangdong were manifold due to a shortage of grain, the need for a massive relief effort to assist the refugees, and the historically corrupt practices. Though the Nationalist government had accepted Communist aid to fight the Japanese, the Communists had to be held in line and watched carefully. Chiang asked my father to work closely with Yu to support the military command.

While my father had concerns over the complexity of Guangdong politics and misgivings about administrating an untenable situation, nevertheless he was still ready to give his home province his best effort in whatever way he could.

In accepting the governorship, my father's career path changed drastically, thus giving up what he was trained for and extremely effective at. Understanding my father as I do now, I believe he welcomed the change as an opportunity to put down the sword, to work for construction instead of destruction, and to preserve life instead of ending it. He was a Buddhist at heart, and his abiding love for his country had made him a courageous soldier. "I have no fear of war when fighting in defense of the Motherland, and when justice and liberty are the call, he wrote. "But I hate wars conducted for conquest and enslavement, for suppression of freedom, and for greed. I believe that some wars have to be fought in order to extinguish war. I would never be the first to attack. I am a soldier. My responsibility is to defend my country with all that I am endowed with and to die if I must."

Before my father began his new duty, he went back to his village to visit his mother and to offer incense at the family ancestral tomb. his mother was getting old, but she radiated happiness, comforted by the fact that her son was serving the Motherland with valor and had risen to a position higher than anyone else in the village. She wanted to have a hardwood coffin ready for her burial, saying that it would give her serenity to know that preparations had been made for her eventual rest. My father obliged her; he bought a fine hardwood coffin and stored it in the back room of her house. In her old age, his mother grew fat and walked with a cane because of her bound feet, leaning on her maidservant for support. From time to time she went to the back room and looked at the coffin with pleasure and a feeling of comfort.

During this and other visits to the village, my father would pay Third Uncle—the relative who had caused my father's having to flee to Guangzhou—the same respect he did to other elders. For all the misery Third Uncle had inflicted on him and his family, my father no longer bore any rancor or hatred for the man, explaining, "Had it not been for this man, I would not have gone to Guangzhou and would still be a peasant."

In his first weeks as governor, my father quickly learned that the provincial administration was even more complex and problematic than he had anticipated. Apparently the military, civil, and financial administrations, as well as the police security, all strove to be independent of one another. On top of this, all the county magistrates had been appointed on *guanxi*, "connections," and, as Chiang Kaishek noted, many were involved in corruption.

Determined that magistrates be selected on merit, my father took on the arduous task of making new magisterial appointments for more than ninety counties, creating animosity for himself with many right at the onset. To set an example, my father refused his younger brother's request of a county appointment. It was a refusal that created tension in their relationship for years to come.

Because of terrible drought, a shortage of grain became a persistent concern to the provincial government and to my father. After Hong Kong fell, the Japanese expelled three quarters of a million Hong Kong residents to lessen the burden of supplying food for the isle. Refugees from Hong Kong and from occupied territories poured into the neighboring interior of Guangdong Province seeking refuge and safety. The already impoverished provincial government found itself in an endless emergency situation dealing with the provision of food and shelter for so many extra people.

My father's job as governor was made even more difficult because the civilian administration was subjugated to military command. While he was vested with responsibilities, nevertheless the military command superseded him at every turn. Salaries for civil servants were far below those of the military.

Throughout the years of his governorship, the provision of grain to the military was an incessant source of conflict between my father and the military commander and his staff. The provincial government had put a tight surveillance on all grain requisitions, but the military wanted the grain administration taken away from the provincial government and given to the military. The conflict reached its peak in 1944, when the military demanded 324,000 sacks of grain for the army. This was 100,000 sacks more than in the previous year, even though the number of troops had remained constant. The province was in a most precarious position, since the drought had led to a severe grain shortage. The fact that army grain had found its way to the market and had been sold for profiteering was an abomination. Father's only recourse was to ask the central government to intervene.

The central government directed the military command not to make the unwarranted requisition. The military command and the provincial government compromised on 300,000 sacks, but the conflict continued, and my father was accused of not supplying the troops in a timely manner. After years of struggle, the military took control of the grain administration on both the provincial and the county levels.

The military exercised control over the civilian government. In the first months of my father's administration, the military command ordered the provincial government to relocate to Lian County in the western part of Guandong Province. Since Lian County lacked communication and transportation facilities, it meant isolation for the provincial government. My father insisted that the provincial government be moved back to Shaoguan, and for a time he succeeded. Two years later, the military command again ordered the provincial government to move all its administrative units to Lian County—ostensibly for reasons of "safety"; but the order specified that the bureaus of finance, administration, education, and police security, as well as the Bank of Guangdong, all remain in Shaoguan.

My father appealed to the central government's Executive Yuan, the highest branch of government legislature, in Chungking for arbitration; the military order was repealed. For the sake of harmony and coexistence with the military command and to save face for the military commander, my father did not make the Executive Yuan's order public, but rather put up a façade by temporarily moving some units of the government to Lian County. It was survival under extraordinary circumstances.

The rumor mill began churning and took on a life of its own. Rumors spread through the military news dailies about plans for reorganizing the provincial government and that the governor was very ill, implying that he might succumb to this illness. At the time, my father was in fact suffering from a severe bout with dysentery. Such rumors inculcated fear in the hearts and minds of the civil servants and swayed the confidence of the civilian population. The slander and accusations of withholding grain supplies from the military reached hysterical proportions when my father, on reports of cannibalism in Toishan County after another severe drought, ordered the release of grain from provincial storage for civilian consumption. Some felt that the release of grain to the population was unwarranted.

Vicious rumors spread that the governor was soft on Communists. When my father first became pacification commissioner of the Eastern District in Shantou, thirteen young teachers and students associated with the leftist People's Front-line were arrested and accused of being Communists. Rather than imprison the students or hand out death penalties to them, he spent an afternoon talking to them and had his chief secretary explain things further to educate them and to give the young people an opportunity to redeem themselves. The students were granted the option of joining the army as propagandists to mobilize public support for the war effort, or being released into the custody of their parents. My father never regretted the action. He believed that the young revolutionaries—the brightest of their generation—were patriots, albeit immature. They needed to be guided and they deserved a second chance for the love they had for their country. Nearly all selected to serve as propagandists to support the war.

The other faction playing the rumor game was headed by my father's predecessor, who also wanted to have someone close to him in the governor's chair. Early in his administration and as director of the Provincial Committee of the Nationalist Party, my father had established a center for the training of party members. Rumors went all the way to Chungking that Father was involved in *tsudang*, "forming a new party group." It was well known that *tsudang* was a thorn in Chiang Kaishek's side. My father gave up the position as head of the provincial Nationalist Party when he realized that two-thirds of the party membership were followers of his predecessor. The rumor mill was further fueled and went non-stop both within the province and in Chunking at National Congress time.

Chiang Kaishek was famous for creating checks and balances, which was his way of preventing any one individual or a single group from becoming too strong or influential. To Chiang, the Guangdong generals were not to be trusted because of historical antecedents and even very recent events, such as Chen Zitang's alliance with Li Zongren on the eve of the Sino-Japan War. Chiang saw to it that the key posts in Guangdong were filled by individuals who were not of the same group in order to spawn conflict.

At times, the military command's staff would withhold important intelligence from my father. During the final retreat to Mei County, in 1944, my father went to the military headquarters for an appointment with the commander in chief. On arrival, he was told that the commander in chief had evacuated his forces and left Shaoguan half an hour earlier. It was only then that Father learned that the Japanese had reached the city outskirts.

Then there were the natural disasters. The most devastating were the three droughts that resulted in severe grain shortages. The provincial government had plans drawn for hydroelectric power and dam constructions to increase irrigation for rice planting and grain production, but the lack of funds hampered their full implementation. Eleven small projects were completed, but these were inefficient during times of severe drought. My father was blamed for negligence in not promoting self-sufficiency in grain supplies through hydroelectrification and the construction of dams.

Historically, Guangdong Province had relied on grain imports to meet its deficit. At the beginning of my father's administration, the provincial government established a plan with neighboring provinces for aid, trading salt for grain. In order to avoid the abuses of private accumulation and profiteering, the provincial government strictly controlled grain regulation and distribution. It forbade any private transport of grain without appropriate clearance. It also prohibited the use of grain for making wine, because wine was an unaffordable luxury.

As the drought continued into its third year, Hubei Province, which had traded Guangdong their rice for salt in a ratio of two to one, demanded that the exchange be in equal weight, even though the price of rice was well below that of salt. The provinces of Guizhou and Guangxi also raised the price of grain for Guangdong's purchases. Adding to the problem, the Japanese and their collaborators were offering high prices to the profiteers for grain purchases.

Following one drought, the people of Hangyang voluntarily donated grain to Guangdong's relief. Their compassion renewed my father's faith in humanity.

The saying "one looks to the sky for human salvation" rang true. For months people in the province looked to the sky for rain. When thunder finally broke the sky, they rejoiced. But they soon worried almost as much when torrential rains poured down, drowning the young shoots and rotting the roots of the tender new rice plants.

"I fought the Japanese with every ounce of my body," my father wrote in his diary, "and I fought the droughts and hunger the best I knew how. At first, I tried to fight the rumors. But it was all too exhausting and time-consuming. I decided to give up fighting the rumors and let events take their own course, for I had given everything I had to my duties, and my conscience was clear."

There were several assessment visits by representatives of the central government, some instigated by the rumor mills. They not only cleared my father completely, but also awarded him a meritorious service commendation.

But my father's problems were not limited to Guangdong Province alone. In 1942 the central government was found to be shipping 700 crates of opium overseas via the Guangdong interior. Concerned that some of the crates might get shipped back to the province and be sold on the black market, he immediately asked the central government to stop shipping the drugs through Guangdong. Chiang Kaishek promised that none of the crates would stay in Guangdong. When there was a second shipment through Guangdong the following year, my father protested again. The Minister of Finance Dr. H. H. Kung explained that China was fighting a war and was in need of money for arms purchases. When a third shipment came through—this time of 2,000 crates—my father made it known that he was ready to resign the governorship in protest if that was what was required.

Knowing what I do now, I wonder how my father weathered his seven years of tenure as Guangdong's wartime governor and withstood the pressure. As a child I only knew him as an ascetic figure, someone who was indifferent to material things, who worked long hours from early morning into night, who had a volcanic temper that exploded from time to time, and who took pleasure in teaching my siblings and me Tang poetry.

Chapter Five
Childhood in Wartime

I was just over four years old when China's War of Resistance against Japan broke out in July 1937. At the time, my younger brother, baby sister, and I were living in Guangzhou with my mother. My father, a lieutenant general with the Sixty-fourth Army, was fighting on the central plains more than two thousand kilometers away.

My earliest memories, dating back to that year, are of our large, two-story house in the city of Guangzhou. My three-year-old brother Shao and I used to play in the walled-in garden under a large cottonwood tree. A talking parrot that lived in the garden used to startle visitors by squawking, "Left foot, right foot, left, right, left, right . . ." We would try to march to its commands, but sometimes it would shout, "Left foot, right foot, left foot, right foot, left, left, wrong foot . . ." and we would get confused and stumble over each other. One day, a Japanese bomb shattered the front gate and killed the parrot.

We also had a vacation home, a farm in an area called Dragon's Eye Cave on the edge of the city. Fields of watermelon and pineapple lay behind the house, and right outside our back door a cellar-like concrete bomb shelter. One day I saw a big black snake there, coiled between two rows of pineapples. Its pointed head and beady eyes terrified me, and I ran, crying all the way, to my nanny, a young woman with a braided queue that reached the seat of her pants, who was standing under the shade of a big tree. She scooped me up with both arms and I hung on to her as tightly as I could.

In January 1939, two months after Guangzhou fell to the Japanese, my father was named governor of the province, and the provincial capital was relocated to Shaoguan, three hundred kilometers to the north of Guangzhou. That spring, my family moved into a rustic house in Huanggong Hill, a small township comprised of several villages, just twenty miles outside of Shaoguan.

Our family residence was a six-room wooden house, its roof and outside walls covered with pine bark, shrouded by trees about a mile up the hill. It could be reached only by foot or on horseback. The kitchen and servants' quarters were separate behind the house, and an annex to the left housed my father's office and those of his aides and assistants. Years later, I found an entry in my father's diaries in which he wrote about the house: "My friends feel that the house isn't worthy of my status, but the house suits me fine and I love it. I'm a farmer at heart, just like my father." I also found a small photo of the house in an old family album, its brown leather cover marked with cracks. Looking at the photo, it surprised me to see just how humble the house was.

I have warm memories of growing up in this home. The tropical sun shone regardless of the season. I awoke to the chirping of birds and fell asleep to the buzzing of the cicadas. I loved springtime, when blooming azaleas and wild berry shrubs blanketed the hillside in pink. There were times when we would come upon female pheasants hidden in the bushes only a few hundred yards from the house: they would stand guard over their aqua-colored eggs while their mates stalked the nesting ground like the sentries guarding our home. Bonsai-shaped branching Chinese pines grew out on the hills and surrounded our home; their fragrance permeated the air all year round. We watched the wild blossoms turn into little berries and mature to a dark purple color, and then we would pick the berries to make jam.

But spring had its special hazard, at least for me. All around, hairy green-and-black caterpillars dangled and fell from the pines, wiggling. I would jump up and run to avoid the caterpillars, or stay indoors. Every morning the servants and the gardeners would sweep away the fallen caterpillars and bury them in a hole, but in no time, hundreds more would creep back onto the footpath around the house. One afternoon while I was playing in the garden, one of the hairy worms fell onto my neck. With arms flailing and screaming at the top of my lungs, I began running around in circles, not knowing what to do.

Seeing that I was completely hysterical, the sentry stationed nearby rushed over and pulled it off. I ran inside the house and splashed water from the enamel basin that sat on the floor of my room. After that, I was always careful whenever I played under the trees.

In the fall, I began my formal schooling as a first grader in the local elementary school at the foot of Huanggong Hill. I felt like a big girl as I walked one kilometer down the hill to school, even though I was accompanied by a maid. Nearly all my classmates were the children of civil servants. The once quiet little township was now filled with buzzing activities, as it had become the main artery of the provincial government. Within months, new office buildings and homes—flat and constructed of wood, bamboo and bark—had sprung up all around the town to accommodate the stream of relocated civil servants and their families.

My school was a complex of several small bamboo wall flats that had dirt floors and thatched windows without glass panes. During class, the teacher would read aloud from her text, and we children would recite after her. When she wrote on the blackboard, we copied in our exercise books. When it rained, the window thatches had to be lowered to keep water out, but this shut off the daylight as well, leaving the room dark and murky. When the bell clanged for recess, before racing out the door we would wait for our teacher's signal to stand up, and then bow to her, just as we did when she came into the room. We would play on the parade ground, which was really just dirt ground packed with a thin layer of tiny rocks and sand. I would join the girls, jumping rope, and kicking feather birdies we had brought from home until the bell clanged again to summon us back into the classroom.

Students were responsible for keeping the classrooms and school grounds clean. At the end of the day, we would have to sweep the classroom, straighten the tables and chairs, wash the blackboard, and then sweep that part of the playground that had been assigned to our class. We would have to pass our homeroom teacher's inspection before going home.

Except for Sundays, my tutor Teacher Lee would come to our house almost as soon as I got home from school. Just out of teacher training school, she was tall and vivacious and was my companion and friend as much as my teacher. Once I finished my homework in calligraphy and arithmetic, which took about an hour, we would play games, tell stories, and sing. Teacher Lee had a soprano voice that made me want to sing like her. Together we sang marching songs, children's songs, and some folk songs.

My father always wore a long olive-green woolen military cape in the winter, with a matching hat that had a blue-and-white twelve-point star, and black boots. He often rode on horseback rather than using his automobile in order to conserve gasoline and to set an example of austerity. China was fighting a war against the Japanese. We had no cigarettes in the house and no one smoked in his presence. He did not ban smoking, but everyone knew how much he detested smoking. The aversion, I believe, had to do with the opium addiction of both his father and father-in-law.

Although I was only six when my father became governor, I knew that he was an important person. I could tell by the way people stood at attention in his presence, by the way that soldiers saluted him, and by the constant presence of the two aides who stood at his elbow, ready to respond to his orders. I knew that he was involved in fighting the Japanese. I also knew that he held a number of different and confusing titles—governor, commander in chief, chairman of the Nationalist Party of Guangdong Province, and several others.

"Papa," I asked him one day, "I don't understand what it is you do. Why do you have so many titles?"

"Because I work for China." He tousled my hair and seemed pleased by my curiosity. "Because I'm a soldier and a civil servant."

"I know that you're fighting the Japanese because you're a soldier. But what do civil servants do?"

"Soldiers and civil servants both work to protect our country's sovereignty and the rights of our people. A soldier's first duty is to his country. As governor, I work for the benefit of the people and try to do what the people want me to and to ease their hardship." He leaned over and looked into my eyes. "A soldier lives and dies for his nation's honor and security. Do you understand that?"

I nodded. I understood a soldier's duty because I had heard all the marching songs, but they also talked about soldiers dying for their country, and the thought that my father could die was unbearable. I didn't want to think about it. I didn't want to hear any more, so I went out to chase and swat at the butterflies in the garden with a woven bamboo fan.

I seldom had a chance to talk with my father. For one thing, he was always busy. For another, in those days well-behaved children were still "seen but not heard." I liked eavesdropping and listening to my parents as they talked between themselves and with their secretaries and visitors. I never knew who might show up at the dinner table because my parents often invited visitors to stay and share our meals.

I knew what was going on, and sometimes I relished the tension and excitement as much as I was overwhelmed by dread, hoping that the Japanese would be defeated. Crises could erupt at any hour of the day or night. Telegrams and phone calls would come in, reporting shortages of food and medicine, orphans in need of shelter, refugees, homes destroyed by bombs, supplies delivered to the front lines, the new conscription of soldiers. We also received frequent reports of natural disasters such as droughts and famine, not just in the province but elsewhere throughout the country.

Because Shaoguan was the wartime provincial capital, the Japanese carried out frequent air raids, sometimes several times a day. Whenever the big bell on the summit of Huanggong Hill began tolling, I could feel my heart start to pound and my muscles tighten, and I could see the worry on the faces of everyone around me. Whether I was at home or at school, I would drop my books, pencil, toys, or whatever else I was doing and follow everyone into the bomb shelters, a series of tunnels hollowed out inside the mountain. One tunnel close to school could accommodate hundreds of people, and a smaller one had been dug into the hill about a hundred yards behind our house. In the summer, the tunnels were hot, humid and stuffy. We tried to fan for air, but that was not always possible because the tunnels were packed with people back-to-back. When we emerged from the tunnels, our clothing could be soaked with perspiration.

Above the tolling bell and the sounds of running footsteps I could sometimes hear people yelling, "Run! Run!" and the voice of the sentry stationed at the top of the hill calling out through his bullhorn, telling us how many enemy planes were approaching. I knew that if the bell tolled a second time, and more rapidly than the first, it meant that the Japanese planes were already over Shaoguan.

Inside the tunnels, the few who had flashlights turned them off to save the batteries. I could hear the droning of the planes coming ever closer, and sometimes the thunder of exploding bombs.

Around me, people would whisper, as if the Japanese pilots could hear their voices if they spoke too loudly. "We're far enough away from the city that the bombs won't hit us. It'll be all right." But then would come more explosions, and more whispers. "How many will die this time? More burning! . . . Maybe we're going to get hit this time . . . !" Finally the bell would toll for a third time to signal that the planes had left. But if we happened to be in the tunnel by our home, sometimes we children would quietly recite poetry that our father had taught us. It helped us pass the time as much as mask our fear.

During the air raids, I always worried about my mother and father because most of the time they were at meetings away from home. I would become especially frightened for their safety if I knew that they were at the Shaoguan Guest House, because it was located in the center of the city and the hub of many official activities. Many bombs were dropped in Shaoguan, killing people and setting the city on fire.

Most of the time, though, I didn't know where my parents were. During all those years, I remember my mother being in the shelter with us only a handful of times—and my father not at all.

My parents were often away from home for weeks at a time. My father was constantly on the road on inspection tours, where a day's journey by car on the narrow and unpaved roads covered only about fifty kilometers. There were long trips to Chungking to attend the Nationalist Party Congress, as well as other top political and military meetings. He went by train to the city of Guilin, and from there he flew to Chungking. My mother was busy with relief organizations rescuing children from the war zones. She was always on the road, too, traveling all the way to Chungking, raising money for food and shelter for the refugee children's homes and schools.

For the greater part of the time, we children were in the care of our nannies, a resident nurse and, of course, Little Granny. Little Granny was our housekeeper and a distant relative, a permanent fixture in our household as far back as I could remember. She was thin as a cane and was related to my paternal grandmother's side of the family. Everybody called her Little Granny, including my father, as a matter of courtesy; she was the second wife and widow of a distant cousin. Little Granny could be stern with the servants as well as with me and my sister and brothers—she was the one person who ever scolded me as a child. Whenever I left a few grain of rice in my bowl, she would warn that the lightning god would strike me down for wasting food. Immediately, I would clean my bowl to avoid her curse.

It was during that first year we lived in Huanggong Hill that my brother Shao died.

I remember it was a hot summer day, and my mother and I were on our way home from an inspection trip. I saw my father's black sedan coming from the opposite direction intercepting our car; Captain Tao, my father's aide, got out, saluted my mother. After a brief pause he said: "Reporting. Brother Shao has died this morning." My heart jumped out of me. I looked at my mother, she was wooden.

Except for that one instant, I have no other recollection of my brother's illness, or his burial. When we got home, Mother went to Shao's room, but I stayed on the porch. Mother was crying when she came to the porch and said to me, "Brother Shao is no more." She held me close to her. After a minute or two, I was able to get away from her. I didn't want to see my mother cry and I wanted to hide myself, so I went out into the garden circling the trees. With my straw fan in hand, I swatted at some butterflies that were flitting around. After a while, I stood there and cried.

Shao was barely five years old when he died. His pleurisy had been misdiagnosed as malaria and mistreated by the doctors until the end. I have only scattered memories of our childhood together. Only the photos reminded me that we danced and sang together on stage in support of the war effort, performing before hundreds of people inside the auditoriums in Shaoguan and in Huanggong.

Shao was dressed in a white linen shirt and pants wearing a white cap, and I wore an organza pinafore and the headpiece of a swallow made of real feathers. When the red curtain opened, we sang:

Shao: Little swallow, little swallow. Where is your mother? Where has she gone?

Me: Where has my mother gone? She hasn't come back. My stomach growls in hunger.

Together: You are my good friend. I am your good friend. We hold hands.

We tap-danced to the applause of the audience. At the finale, Shao, dressed in a soldier's uniform much like our father's, and, looking very serious and smart, gave a patriotic speech rallying the audience to a standing ovation.

Shortly after Shao's death, the doctor came to our house to give my sister and me immunization shots. My three-year-old sister accepted her shot without a murmur. But I cried hysterically, refusing the shot and rejecting my mother's plea that it was for my protection. I kicked and screamed, and no one could hold me down. I was rebelling not so much out of the fear of the needle, but rather I was upset that my brother had died and I was scared. It felt as if my arms and legs were torn from my body.

In spite of the war, life in Huanggong was orderly, and I felt very grown up. My sister and I ate most of our meals at the big round dining table with our parents and their aides and secretaries. I always sat next to my mother and my sister next to me. We did not speak at the table unless spoken to. We were taught to approach food with a gladness bordering reverence. Even before the first grade, children were taught that the farmer cultivates the grain and that every kernel grew by the backbreaking labor and sweat of the farmer's brow. We learned never to waste food.

The servants would announce when the meal was ready. But my father would keep working, and that kept everyone waiting at the table. After two or three such announcements, my sister and I would run to his office in the annex to fetch him. It was one of the very few moments when we could have fun interrupting our father. We would take away his pen, put aside his ink plate, or make him give up his reading. We would take him by his hands, pulling him into the dining room. We would try to be playful and see how fast we could pull him, both of us straining with all our weight. Of course, he would put up a fight, but gradually yielding, while feigning a stern, displeased countenance. Inevitably, his face would break into a smile, as we dragged him all the way to the dining room. All around, servants and aides smiled approvingly.

At the table, meals were often eaten in silence, except when there was company or when my father conversed with my mother, their aides, or visitors. This was the only time of the day when my father could have a few quiet moments to himself, and he was usually deep in thought. But our dining table was an educational seminar for my sister and me. We heard briefings on decisions that concerned people's lives and learned about the operations of a multitude of agencies. Mother often invited a professor or two from Sun Yatsen University to have lunch at home and picked their brains for the educational programs of the refugee children's homes and schools.

When drought came and there was a shortage of food, my father would eat only two meals of thin gruel a day. She kept telling him that he should eat three regular meals a day so that he could maintain his health and his one-hundred-pound frame. My mother got very upset, telling him: "You're already so thin and sick with chronic dysentery. How long can you last if you don't have proper nourishment?" My father refused to listen.

Except for soy bean sprouts, my father would eat anything placed before him, never complaining about his food. During all the years he commanded troops at the front, soy sprouts were the one constant item in his diet. He had eaten so many rotten sprouts and sprouts peppered with sand that for the rest of his life he intensely disliked them. His favorite item was salted fish. The cook often had a small piece in a dish prepared especially for him. My mother said it was easy to be his cook because it was so easy to please him, but hard to be his secretary because the documents and memoranda prepared by his aides seldom satisfied him. He was a man of letters who looked at all writings with a critical eye and would pick up his brush pen to edit the piece.

When my father could spare the time, he taught my sister and me Tang poetry. I felt happiness at such times, pleased with the attention he gave me. After supper, under the kerosene lamp that hung from the ceiling, we stood by his side and listened to his recitation and the interpretation he rendered. Flying moths and bugs hovered over the light. The recitation and interpretation were often interrupted by the slapping at the blood-sucking mosquitoes that stung our arms, legs, necks, and faces. I could smell the foul sulfur sticks that were supposed to drive away the mosquitoes. But the mosquitoes were always there.

"Poetry is not only a reflection of the inner self, but also of the external world and life itself," my father explained. When read out loud, a poem was melodious singing. The recitations we rendered by rote always pleased him and he tousled our hair to show his affection, complimenting us, "Well done. We'll continue next time," as he hurried off to his office.

My sister and I learned the "Song of the Conscripts" by the seventh-century poet Du Pu. I can still recite the poem by rote almost fifty years later:

> Chariots rumbling
> Horses howling.
> The conscripts march with bow and arrows at the waist.
> Their fathers, mothers, wives and children run in haste to
>   see them off,
> The bridge is shrouded in the dust they've raised.
> They clutch their coats, stamp their feet and bar their way,
> Their grief cries loud all the way to the clouds, straight away.

The remainder of the poem told the story of conscription to send men off to war. The emperor's greed had made the faraway field a sea of blood, leaving the women to till the fields. The soldiers, the poem went on, were reluctant to speak of their hardships and the bloody battles they fought, of the comrades-in-arms who die in strange lands. The anguish of parents was such that going against both desire and tradition, they preferred the birth of a girl to a boy because a daughter could be married off in a neighboring state and thus spared. But a son would surely be fighting a war, his bones turning white and brittle beneath the grass in faraway soil. Telling the story in the "Song of the Conscripts," my father said that even though modern warfare had replaced bows and arrows with guns and artillery, and with bombs dropping from the sky and mines planted under the ground or beneath the sea, the unchangeable constant in war through the centuries was human grief and the untold suffering of those dying as well as those living, then as now.

I wanted to be close to my father when he was home, yet I was afraid that I would only be a nuisance. I watched him do his early morning *tai chi* exercises in the garden, one foot firmly planted forward on the ground, the other foot slightly bent in a self-protective position, his body slightly turned to the right and then to the left, the palms of his hands one above the other at nose level. He would kick forward with one foot, then the other foot. When he finished, he would walk toward me and I would greet him, "Good morning,

Papa," and bow. He would acknowledge my presence, but I could see his mind was elsewhere. Sometimes he would tousle my hair or slightly pinch my cheek. I would quickly disappear so as not to be late for school. Chinese fathers were known to be *yan*—strict—disciplinarians. My father wasn't *yan* with me, he was just busy and I knew he loved me. Before I went to school, I would look through the window in his study and see him reading, a book or a document in his hand. He kept his classics and poetry collection in there. He always took along some books when he traveled.

I understood that his long trips away from home had to do with county inspections, and he would visit several counties at a time. These visits allowed him to meet with the local administrators and civilian leaders on local governance, to hear their petitions or grievances that dealt with drought, banditry and shortages, and to look into the coordination between civilian and military activities, especially in matters dealing with security and defense. Because of his interest in education, he would visit the local schools. Frequently, classrooms would temporarily become sleeping quarters for him and his entourage at night time, since there were no hotels or guest houses to be found in the counties.

The birth of my brother Pei, in May 1940, was a particularly joyful occasion. My mother gave birth at home, assisted by two women obstetricians. When I came home from school and went into my mother's room, I saw my new baby brother, big and chubby, wrapped in a bundle inside the crib next to her bed. Mother looked very happy and excited. Then she told me that my brother would have the service of my nanny and that I would share her maid until a new one would come on board. I felt very grown up to let my new baby brother have my nanny.

Brother Pei could bawl so loudly that I could hear him even in the garden. I heard whispers that my baby brother had turned blue at the time of his birth; the nurse held him by his feet and gave his bottom two solid whacks before he started to cry and a pink color came over him. But he sure was cuddly and didn't cry that much. Everybody said he looked just like Shao.

The next year, I had another new brother named Hao. Because

of the near mishap in Pei's birth, my mother decided to go to Hong Kong for Hao's birth. Her tummy was very big when she took my sister and brother and me, along with our nannies, to Hong Kong in August. We first went to Guilin by train to fly on to Hong Kong.

My first memories of Hong Kong were the ice cream cups and the movie *Snow White and the Seven Dwarfs*. Every evening, the nannies would walk my sister and me to the store three blocks down the street to buy cups of orange and vanilla ice cream. I enjoyed the dwarfs merrily singing, "Hi ho, hi ho . . ." as they marched to work. Even today, I enjoy watching the video with my little grandchildren.

During our two-month stay in Hong Kong, my mother arranged for a dance teacher to come to our home to give tap-dancing lessons to my sister and me, as well as three daughters of her friends, who were my age. My father had bought the three-story house on King's Road for my mother shortly after their marriage. We had a great deal of fun driving the metal tips and heels of our dance shoes into the wood parquet floor in our living room, competing with each other to see who could make the most marks.

Brother Hao was born in the Queen's Hospital in September. He, too, was a big baby, very pink, and he cried very loud. "When Hao was one month old, we returned to Shaoguan via Guilin," my mother told me. "The British Colonial Government had made available an aircraft for our flight to Guilin. The day before the flight, I ran a fever of 102 degrees, but against the doctor's advice I decided to leave anyway. I was afraid that another plane might not be available for a long time if I missed this one. It ended up being a fortunate decision because, two months later, Hong Kong fell under Japanese occupation.

I have very happy memories of Hong Kong except for one incident. One afternoon when my sister and I were on our way to a Laurel and Hardy movie with a nanny, our chauffeur stopped the car at an intersection to let a British military parade pass by. I was on the front seat and my hand accidentally touched the horn. A startled British soldier in white uniform appeared by the car widow and spoke sternly to the chauffeur. I couldn't understand what he was saying, but I didn't like the manner in which he spoke. He was rude and arrogant as he pointed and shook his finger at me. When he turned to leave, the chauffeur just shrugged his shoulders and told me, "Don't pay him any attention—but don't touch the horn again."

That winter and spring, a stream of visitors came to our home including many dignitaries and friends who had fled Hong Kong. Whenever visitors called on my mother, I would go into the living room, bow to the visitors, greet each one by his or her surname with a kin term attached such as "Uncle Chen" or "Auntie Lu," and then leave the room quietly. Once in a while, my mother would ask me to sit down to listen so that I would learn something.

Grandmother Zhou was the wife of the former president of Sun Yatsen University where my mother had studied. When I came into the room, I saw Grandmother Zhou sniffing into a handkerchief, her eyes red from crying. I bowed to her, curious about what had made her shed tears, hoping my mother would tell me to sit down so that I could learn something. To my disappointment, she told me to go outside to play. I left the room, but I eavesdropped by the door, leaning against the wall.

I heard Grandmother Zhou tell my mother, "I was hiding on the second floor and heard the sound of the Japanese soldiers' boots coming through the garden. . . . Ghok, ghok, ghok . . ." Grandmother Zhou sobbed as she uttered the words so that she sounded like a hen hatching her chicks. "They banged on the door ghok, ghok . . . came into the living room . . . and shouted . . . ghok, ghok, ghok . . . I heard my son scream once, twice, three times . . . six loud screams. Then his screams stopped. Ghok . . . ghok . . . ghok. I knew the Japanese soldiers were bayoneting him . . . ghok . . . ghok . . . ghok. . . ." Old Grandmother Zhou said her son was lying dead in a pool of blood by the time the Japanese soldiers left and she was able to rush downstairs. The Japanese soldiers were searching for her husband who had escaped and left Hong Kong.

I peeked from behind the door and saw my mother holding Grandmother Zhou's hand. Little Granny spotted me and whispered to me not to eavesdrop. Old Grandmother Zhou's account was so sad that I was glad that she told me to go play. I just walked around the garden and pulled bark from the trees.

The United States entered the Pacific theater after Pearl Harbor and declared war on Japan. Great Britain and France also declared war against Japan over Japan's occupation of Hong Kong and the invasion of Java. We rejoiced, because it meant the United States, Great Britain, and China would all become allies fighting militarist Japan. The Second World War had exploded!

I learned such events not only at home, but also at school, where important news of the day was written in white chalk on a big blackboard for all the students to see. Each morning at the school assembly, the principal spoke to students, explaining the engagement of the Allied forces in Europe, Africa, and Australia, as well as in the Pacific stretching from the Philippines to Burma and all the way to Java.

Our parents and teachers reminded us of our duty as good citizens. We should study hard, be frugal and willing to aid others, especially little children and older people. Everybody had a responsibility to help win the war, and we children were to contribute to the reconstruction of China when we grew up, making her free and strong among nations.

Even at that age, my love for China was genuine, and I knew I was privileged because of my parents' positions. Dreaming of the future, I aspired to become a teacher, a writer, a scientist, or a legislator.

Two to three times a year, my sister and I went with our father to Nanhua Temple in the outskirts of Shaoguan. This is where my father would go whenever possible for reflection and prayer.

Although it gave me the chance to be with my father, I never enjoyed the visits to Nanhua Temple. I was frightened of the huge temple gods guarding the main entrance, their bulging eyes staring at me every time I passed through. Even worse was the eerie feeling that Brother Shao was buried beneath the small open pavilion on the temple grounds, and I always wondered if his ghost was following me around. I had heard many ghost stories from the servants who told tales based on their own encounters or from old village tales. When my parents traveled, Little Granny presided at telling ghost stories after supper with the household servants and aides around the table. My fists tight, eyes opened wide, and legs dangling from the chair, I would sit next to Little Granny or my maidservant, Spring Grace, relishing the tales. I didn't want to miss a word. There were tales of ghosts who were hungry and lacking money and warmth, ghosts who came back to haunt because no offering of food or paper money had been made for their passage to the underworld of the dead. Ghosts wailed, cried or howled for the wrongs they had suffered, wanting to be understood and looking for someone to redress their wrongs. Ghosts sullenly blew in and out with the breeze, walked under the shadow of the fog and by the light of the moon. Women ghosts had a way of holding their heads in their hands, combing and braiding their hair under dim oil lamps.

So frightened by ghost stories was I that the shadows of the flickering oil lamp on the wall and the fluttering moths and bugs that circled the room gave me the shivers. At night I insisted that Spring Grace sit by me as I went to sleep, pulling the sheet over my head even as I was sweating in the humid summer heat.

Spring Grace was a young maidservant whose main job was to take care of me now that I no longer needed a nanny. She was my closest companion and friend for the greater part of my childhood. The first time I saw her she was standing by the door of my room with her eyes looking down, as if searching for something on the floor. She was tall and dark-skinned, her eyebrows heavily set on her angular face, and she wore a loose pajama-style top and pants.

Little Granny had brought Spring Grace to meet me, saying that she would attend to me from now on. She was to get water for my washing in the morning, serve me breakfast, be sure I dressed warmly for school when the weather turned cold, and fill a hot water bag for my bed at night. She would also attend to my bathing at night. Spring Grace had other duties. She waited on tables with the other servants and served tea when guests came to call. But her main place was with me whenever I needed her.

I learned that she was thirteen years old, just five years older than I was. Spring Grace had been bonded as a young maidservant to my paternal grandmother back in the village when she was barely six years old. She was the youngest of three children and the only girl. There was a drought that year and her parents were unable to farm enough to feed the family. To make certain the sons would not starve, her parents took her to my grandmother and pleaded with her to do a "good deed" and take their daughter for a price. Someday, when they saved some money, they would redeem their daughter.

Although the old custom of purchasing or bonding young girls as maidservants was legally abolished, the practice had continued in villages. For centuries, the bonding of poor people's daughters as maidservants had been looked upon as a charitable deed by many. Custom demanded that the young maidservants would be well treated, and, when they passed into their later teen or twenties, suitable husbands be found for them. During holidays, they would return to the home of their mistress for the festivities as if they were married daughters.

Spring Grace always had a piece of cake or a bowl of sweet gruel made of lotus roots or mung beans ready for me when I came home from school in the afternoon. Our favorite pastime was kicking feather birdies. We made the birdies ourselves with thin round rubber pieces fastened together and decorated with lustrous rooster feathers. The birdie was kicked up and inward with the right foot in rapid succession. Another way to play was to kick it up and inward with the right foot, let the birdie land on the tip of the left foot, then toss it into the air and kick it again with the right foot. There were many ways to play this game; a skillful player could kick the birdie into the air hundreds of times without letting it fall to the ground.

Every afternoon except for Sunday, our tutor Teacher Lee reviewed my sister's and my homework. When the tutor was not occupied with my sister or me, Spring Grace would ask her to explain the meaning of something she had read, or she would present her with a vocabulary list she had compiled. Realizing the interest she had in learning, my sister and I made it our responsibility to teach Spring Grace arithmetic. We made up problems for her to solve, then checked the answers. Teaching Spring Grace became a mission for us, and we both felt good about our efforts in doing this for her.

The Lunar New Year celebration was always fun because school was in recess and I had only calligraphy for homework. I loved the crackling sound of firecrackers, the dragon dance, the holiday candies and cakes and, best of all, the traditional red envelope with money. On the morning of New Year's Day, I would receive ten yuan from my parents when I greeted them with a "Happy New Year" and a bow, and one or two yuan from relatives as well as some of the guests who came to wish my parents a joyous year ahead. As the day progressed, the money from the red envelopes would accumulate adding up to more than one hundred yuan, not a small sum at that time, particularly in the eyes of a child. Mother told us children that the soldiers fighting in the front needed money for blankets and medicine, and that we should donate the money from our red envelopes to the war chest for the soldiers. My siblings and I rode with our mother to Shaoguan to drop the money in a big collection box. We felt proud and happy that we were doing something to help fight the war.

The other fun part of New Year was having my older (half) brothers Huon and Kam home for the holidays. I adored my older brothers, who were boarders in middle school away from Shaoguan. They also came home during summer recess. I loved the stories they told and the riddles they had me guessing, and I marveled at their quick wit in solving arithmetic problems in the blink of an eye. My eldest (half) brother Ban rarely came home, and I always regarded his homecoming as particularly special. He was already in an army officer's uniform, having spent two years first Germany and then in Czechoslovakia where he studied military science. Everybody always commented that Brother Ban looked like our father.

We lived on Huanggong Hill from 1939 to 1943, then we moved into a larger house and compound that faced Black Dragon Pond. My father renamed it Mirror Pond because of the way the water reflected light under the sun. Our new home was only a few kilometers from our old house, but because it stood on flat ground with another hill behind it, trucks and cars could drive right into the compound and all the way to the front of the house. Hired workers tended the chicken coops and the vegetable and watermelon patches behind the house. Barracks large enough to house about sixty troops stood near the entrance to the compound.

Summertime was the most carefree and fun, picking and eating the tomatoes from the garden, twice the size of my fist and watermelons red and yellow. The butterflies we caught were mounted into specimens. We had two little boats in the pond. After sundown my sister and I, along with Spring Grace and sometimes a schoolmate or two, paddled the boat, landing on the inlet searching for nests in hope of catching a fledgling bird. One time we caught two baby magpies and placed them in a bamboo cage. For two whole weeks we fed them with grain and worms and saw their wobbly legs grow strong and their feathers thicken. The little birds cried day and night. We decided the birds wanted their mother, so we took them back to the inlet and put them in the nest where we found them.

On hearing the sound of the galloping horses or the sound of his automobile engine, we children would race to greet Papa with a bow at the front entrance. "Papa!" we would scream at the top of our lungs because he was hard of hearing. Our father would be playful with each of us, giving us mock orders and coming up to tousle our hair. Neat and smart in our smocks and togs, we happily hopped behind him, stamping our leather shoes on the graveled ground pretending to be part of his retinue.

On occasion the whole family sang marching songs together. My little cherubic brother Pei learned to sing along, but my youngest brother Hao just bounced around, jumping and laughing. My sister Chi and I tried to harmonize, she the alto and I the soprano. We could easily outsing our parents. My sister had big eyes and fair skin. Everybody said she looked like the American child movie star Shirley Temple. I felt envious whenever I heard that, because she had all the attention from the adults. I had seen Shirley Temple movies in Hong Kong. Shirley Temple was very pretty and cute. My sister was very pretty and cute.

I never quite got used to my parents traveling and staying away from home, especially my mother. Sometimes I cried under my bedcovers, feeling sorry for myself. I knew we were fighting the Japanese after the invasion, and my parents were doing their duty. I knew that I should be patriotic and not think only of myself. But I felt very lonely and wished they had taken me along. On one occasion I cried without shame when my mother was leaving for Chungking. I was a very happy girl when an aide returned with a letter from my mother, the first letter I had ever received. She told me that she missed me and thought of me all the time, and that I should be good and diligent with my schoolwork and a caring sister to my younger siblings.

Another time a military representative of the United States forces came to our home to discuss with my father the possibility of a marine landing in the Japanese-occupied territories along the shores of Guangdong. That evening, while my sister, brothers, and I were playing in our parents' bedroom, Father was in his pajamas sitting on the bed, Mother next to him. Father told us solemnly and proudly that he had volunteered to lead the guerrillas for the preparation of the U.S. marine landing in the southern coastal region. He was so full of patriotism and pride when he told us that he would be happy to take up arms and lead the fighting men, just as he had done before his appointment as governor.

Having said that he was ready to give his life for his country, if that was wanted of him, he looked at my mother and tried to smile. But I knew his smile wasn't real. Then he patted us on the head one by one—me, my sister, and my two little brothers. Mother was quiet. She turned her head, her eyes looking out the window into the darkness. I wanted to cry but I pretended to be brave and I smiled, too. I was worried and scared. I understood that thousands of combat troops and civilians would be sacrificed. I didn't want my father to die, and secretly I hoped there would be no marine landing.

Chapter Six

"All My Children, All My Sisters"

During the war, my mother wore her hair short and never any make-up; a pair of gold-rimmed glasses rested on her nose. She often wore pants and a white shirt, or a mustard green uniform like my father's. My mother took my sister and me to visit the refugee children's homes and schools and the women's brigade camp whenever this didn't interfere with our schooling—which meant only on Sundays or during summer vacation. I was about six years old when she first worked with the refugee children and the soldiers' widows. Already I had formed two distinct impressions: My mother was consumed with her work because these people were "all my children, all my sisters," and, on that account, the children and the women were kindred to me in some way and I would have to share my mother with them.

"You must think of them as brothers and sisters," my mother told me about the refugee children. "I and all the teachers caring for them are now their parents. We are family." I thought it was neat to claim so many brothers and sisters and hoped that nobody would ever ask me their names. I didn't mind sharing my mother as long as she wasn't away all the time. I wanted to go with her to the children's homes and schools more often and get to know some of the children, wondering how many were older than I and how many were younger.

The receiving center in the town of Shayuan was an hour from Shaoguan, and the Children's Home and School in Nanxiong was within three or four hours by car, so I got to visit these from time to time. I have the vivid memory of seeing all the children in unisex scout uniforms, and the way to tell the girls apart from the boys was their haircut. The boys had crew cuts, and the girls had short hair cut ear-length. When a whistle was blown, one thousand children would march in formation onto the parade ground. The centers looked like schools—except that they were much bigger—in which the buildings were constructed of bamboo mats and poles, wood, and pine bark, and had a parade ground that would accommodate a thousand. On the review platform, my sister and I would join my mother and others watching the children in game competitions or in exercise.

Afterward we would sit on short wood stools and eat with hundreds of children and their teachers in a big hall that had a thatch roof but no walls. The older children on kitchen duty would scoop the rice and vegetables mixed with legumes into the enamel cups held outstretched from the long line. When the children finished eating, they were given their boiled water the same way, also scooped from a big cauldron. We had our food from the cauldron, too, but it came in bowls brought to us with a salute. I ate heartily, excited by the novelty of it all, looking at the children gobbling down their food and smiling with their stomachs full. I knew I was a very privileged person. These visits undoubtedly taught me something about duty and service, watching the dedication with which my mother went about her tasks, speaking with the teachers and the children, inspecting the dormitories and spending hours in meetings.

I knew the story of the refugee children and the war widows in the Women's Production Brigade from my own witnessing, as well as from the tales of many who were participants in these brigades, and from published accounts in journals, newspapers, and books. In the course of gathering material for this book, I asked my mother to use her own words to tell her story and gave her a tape recorder and some cassettes. Several months later, in the summer of 1997, my mother handed back to me seven two-hour cassettes she had recorded.

My mother was approaching her eighty-seventh year, but her voice was steady and strong in her narration:

> I was pulled into the rescue operations early in the War of Resistance against Japan. In early spring 1938, the first group of war

orphans arrived shortly after the fall of Guangzhou. At the time, the provincial government appointed the New Life Women's Commission as the coordinating agency to rescue children who were trapped in the occupied territories and fighting zones. The Women's Commission was given the task of forming a network with the county governments, civic agencies, and guerrilla groups. The operation of the mission was charged to the counties. The refugee children, once rescued, were transported to a central site in Shayuan outside of Shaoguan.

At the time, I was head of the New Life Women's Commission, so I took responsibility for organizing the rescue teams and taking care of the children afterward. In my speech to the rescue workers departing for the occupied territories, I entreated them to go about their mission caring for the children as if they were family kin. "Attend to the children's safety and to their food and hygiene needs. Be the children's confidante, breathe with them and share your fate with them," I told them. I reminded them that the mission would certainly involve personal risks and that the stakes were high. They would face hardship could even encounter and enemy gunfire, all the while encumbered with frightened and sick children. The rescuers had to penetrate behind the enemy lines, locate and round up the children, and get them inland by whatever means possible. So many things were unpredictable in war. The rescuers had to face the fact that all the plans and logistics that had been carefully laid out could become inoperable at any moment. In such instances, they had to be quick and resourceful in transporting the children out of the fighting zones by whatever means possible.

Chen Mingsu led the first group of forty-six young teens out of Guangzhou after it fell. She was a remarkable and energetic woman who was already involved with youth work in Guangzhou at the onset of the war. Chen—tall, her hair short, her posture erect—was ten years older than I was. She was my mentor who taught me a great deal about organization. Within months, these teens became junior rescue volunteers in the operations. Because of their own experience of losing parents, family, and home, they had an especially keen sense of the mission and shouldered their responsibilities like adults. These young rescuers were incredibly determined. Their will was like steel as they pitched in and did their part. They were dependable, alert, and patriotic.

The rescuers wore plain everyday clothes to remain inconspicuous. They went inside the occupied territories by whatever vehicles were available, and often on foot. They picked up abandoned children on streets and along railroad tracks and highways, some of them crying beside their dead parents. The children were brought to a designated location and transported by trucks if available, or by boat to the receiving center in Shayuan.

The refugee children came by tens and sometimes hundreds. Some were the children of soldiers who had perished in battle. On arrival, the children all looked bewildered, their clothes soiled and torn, their heads full of lice and scabs. They had skin infections and many were skeletally thin. Many were sick with fever and diarrhea-inducing diseases. The children had been through the merciless experience of seeing their homes burned and destroyed and their parents and kin mutilated and killed before their very own eyes. These children lost their ability to smile and laugh. They made hardly a sound, even when crying.

When the children assembled at the Shayuan center, our first task was to feed and clean them, change their clothes, and give them a physical check-up. The sick ones were housed in the infirmary and fed liquids before solids until they regained sufficient strength to join the healthy ones. We separated those eight years old and older from the younger ones. The younger ones were transferred to the Baoyu Yuan—Caring Centers—and the older ones to the *Guangdong Ertung Jiaoyong Yuan*, the Guangdong Children's Homes and Schools. We had a dedicated staff. They were tireless. With care and some pampering from the staff, the children's smiles and laughter returned. Their healing began as they shared their sorrow and hardship, and then the joy and achievement in their new family. Because of their remarkable resilience, the children recovered from the most devastating personal traumas a person could face.

Within the first twelve months, over eleven thousand children were rescued. At the fall of Guanghou and later Hong Kong, we received eight children, four boys and four girls, from one family alone. This necessitated the founding of seven homes and schools, a thousand children each, for their shelter and education. They were known as Number One Home and School, Number Two Home and School, all the way to Number Seven. I became the president of the organization, and each center had a director in charge of operations. We selected sites that were close by the river and the hills. The river provided a natural place for bathing, and the hills gave protection during air raids. Being close to the river also made it easier to ship grain and supplies.

I had never dreamed of nor for a moment had I thought that I would have the inner strength or resourcefulness to become involved with the lives of thousands of children who had lost their parents—and another thousand more women whose soldier husbands had perished. I did not want to be the organization's head in name only. There was work to be done that ranged from organizing rescues in the occupied territories to finding shelter, food, and medicine, and creating an opportunity for the education of the rescued children. Each step involved planning, staffing, raising funds, and procuring supplies. I presented the case of war relief work, begging and cajoling, trying to persuade those who had money and influence to help. It was an endless cycle, with more and more children arriving week after week.

At times my mother was emotional as she told her story, but her voice remained steady:

I was not quite thirty years old. What pushed me forward was the tragedy of the time, a commitment to do my part for Guangdong and for the country, and my youthful energy and naiveté. I lost my five-year-old son to illness within months of assuming the responsibilities for the war orphans. I thought to myself, my son had the best of care at that time, but we were not able to save him. These refugee children have no parents. That thought gave me resolve and courage so I worked and smiled, but often I was crying inside. I understood the anguish of parents who lost their precious children, and of children who had no parents, because I had lost my own mother before age two. I pulled myself together to do what had to be done and did my best for them. The Guangdong Children's Homes and Schools Incorporation was formally established in a ceremony at the Sun Yatsen Park one week after my son Shao's burial.

The first time I went to Chungking was to present the plan for the children's homes and schools for Guangdong Province. I met with the minister of finance, Dr. H. H. Kung, in order to procure the necessary funds. My original plan requested 100,000 yuan and a quota of 10,000 refugee children. Dr. Kung was surprised at the modest budget and asked me many questions about the plan. I explained that we would watch our spending very carefully and would work very hard on voluntary contributions to supplement government funding. At the end of our hour-long meeting, Dr. Kung signed an executive order for the allocation of the 100,000 yuan that I requested, but he set a quota of 1,000 orphans instead of 10,000. "The work will require lot more money than your plan projects," Kung warned. He was right. Inexperienced and a neophyte, I had no idea of the cost it would take to shelter, clothe, feed, and educate the children, and over the years, to train and maintain a staff of 4,500 people for the operations. Three months later, I went to Chungking again to petition for enlarging the quota and for more funds to accommodate the steady stream of incoming refugee children. The quota was increased to 3,000. Kung explained that this was the most the central government could do for Guangdong. But the children kept on coming. Fortunately, the provincial government came to our aid and funded four more centers with one thousand children each. Resources were hard to come by, even to have enough grain for daily consumption. Every sack of rice, every crate of medicine, and every yuan for salary, shelter, blankets, and clothing was precious and had to be raised or negotiated. I learned to speak in front of groups and in the presence of ministers, and even before the Generalissimo and with Madame Chiang Kaishek.

I went to Chungking two to three times a year. In those days, transportation was difficult; I had first to go to Guilin by overnight train and then wait there for a flight to Chungking. The flights were seldom on schedule and often canceled. The planes were small with two rows of seats facing each other and accommodated about twenty people. The metal seats were so cold that I felt frozen in the air.

Your father was governor of Guangdong Province at the time. It was his order that second only to the military, the Children's Homes and Schools would be next in line for the grain allotment. As a result, the children never suffered hunger in times of drought and food shortage. Medicine and funds were also in short supply. When we went around to search and beg for them, some turned the other way, unimpressed by the dire needs and fate of the refugee children. But there were many who were generous and helpful. Whatever assistance we received was like being given coal during a snowstorm. But the contributions simply could not match the need.

I was often away from home for planning and inspections, thus leaving you children to the care of our nannies. I paid the price of losing Shao. But, then, when your father returned from a conference in Guilin, he told me that he had heard much talk about "Madame's Clique"—referring to my work with the refugee children and the brigade women. Guangdong's rescue work attracted journalists from all over, including the foreign press and top officials from the central government. Such visits gave our work both visibility and recognition for achievement. The gossips were most unkind and upsetting. My work with the orphans and the women bothered many people out of envy. Most of it came from men who were unable to accept a woman as a partner in matters that counted. The defense minister Chen Cheng told your father that he thought I should "slow down." I felt so hurt. I had to make a decision either to go head-on with the work I was doing or to retreat into the background. I decided to continue meeting the rescue tasks head-on. To avoid further insinuations that I dominated the provincial government politics and to make your father's position easier, I relegated the women's production brigade to Chen Mingsu, resigned from most of the committee memberships, and concentrated all my energy on directing the Children's Homes and Schools.

Here my mother's voice grew strong and animated, as if she were speaking to an audience:

The Guangdong Children's Homes and Schools combined *guan*, discipline, *jiao*, education, *yong*, nurturing, and *wai*, guardianship, as the organizing principles in carrying out their mission. These, in turn, formed the framework for *jia*, family, *hsiao*, school, *yean*, camp, *tien*, farm. *Guan* taught the children to become self-reliant, to conduct themselves with moral fortitude and to behave as responsible citizens. *Jiao* embodied the principle of teaching oneself and teaching others that included writing, reading, arithmetic, music, and art. *Yong* emphasized self sufficiency, attended to learning about the economy and livelihood, and showed the children the importance of productive work through their study of nature in relation to planting, garden-farming as well as handicrafts. *Wai* involved guardianship of the Motherland, emphasized health and physical education, and applied the survival skills of boy scouts to war situations. The Homes and Schools embodied family, school, camp, and farms that protected and sheltered, as well as teaching the children that they were valued and loved and that they were assets to their country.

Professor Chiu Jai-Young, who was the dean of the College of Education at the Sun Yatsen University, became our advisor. As I was an alumna of the university, it gave me easy access to tap into the academic talent pool. Many of the professors and graduates rallied around me and offered their support, not because I was the governor's lady, but because I was an alumna and a schoolmate.

One of the most significant contributions to the refugee children was made by Professor Chui. He formulated a national-ethnic awareness curriculum and designed a four-year system for the primary grades in lieu of the normal six-year curriculum in that he added the summer months for regular school work. Chui laid out a teaching theme for the four years of primary education. The first year emphasized homeland in the context of village, town, and city; the second year the present and the future of China; the third year the history of the Chinese people; and the fourth year China and the world today. The lesson plans were organized into weekly learning modules. The children were also involved in extracurricular competitions in writing, art, singing, track and field, games, and drama—activities that challenged their minds and physical dexterity. The curriculum worked very well for our children, since they were older than the ordinary children of those grades. They were even taught how to build a suspension bridge.

The children made their own jute-and-straw sandals. In the early years, there were wooden peg benches that held the leather straps to wooden soles and nails to fasten the soles. Then leather straps and nails became unattainable. As funds became scarcer, we were no longer able to replace the old benches that were lost during evacuations. Several children had the ingenuity to braid the jute and straw for use as straps and soles by sitting on the ground and using their two big toes as pegs.

We recruited young women from the counties who were graduates of normal and middle schools with several years of work experience as teachers. Each teacher was responsible for twelve children. We trained over five hundred teachers in groups of one hundred in three-week sessions. Health, academic excellence, and creativity were what we strove to cultivate in our children. Our teachers were the children's confidantes. They shared their meals, lived in the same dormitory, attended the classes, worked in the fields, and engaged in recreation with the children. In the classroom, they were teachers. After recess, they became parents. They acted as group leaders when laboring in the fields, and as older brothers and sisters in the playground. They were young, energetic, patriotic, willing to give, and had a sense of mission for the country and for the children.

The teachers organized the children to help soldiers write letters home and assist the neighboring peasants harvesting their crops. Some bought postage with their meager pay for their young charges so that they could send letters to relatives. They led the older children in building roads and clearing the fields for a parade ground; they even helped with erecting the dormitories. There were many deeds that were beyond the call of duty. At the Number Six Home and School, its director asked each teacher and staff member to adopt one or two of the children as their godchildren for the New Year's holiday in honor of New Year's Day 1942, and give a small gift to each child. Everyone did.

To encourage the teachers to further their own learning, we set up a special fund to pay the tuition for those who got themselves admitted to normal schools or universities. The Homes and Schools organized troops of young volunteers to go to the counties that were close to the front line in order to promote China's efforts in the war. They wanted to arouse people's patriotism to become fighting guerrillas and intelligence gatherers to report on the traitors and enemy movements.

When we first started the Homes and Schools, we were able to give the sick children cod liver oil and feed them soup cooked with pork liver and beans as a nutritional supplement. All other children were fed two ounces of meat twice a week. But when the war dragged on and meat became more and more scarce and there were more children to feed, we improvised a way to give the children the needed protein. For no fee, the Homes and Schools borrowed ox bones from factories that collected the bones for making tooth brush handles and fertilizer. The bones were cooked in giant iron cauldrons with lentils. The nutrients from the marrow mixed with lentils provided nourishment to children. The bones were then returned to the factories for their original intended use. The merchants were happy that they had saved the cost of firewood for boiling the bones to be sawed into toothbrush handles. Later, when ox bones were not longer available, we had to ration the legumes by the spoonful for protein. To save on salary and to conserve the funds for food, we dismissed the cooks and then trained and rotated the older children for kitchen duties. The children raised their own vegetables and yams, gathered firewood, and prepared meals to feed over one thousand hungry mouths every day. Those who had kitchen duties during the day would make up their classroom studies at night under the watchful eyes of their teachers.

The United States had donated some cloth to China, which was dubbed Roosevelt cloth. The cloth had been stuck in storage in

Chungking. The central government had not been able to get the cloth distributed to the organizations that could made use of it due to the lack of transportation. When we heard about the "Roosevelt" cloth, we looked for ways to get some for the children's use. We were lucky to obtain an allotment of the cloth for the children's uniforms. It happened that the central government was printing paper currency in Hong Kong, and the Bank of Guangdong was responsible for transporting the paper currency to Chungking. The provincial government had trucks assigned for the transport. Since the trucks normally returned home empty after the paper currency had been unloaded in the central government treasury, they were able to bring the Roosevelt cloth back to us free of charge. The Roosevelt cloth was of a higher quality than homespun cloth. Afterward, our children were dressed smartly in unisex shirts and shorts sewn by the women in the production brigade.

We didn't have basketballs, volleyballs, or ping-pong balls, or musical instruments for the children's recreation. Those were rare luxury items that were hard to come by. The children carved wood and bamboo pieces into checkers sets. They made feather birdies from old newspaper and bits of rubber for kicking, jump ropes from jute and straw that the peasants found too tedious to gather, and long bamboo poles cut from the wild groves along the rivers or on the hillsides for high jumping. Together with their teachers, they built swings and turned the parade ground into a recreation field.

But just as soon as we had the operations under control, the Japanese came. During the retreat to Lian County in 1940, the children—some as young as ten years old—walked 350 kilometers over fields and mountains. They backpacked their bedding and clothes and grain and marched like soldiers. The older children had the additional burden of carrying the cooking cauldrons and supplies, as well as the sick ones in large straw baskets on poles shouldered by teams of two. On the paths along narrow rice paddies and on mountainous roads, the children sang. As the days became longer and longer and they grew tired, their feet covered with painful blisters. They moaned and cried. "How much farther do we have to go?" the children asked. "Ten more miles," responded the teachers. It was ten more miles and another ten more miles that finally got everyone to our destination.

Almost immediately after the Homes and Schools settled in their new sites in Lian County, three children from the Number One Home and School died in a meningitis epidemic. Its director immediately isolated the sick children, canceled all classes, and ordered all the others to stay in their dormitories. Other centers followed suit. We appealed to Guangxi Province for medicine, gave the children vaccination shots, and had everyone wear a cotton face mask. Two more children died in the epidemic. The measures taken were able to reduce the spread of the disease and arrest the epidemic. Sadly, Director Liang himself died of a viral infection the following year.

We established an experimental middle school for talented children who had finished their primary education. At the experimental school, we hired two renowned teachers to train young opera singers, musicians, and acrobats. With donated funds, we had costumes and musical instruments ordered from Guilin. These young actors and singers entertained troops and performed for the public just like real professionals. The most talented of the children entered Lixing Middle School, and the others went to the vocational schools or Beijiang Normal School for teacher training. We founded factories that produced paper, soap, woodcrafts, printing, and bricks to give work to those past the age of eighteen. Our aim was to have them gainfully employed and able to have a livelihood as young adults. Some children were likely to reconnect with their families and kin. We also had a school for delinquents who required extra attention in their schooling and development. The one thing they did that caused the most trouble was stealing the peasants' hogs and roasting them for feasting in the hillsides.

Each year, some twenty children passed the national examinations and gained entrance to the air force and naval cadet schools. All together, over a thousand volunteered for those branches of the armed service that recruited students. Some of the teens who failed to meet the weight requirement put rocks in their pockets, hoping that they could sneak through the examination in order to have the opportunity to fight the enemy. I was proud of them. They were true sons and daughters of China. But it broke my heart to see them go, and I wept every time a group took leave. For I knew that most if not all of them would be incinerated by bombs and explosions in crossfire with the enemy in defense of China.

My mother's voice was full of pride and very emotional at times. I remember well many of the sounds and sights of the refugee children at the Shayuan center and the Number Three Home and School in Nanxiong. The children sang songs about China and about their Homes and Schools, and I learned to sing along with them.

There were songs specially written for the children, "At our homestead, we have thatch houses in the shaded forest, next to the stream, behind the hills. We have no fear of wind and rain, no fear of air raids. The river is our friend, the plain our home. . . ." They sang the Song of the Yellow River, "The wind howled, the war horse growled. . . ." They sang when they got up in the morning, during exercise on the parade ground, before taking their meals, during play, and when retiring for the night. The songs raised our spirits, enhanced the sense of camaraderie, and reminded everyone to persevere and win the war for the Motherland.

The visits to the experimental school were always fun. I liked watching the theatrical group practice singing opera, playing the drums and *huchins*, which is a Chinese string instrument, and doing acrobatics. They dressed in colorful costumes, painted their faces like real opera singers and actors and performed on stage for the civil servants, the public, and the soldiers. Behind our home in Mirror Pond the Lixing Middle School. I was a first-year student there in seventh grade. Each year, many of the upper-grade students passed the scholastic and physical examinations for admittance into the youth air force and naval cadet schools. My parents would send them off with a dinner at our home. I was given the honor to present each one with a Chinese-English dictionary. My mother was learning English with a tutor, and students in Lixing received English instruction. "Language is a tool. We must prepare for the future when English will certainly facilitate exchange and communication with other nations," said Mother in her farewell to the departing teens. On these occasions, my mother's eyes became very red and moist when she said good bye to them.

Recalling the old days as I listened to my mother's narration, I felt immensely proud and was glad that I had shared her with the refugee children. Although I was not yet a teenager during those days, I recognized my special standing as the daughter of the governor of Guangdong. I felt good whenever I was able to be a part of her work with the other children. I learned and sang songs, attended flag raisings and parades in review, and even marched with the children on occasions. My mother never lectured me on what was going on around us, but would bring me along with her to "watch and learn something." The impact of her dedication to duty has stuck with me throughout my professional life.

In the next segment of her recording, my mother continued in her zestful voice:

My other involvement was with the Women's Production Brigade that was founded to accommodate the war widows and women who had been rescued past the age of eighteen. There were over one thousand of them. The brigade was located in town of Shielieting, about midway between Shaoguan and Huanggong. The women wore soldiers' uniforms and received military training to enable them to function as a security force in times of emergency. Among the aims of the brigade were that every woman should achieve literacy, contribute to production, and acquire some skills so that she would be able to support herself when she returned to her hometown or village when the war ends. The women made straw sandals and sewed uniforms to supply the troops. We referred to all the women in the brigade as "students." Their mornings were spent in military training, afternoons in farming, sewing, and crafts, and evenings in adult education classes. Since some of the women had young children, we added a nursery for their care.

Chen Mingsu, commandant of the brigade, was my right arm. I depended on her and I learned so much about group work and planning from her. Until her tragic death in a car accident in the early months of the war, she took charge of the brigade organization. Chen always wore a soldier's uniform. Her gentle nature, enthusiasm, quick deliberating mind, and her capacity to shoulder responsibility and work made her a most attractive person to anyone who came into contact with her. When she died, I lost a close friend and mentor, and the women of Guangdong lost an irreplaceable leader.

When I became the brigade commandant, I followed the lead of my predecessor and wore a soldier's uniform whenever I came to the camp or visited the Children's Homes and Schools. It was never my desire to be the women's brigade commandant. The gossips and all the talk about "Madame's Clique" hurt me deeply and had made me weary. But the women came in delegations and pleaded. It was a challenge for me to assume the post. My deputy Chen Waizhen was a twenty-six-year-old woman, and I delegated to her the tasks of the brigade's daily operations. We vowed that we would work together to develop and expand the work that Chen Mingsu had given such a solid foundation. Soon we added a dye shop and machine- and hand-weaving shops for making towels, socks, and uniforms. We also acquired animal husbandry and developed aquaculture. We recruited vocational school teachers and specialists, and each shop was supervised by a director of operations. The shop products were sold in the market to meet the shortage of consumer goods, and they also provided a source of revenue for the brigade organization. The brigade also published the magazine *Guangdong's Women,* as well as adult literacy texts for the general population.

Troops from other provinces were often transported through Shaoguan; the brigade women greeted the troops with congee—a thin gruel—cooked with gluten rice and cane sugar to boost their moral. The congee was such a luxury that many soldiers had tears in their eyes while savoring it. "We have not tasted anything so good in a long time. This is our victory congee. We will fight unto death for our Motherland," said the grateful soldiers.

In the final days of evacuation, in 1941, and again in 1945, when the enemy was pressing closer, the women patrolled the city and participated in the evacuation. Their presence helped calm the population and gave people courage. . . . Out of colossal tragedy in the young lives of these women, the brigade rose like a phoenix from the broken hearts and ashes. Our women were strong, solid and fearless.

I visited the brigade with Mother often, since it was located in Shaoguan, only about an hour from home. I saw women in soldiers' uniforms marching and drilling, sewing uniforms, making straw sandals, and farming. During one visit, I sat next to my mother eating supper with eight teachers. A gasoline lamp hung on a tree and buzzing little bugs fluttered around it. My mother was busy talking with the teachers at the table. I ate the food quietly while the mosquitoes feasted on me. The second time my chopsticks reached for the dish of chicken in front of me, I felt my mother's hand tapping my knee. I looked at her, but she did not look back or say anything. The third time I reached for the chicken, she leaned over to whisper close into my ear, "Eat some vegetables and squash instead. Save the meat for others." On our way home, she explained that the women in the brigade seldom had chicken with their meals, far less so than we did at home, and that I should be thoughtful of them when we ate together.

In January 1945, as the Japanese advanced toward Shaoguan, the provincial government evacuated once more; this time to Mei

County further north of Shaoguan bordering Fujian Province. The night before the retreat, our house was eerily quiet. The aides and servants all spoke in whispers. The living room was lined with suitcases, canvas bags stuffed with bedding and clothes, and tied bundles. After breakfast the next morning, I came into my mother's study, curious about what was going on. My mother was talking on the phone when the telephone operator interrupted to announce that the enemy had advanced to the city of Nanxiong. Then the line was cut. I could see the worry in my mother's face, and in the faces of all those secretaries and aides who were present. I could feel my heart pounding. I knew Nanxiong was only seventy kilometers from Shaoguan, three hours by car or train, because I had visited the refugee Children's Home and School there with my mother. We children were sent away immediately. My mother was to follow, but my father stayed behind in Shaoguan.

Our four-door sedan was piled with bags and bundles tied with ropes, thirteen people packed inside—children on the laps of adults—and two guards standing on the running board on each side holding onto the doors. My mother, stoic and in control, saw us off and then went back inside the house with an aide. The car jerked and moved slowly on the unpaved dirt road and winding mountain path. My head nearly hit the ceiling as the car bounced and bounced. At one point I threw up into a can from motion sickness. Then I saw refugees limping along; they were carrying nursing babies, young children, old parents, and whatever bundles they could manage on their backs or in bamboo baskets carried on shoulder poles. Children of my age and younger sat on the roadside with their little brothers and sisters crying, their parents helplessly looked on.

I started to sing "By the Jialing River, enemies invaded my village, I lost my farm, my home, my family and the cows and sheep. . . ." My sister joined in singing, " I lost my laughter and my dreams. . . . I must go back amidst enemy bullets and bayonets. . . ." We sang "Song of the Yellow River. . . . Winds howling, horses growling . . . ," and "Defend our China. . . . We will all arise to defend our China." We sang from our hearts with sadness, anger, hope, and the determination to annihilate the enemy.

During the next twenty-four hours, we were not certain whether or not our parents had made it to the escape route. I desperately hoped my parents would be safe and that I wouldn't become an orphan. I was only ten years old. What would I do with my younger sister and brothers? Later, Captain Tao told us that my mother retreated when the Japanese got as close as fifteen kilometers away. She had set up an emergency command post in Shaoguan, directing the movement of brigade women patrolling the city and assisting in the evacuation. My father finally retreated when the Japanese had advanced to five kilometers outside of Shaoguan. He held a sub-machine gun in his hand while his vehicle made its way out.

From Shaoguan, the civil servants and their families, including ours, retreated to Mei County to the east. I was sorry to leave our new home at Mirror Pond, which we had moved into only a year earlier. Spring Grace and several of my school friends used to fish in the pond with bamboo rods that we had made ourselves. Sometimes my sister would trail along. We tied long strings to the rod with wire hooks our cook had bought at the market. We dug worms for bait along the edge of the pond. We rarely caught any fish, but it was fun seeing the little fish swimming and fighting for the bait as soon as it was dropped into the water. I had to leave my collection of forty-some mounted butterflies behind. They were a medley of sun-bright orange, peacock blue, yellow, snow white, and midnight black—caught with the swat of a woven straw fan and pinned to a piece of cardboard. Within my precious collection of specimens were two marigold-colored ones bigger than my hands, given to me by one of the guards. All the while I kept thinking about the butterflies, until I saw the refugees retreating on foot.

My mother's voice was shaky when recalling the eve of victory and what happened to her children and the fruits of her labor:

"Your father's departure as governor affected me, too. Except for the Lixing Middle School that Bohao and I took over and supported as a private school, the three children's homes and schools supported by the central government were passed on to one of my able assistants, Xu Waiye, director of the Number Three Home and School. The other four supported by the provincial government were handed to the new governor's wife. The Women's Production Brigade was dissolved under the new administration. Bohao and I were hopeful that Lixing Middle School would become an institute of higher learning in the future. . . ."

Chapter Seven
Postvictory

I jumped with an unbound joy I had never felt before at the news of Japan's surrender to the Allied forces on September 2, after the atom bombs were dropped on Hiroshima and Nagasaki in August of 1945. We had won the war! Peace had come! And we could now return to our home in Guangzhou!

Throughout the night, the sound of explosions filled the air. But this time, they were firecrackers being popped in celebration. Everybody laughed and talked all at once, in a rush of excitement and unrestricted happiness. Some thanked Buddha. Others talked about taking time off to visit parents back in their home villages. And still others spoke of reclaiming lost properties. The electrifying atmosphere was like ushering in a new year.

Little Granny immediately supervised the packing of the household, and we children were taken to join our parents in Guangzhou. After the retreat from Shaoguan, the provincial government, along with my parents, was relocated in Longchuan, seventy kilometers from Mei County. My brothers, sister, and I lived in Mei County for our schooling, but our parents resided in Longchuan to be close to the government; commuting was impossible due to the shortage of gasoline and poor road conditions. My mother came to visit us every two to three months.

At the dawn of victory, the central government released my father from his governorship. He had tendered his resignation twice before, in 1942 and 1944, and both times it was denied. His third resignation was accepted, ironically, just one day before Japan's unconditional surrender.

My father handed over his duties as governor on September 1. From his inauguration as governor on New Year's Day, in 1939, to the day of the transition, it had been six years and eight months, the longest tenure on record of any governor in the province. My father weighed only ninety-eight pounds at the end of the war.

In his farewell address to an assembly of three thousand men and women who had served in his administration, my father thanked them for their support in fighting the war. He urged them to remain faithful to the Nationalist Party founded by Sun Yatsen, and encouraged them to help build a prosperous Guangdong and a strong China. "Everyone in the auditorium shed tears," an aide told me later. "We have come through the hard times together and now someone else will enjoy the fruits of our labor. Among the many feelings and thoughts we held that day, that's what we all knew."

On leaving, the toughest thing for my father was the knowledge that all the men and women gathered together before him would become unemployed under a new administration. He expressed his anguish in his diaries, writing: "These loyal civil servants have subsisted on their government salary. During wartime, grain and oil were rationed to them to supplement their meager pay. In some cases, one person's pay fed the mouths of three generations in the family. Most of them have no savings to tide them over while they search for new jobs and will have to rely on family and relatives for support."

From Longchuan we boarded a large barge propelled by a noisy antiquated engine. There were my parents; my eight-year-old sister, Chi; my four-year-old brother, Pei; and my three-year-old brother, Hao. A thousand or more well-wishers lined the pier and stood along the banks waving good-bye. Also on board was the rest of the household, which included Little Granny, our servants, and my parents' aides and secretaries. We slept and ate on the upper deck for the three-day sail. Bed fleas kept us awake at night, but that hardly mattered because we were going back to our home in Guangzhou. The boat navigated through Dongjiang southward. When we reached the town of Shilong near the now flourishing economic zone Shenzhen, we boarded the train to Guangzhou.

Zhang Fakui, who was the newly appointed commander in chief

of Guangdong's Post-War Operation Zone, sent vehicles to meet us at the train station. We were taken to a big house in Shamien adjoining the garden of his home. The three-story house was loaned to my parents, courtesy of Zhang.

The next day, my father went to look at his city residence in the eastern part of the city and his farm in the Dragon's Eye Cave. My parents' dreams had once been to retire to experimental farming, growing fruit trees, and devoting themselves to the improvement of agriculture. When my mother entered Sun Yatsen University, the farm was loaned to the agriculture college to use as an experimental station free of charge. Students, my mother included, spent many hours working with new seeds, testing the hybrid varieties to grow pineapples, watermelons, guavas, plums, tangerines, and figs.

When my father arrived, the New First Army soldiers who stood guard refused his entry to both his farm and his city residence. The New First Army was among the central government's elites. Equipped with American arms and supplies and commanded by Chiang's trusted generals, it was as a cut above other armies.

The residence had been occupied by Japanese army medical personnel who had yet to move out, and the farm had been taken over by the New First Army. My father's aide persuaded the guards to let him go inside the garden of the residence and the farm. But my father only stood at the gate and stared in disbelief at his now-dilapidated home. The garden was devoid of flowers and shrubs and had been used as a dump. Only three cottonwood trees remained standing. In the farm, soldiers were living in the house as well as the quarters that had once housed the farmhands. My father was told that the Japanese-occupied properties would not be automatically returned to their owners, but rather would have to be negotiated for with the repossession authority.

"If they're treating *me* this shabbily, I can't imagine what ordinary people are experiencing," my father angrily told my mother afterward.

My father stayed in Guangzhou for only seventy-two hours. He then left for Shanghai to report for his new assignment as deputy commander in chief of the Third War Zone, which was still in operation for peace maintenance, with its headquarter located in the famous scenic city of Hengzhou. His hurried exit was an escape from the painful experience of his departure as governor and from the unpleasant encounters he had while visiting his home and farm. He was in need of medical treatment for his health, having suffered from chronic dysentery ever since the Northern Expedition. Soon, my mother also left for Shanghai to be with him.

At the age of eleven, I was fully aware of my father's departure as governor. No one needed to explain to me what was happening. I learned what was going on by listening to the steady stream of visitors who came to our home. Under the new administration, dismissal of my father's former subordinates in the rank and file of the provincial government reached down to the counties. I heard their complaints: The central government was unjustly shifting assignments at war's end; the thousands who had served the country with my father during the difficult war years were left without employment, while the new governor was replacing the civil servants in the old administration with his own.

The change of guard was not limited to Guangdong alone, but had occurred all over. In a symbolic gesture, some two thousand military commanders who were dismissed and became unemployed at the end of the war gathered before Sun Yatsen's Mausoleum as a form of protest. Around the country, there were angry cries that the new administration was enjoying the repossession of properties from the defeated Japanese and the traitors.

In Chinese, the word *jieshou* has two dramatically different meanings, depending on how it is said. *Jieshou*(1) said with an upward inflection means reclaiming possession. *Jieshou*(2) said with a flat tone means stealing possessions. In postwar China, *jieshou*(1) had become *jieshou*(2) in all too many cases.

It was at this moment that China's civil war erupted between the Nationalists and Communists. Within months of the War of Resistance's end, students were demonstrating, angry that postwar reconstruction efforts had turned into widespread corruption and authority into self-indulgence. Rather than governing for and serving the people, the Nationalist government had become the personal property of the chief commander, where loyalty to the chief was supreme. Power and corruption in China were growing to majestic proportion. As inflation grew, the government printed more paper money, which only further reduced the value of the currency. Thousands died from hunger and cold in the streets in cities and towns everywhere. All this happened as victory over Japan was celebrated with hope and fervor at a time when there were ample opportunities and great enthusiasm for reconstruction and renewal.

When my mother returned to Guangzhou in the early spring of 1945, she exchanged the uniform she had worn during wartime for a more fitted and fashionable style. She now had a permanent and wore a light coloring of rouge on her lips and cheeks.

My mother told us that our family would now make its home in Shanghai, and our two little brothers and their nannies would leave with her immediately. My sister and I would remain in Guangzhou to finish the school year. I didn't see my father again until I went to Shanghai the following July.

Mother came back to Guangzhou once more to check on my sister and me. During her visit she gave a dinner party at home. The guests of honor were General and Madame Zhang Fakui, or Uncle and Auntie Zhang to us children. From the hallway, I could hear the laughter of the dozen or so guests at the table clinking their glasses in one "bottoms up" round of *ganbei* after another. "I want the bloody Japanese to know I'm mad as hell that they killed over five million Chinese people." Uncle Zhang bellowed. He was loud and animated, proudly telling the story of the ceremony of the Japanese surrender. He had directed his aide to receive the sword presented by the Japanese general, instead of receiving the sword himself. Many such ceremonies were held throughout China. I had heard the account many times before from my parents' friends and had read in the newspaper about the ceremony that was held in the Sun Yatsen Memorial auditorium in Guangzhou. But it was great to hear Uncle Zhang telling it in his thunderous voice.

Suddenly, I saw my mother climb up on the table with a glass in her hand. "What are you doing? You'll hurt yourself." Uncle Zhang reached out his hand to my mother and tried to lead her down from the table. But my mother ignored him. Then, she looked straight at him, and in a tone and voice I had never heard from her before, yelled, "General Zhang, your heart is tilted to one side! You are very unfair!"

In an instant, the whole room went deathly silent. Eyes were wide and mouths agape around the table. Wobbling slightly, my mother yelled again, this time shaking her finger at the bewildered

General, "I say your heart is tilted to one side! Does everybody hear me?" Uncle Zhang's face went white. "Get down before you get hurt," implored Auntie Zhang in her high pitched voice, as she extended her hands toward my mother. But my mother ignored her, too. The other guests began saying to one another that my mother was drunk and also tried to persuade her to get down from the table. "General Zhang's heart is tilted to one side and unfair! Do all of you hear me?"

My mother stomped her feet on the table and clapped her hands repeating even louder, "General Zhang's heart is tilted to one side and unfair! Do all of you hear me?" She repeated this chant over and over again.

I had never seen my mother out of control like this before. I had no idea what to do. So I just stood by the dining-room door staring at her. I glanced over and saw Uncle Zhang get up from his seat, whisper something into Auntie Zhang's ear, and then rush out of the dining room. He looked both confused and embarrassed. At this moment my mother climbed down from the table and ran after Uncle Zhang, following him down the stairs and out the door, all the while yelling, "General Zhang's heart is tilted to one side and unfair! All of you hear me?"

I ran out to the balcony overlooking the garden of the Zhang residence next door and saw my mother chasing Uncle Zhang, even following him into his house. The moon was round and bright, its beams shone on the peonies and shrubs, casting a shadow on the ground that wavered with the breeze. My sister had also come out onto the balcony. We looked at each other in bemusement at what our mother had just done.

"Too many *ganbei*," said my sister.

"Too many drinks for Mama," I said and nodded in agreement.

Neither of us could make any sense out of what our mother was saying about Uncle Zhang's heart.

Auntie Zhang and the other guests began to leave. My sister and I stayed on the balcony looking out for our mother. After what seemed to be a long time, we saw Auntie Zhang walk her out of the house and into the garden and then bring her back to our home. She told Little Granny to serve my mother some tea and put her to bed. But once back inside, my mother didn't want to go to bed. She put her arms around my sister and me and was gleeful. "Daughters, I was not drunk just now as I know everyone thinks. I just pretended to be, so that I could say what I said to Uncle Zhang."

"Why did you say his heart was tilted to one side?" I asked.

My mother turned to look at me. "I said that because he is partial and unfair. He wasn't fair to Papa. Uncle Zhang and Papa were close colleagues from the time of the Northern Expedition as far back as twenty years ago when they were in the Fourth Army together. He never spoke up for Papa when he could have. Now he sees Guangzhou in a mess, with hundreds of people dying of hunger every day, and he doesn't speak out. That's why I wanted to scold him and tell him and everyone else how unfair he is. He deserves it."

Then for a few moments, my mother was silent, as if lost in her own thoughts. Finally, she turned to my sister and me and, with a mischievous smile, leaned over and whispered, "You know, your Mama has a pretty good capacity for alcohol." She proceeded to tell us, that in the days before the War of Resistance, she and two of her chums, wives of my father's colleagues, used to play a game to entertain themselves by targeting one of the men at dinner parties. They would take turns challenging the unsuspecting victim to *ganbei*, until he was down and out. Then they went on and took on their next target.

I thought our mother was brave to take on Uncle Zhang and make him run. Uncle Zhang was a funny man. He liked to tease us children and thunder out, "Are you afraid of me?" We would say "No." "Well, Uncle Zhang has killed countless people," said the general of the Iron Army without blinking an eye, back straight and chest out as if he were posing for a portrait.

For the rest of the night, the three of us giggled and laughed at my mother's scene at the dinner table, with my sister and I doing imitations of my mother swaying and yelling at the top of her lungs. "Don't tell anyone about our little secret," she said softly to us just before tucking us into bed. I felt both proud of my mother and special that I was part of something that only three of us in the world knew about.

Shamien, a little islet with a small canal on one side and the Pearl River on the other and joined to Guangzhou by a small bridge, was once a British concession. The British erected magnificent villas with gardens along the riverbank, which housed several hundred foreigners: British, French, Americans, Dutch, Italians, Germans, Japanese, and Portuguese. The Protestant church built by the British and a Catholic church built by the French excluded the Chinese, since Chinese were not allowed to enter Shamein.

Every morning on my way to school, I saw two white nuns in gray habits stepping in and out of rickshaws pulled by coolies, Chinese human beasts of burden. I didn't like seeing missionary nuns, women who preached the gospel of Jesus Christ and professed to help the poor, riding in rickshaws. The nuns taught in a small English-speaking girls' school.

Guangzhou was a buzzing city. The restaurants and shops were crowded with people, and food vendors manning makeshift stalls packed the sidewalks. Passing to and from school, I smelled the aroma of the stir-fried rice noodles with meats, fish, and vegetables, and fresh bowls of wonton as customers shouted their orders against the cacophony of honking cars and the clacking of wooden sandals on the cement ground. Men and women elbowed their way into the stores or hovered over the merchandise spread out on streets, bargaining for a better price. Postwar euphoria gave the city the appearance of prosperity and the longed-for peace.

Amidst the shoppers and pedestrians were beggars—men, women, and children—their hungry and unwashed faces smeared with snot and filth; they stood by the street corners or close to the food stands staring and holding out their cans for a drop of anything. My heart pumped faster and faster when the beggars were following me.

One time, I went inside a bakery with Spring Grace and bought several buns. The clerk put the buns inside a little paper bag, which Spring Grace held. No sooner had we stepped outside the bakery, when a young boy, no more than eight years old, snatched the bag from Spring Grace's hand and ran. Less than ten yards away, he opened the bag and started stuffing the buns into his mouth. "He was starving," Spring Grace and I said to each other simultaneously. We walked home in silence the rest of the way.

My mother had always been somewhat apologetic that Ahnai, my grandmother, had bonded Spring Grace, even though it was at the begging of Spring Grace's parents. Mother was delighted at Spring Grace's desire to learn and to study and had encouraged her to strive forward. Now that the war was over, she offered Spring Grace the opportunity to obtain a formal education and to become a teacher, making it a type of postwar victory present. But first Spring Grace had to pass the entrance examination to the Girls' Normal Middle School. To give Spring Grace a fighting chance in the highly competitive entrance examination, my mother directed the tutor to give Spring Grace one hour of instruction after my sister and I had finished our lessons.

Spring Grace took her entrance examination in summer of 1946. For three hours she wrote and tested. For her this was the chance of a lifetime; she would give all she had to be educated and to become a teacher. Then, she would go back to the village where she was born and teach school. She would be a good daughter and help provide for her poor, aging parents. She had never blamed her parents for bonding her into servitude or thought that it was their fault that they were poor.

The morning the school posted the names of those who would be admitted, Spring Grace and Little Granny got up before dawn, arriving at the school even before the gate opened. A flock was already eagerly waiting, with hopeful girls accompanied by family or friends. As soon as the gate opened, Spring Grace and Little Granny rushed toward the bulletin board. They pushed their way forward, but had to wait their turn to get close to the list of names.

Spring Grace was trembling and had to read the black characters dancing before her through her tears. Jostling closer to the bulletin board, she saw faces instantly brighten with joy and others go slack, and then wet with tears. Little Granny, too, searched the long columns, her eyes moving up and down. At last, there it was. Spring Grace spotted her name at the bottom of the list. She jumped up and shouted, "There's my name! There's my name!" Her shaking finger pointed to the last column on the bulletin board. Tears of relief and happiness came streaming down her face.

Little Granny began to cry. Like a proud mother, she also had spent hours teaching Spring Grace to read and write. She was fond of this maidservant, and had treated her as a kindred spirit. Little Granny had never studied in school, but she had learned to read and write, and her fingers were quick with the abacus.

When school ended for summer recess, my sister and I prepared to leave for Shanghai. Mother instructed Little Granny to pay Spring Grace's tuition and to have two Girl Scout uniforms made for her so that she wouldn't look different from the other students. The last night in Guangzhou was a sad one for me because I would have to leave Spring Grace. That evening, when all the packing was done, I stepped out onto the balcony to pull myself together and say good-bye. Spring Grace found me there. She stood leaning against the balcony and handed me a dish of grapes. We were both very still, looking at the stars, each waiting for the other to speak first.

"You'll be a teacher in a few years," I said.

"Someday, you'll go to college and then study in America," she told me. "You'll be successful and famous."

I offered her the grapes she had brought me. She took one and held it in her hand for a while before putting it in her mouth. The night air was sticky humid with the fragrance of jasmine from the garden. Suddenly, she stood erect and looked straight into my eyes. I could see she was trembling.

Then suddenly and without warning, the words came flowing out. "Why should some people be so privileged and have everything? Your parents are able to take care of you and provide you with comfort and the best of things. My parents are poor." Spring Grace almost shouted this, her face contorted as she began crying, wiping her tears with her sleeves. "They were so poor they had to sell me as a maidservant to your grandmother to stay alive. They had no grain in the house and had to give me up so they could feed my brothers. Why is society so unjust? Why are you a mistress and I a slave?"

I stared at her, stunned by her outburst. Spring Grace was always a strong person and I had never seen her cry before. Not knowing what to say to her or how to comfort her, I offered her more grapes. She shook her head and did not want any.

"You never have to worry about having oil and grain in the house or firewood for the stove. You always have a full stomach and warm clothes. How can you understand what it's like to be poor? What do you know about how I feel being little more than a slave? Every time you beckoned, I obeyed!" Calming down but still sobbing, Spring Grace blew her nose so hard it was as if she were trying to get rid of all the anger that had lodged inside her.

I tried to avoid looking at her. Awkwardly, I ate the grapes one by one until they were all gone. We were silent for a long time.

"You'll study hard. Maybe someday we can change society," she whispered, as she began to calm down. She wiped her tears on her sleeve.

Li Hanhun, pacification commissioner of the Northwest District of Guangdong Province and commander of the Third Independent Division, 1931

Wu Chufang in Yichang, Hubei, 1928

Li-Wu wedding in Shaoguan, 1932

Back view of the Nanhua Temple taken from a hilltop, 1934

Family portrait in Hong Kong,
1936

Li and comrades at De-an front line, 1938

Wu visiting the troops at war front, 1938

Governor Li, 1939

Peasants celebrating Governor Li's visit, 1939

Wu inspecting refugee children from Japanese territories, 1939

Wu with children visiting Guangdong Children's Home and School in Nanxiong, 1940

Children helping to build their classroom, 1940

Children studying using their beds as desks, 1941

Women's Brigade in military exercise in Shielieting, 1941

Women's Brigade in production, 1942

Li and Wu with rescued war orphans in the Guangdong Children's Homes and Schools, 1941. Children wore uniforms made of "Roosevelt cloth" donated to the Chinese Central Government

Wu visiting youth air force academy cadets transferred from the Guangdong Children's Homes and Schools in Chungking, 1944

Family portrait at Pond Mirror home in Huanggong, 1943

Portrait of Li and Wu in Shanghai,1946

On arrival in New York City, 1947

Wu's arrival in Guangzhou as delegate to the National Congress for the first postwar presidential election, 1948

Li with his gift of a rare book collection to the East Asian Institute of
Columbia University, 1967

Li in front of himself as a young soldier, 1981

The old soldier's last portrait, 1982

Fiftieth wedding anniversary
portrait of Li and Wu with
their children, 1982

Li, Wu, and daughter Virginia meeting Deng Xiaoping, 1982

Wu with President Li Dunfei in Taiwan, 1993

Li siblings at family reunion in San Diego, California, 2002

Wu at China Garden Restaurant in White Plains, 1965

Virginia and officers of the Guangdong Children's Homes and Schools Alumni Association, at the 2003 reunion in Guangzhou.

"Things can change," I said. "You will be a teacher."

"I will take apart the two sweaters you gave me, wash the yarn clean, and knit myself a sweater for school."

She took the empty dish from my hand and left me alone on the balcony. I did not look at her. I did not know what else to say. I felt hurt that she had questioned the relationship we had had for so many years. But in my heart I knew what she said was true. Society was unjust. There were the "haves" and the "have-nots." I had seen beggars all over in Guangzhou. I knew poverty was what had brought Spring Grace to my family. I loved Spring Grace, but I knew little about her world and the suffering imposed by it. I had always assumed it was my right to have her service and loyalty and that it was also my duty to help her become educated. I had not given much thought before to her deprivation and sufferings, until that moment. I was hoping that Spring Grace would not hate me, and I hoped that someday we could reform society together.

I was eager to leave Guangzhou and join my family in Shanghai. Another reason for wanting to leave Guangzhou was that I dreaded walking to school in the morning, for I had to pass many beggars crouching in the streets past the little bridge that connected Shamien and the city proper. Beggars, old and young, all of them desperate, stretching out their emaciated hands. Some held cans, all of them cried out for mercy, even from a young girl like me. Every morning a white truck with a red cross came by and stopped to collect the corpses of the ones who had died during the night. Once, I saw two men who got out of the truck, picked up two motionless bodies, one after the other, and tossed them into the truck, like sacks of garbage. The third one they picked up was still moving feebly when they threw it in with the dead. My own body shook violently. I looked the other way, wondering why such misery existed, and why so many people were suffering more in peace than in war.

In July, my sister and I left for Shanghai to join our parents. By then the central government had disbanded the Post War Operation Zones. At one point, Chiang Kaishek offered my father the governorship of Xinjiang Province in northwestern China. It wasn't a desirable position, but certainly a challenge for anyone who tried to govern. Xinjiang was extremely impoverished, and because of its wide range of minority Chinese cultures, there was widespread ethnic unrest. A few weeks later, my father saw the appointment of General Zhang Zhizhong as governor of Xinjiang announced in the dailies. When Father offered Zhang his good wishes, he mentioned that the governorship had been offered to him by the Generalissimo. Afterward, Zhang cynically joked with my father that any daughter of Chiang Kaishek would be given in marriage to two men at the same time, and that he would stretch every prize he had and pawn it as merchandise as long as it was advantageous.

My father was assigned to another unrewarding position as Deputy Pacification Commissioner of Xuzhou District, which covered the provinces of Jeijiang and Jiangsu. Posts such as these were created to accommodate the many generals who had contributed to the resistance war. These posts had little real power militarily or administratively, especially for the second in command.

In the absence of any meaningful work, my father set out to research historical documents on the life of Yue Fei, a twelfth-century general who fought the Mongol invaders during the decline of the Soong dynasty. Father visited Yue Fei's tomb in Hongzhou and the temple that had housed the prison in which he was held and put to death. Father spent the next eight months researching and writing the *Chronology of Yue Fei, His Life and Time.*

Ever since his youth, Yue Fei was my father's hero. Yue Fei was known for his devotion to his mother, his fidelity to his emperor, and his honesty and honorableness in all his actions. Yue's mother tattooed on her son's back the characters *jinzhong bouquo*—serve the country with the utmost honor and fidelity—as a reminder of his purpose in life. A true patriot, Yue was adamant in fighting the invaders until all the lost territories had been reclaimed. Though he was in the midst of winning many battles against the Mongols, he was recalled by the emperor at the urging of the prime minister, who feared the general as a rival. The prime minister accused the general of insubordination and treason, and Yue was cruelly whipped to death. Through the centuries, Yue Fei was venerated as the most honorable and revered as the holiest of Chinese martyrs.

My father admired Yue Fei for his noble character. Yue's poem "The Flowing Red River," written at the time he received the emperor's order to return to the capital, was an expression of his anguish at the betrayal and treachery he suffered, his unbending loyalty to his emperor, and his hope for a victorious future. "The Flowing Red River" has touched Chinese souls through the centuries and has been sung in popular songs and operas.

In Shanghai, my father exchanged his uniform for a Western-style suit and even took up dancing lessons. He never managed to become a good dancer, because he couldn't hear the music to follow its rhythm. He thought about a study tour to America and Europe and began to learn English with a tutor. At the cadet school, he had learned some German. Now, at age fifty-three, he studied English two hours daily with the modest goal of acquiring the proficiency to read the newspapers and to participate in basic conversations. For the first time, he was attracted to American movies and actually had the time to go to the theater. These movies gave him a glimpse of American customs and manners. My parents often took us children along with them to the movies. I liked the water ballets starring Esther Williams the best; my brothers liked Lassie and Tarzan.

When my father inquired about permission to leave on a study tour, he was told that Chiang Kaishek would not look upon it favorably. On the other hand, a medical leave might meet Chiang's approval. My father's desire to seek help for his hearing problem was rekindled when he learned that a Doctor Julius Lempert in New York had invented a new technique, drilling an aperture in the mastoid bone to restore hearing loss. Since he had been put out to pasture, my father wanted to use this time for his physical and mental renewal, and my mother would accompany him abroad. Together, they would fulfill a desire they had shared from the time of their betrothal. While he underwent treatment and rehabilitation to regain his hearing, she would study for her advanced degree in education. It was all a part of my parents' dream, which *was* to expand Lixing Middle School into a college and, eventually, a university.

Twice, my father's request for leave was denied. Finally, he cornered Chiang at the conference of the Nationalist Party Youth League and appealed to him directly. The Generalissimo nodded his head, signaling his approval.

When my parents went to the Foreign Ministry for their passports, they learned that, according to American government regulations for diplomatic passport holders, children below the age of sixteen were allowed to enter the United States under their mother's passport. When the American consulate confirmed this information, my mother insisted on bringing her four children along, since my siblings and I were between the ages of five and thirteen. My father was against it, but my mother said she had already lost one son during the war and she would not want to leave her children ten thousand miles away, if she could help it. She argued that two years in the United States would give us the opportunity to acquire English language skills, and that would serve us well in our adult lives. Also, in light of the raging inflation in Shanghai, it would be cheaper for the family to live in America than to maintain two households. She gave my father the ultimatum that either the children come along or he would have to go abroad without her.

In the end, my father gave in to my mother.

Part II
NEW WORLD

Chapter Eight
Beautiful Country

"*B*eautiful Country" is what the Chinese called the United States of America. In January 1947, we sailed from the port of Shanghai to America on *General Gordon*, a converted troop carrier during World War II. We were a party of eight. There were my parents, my sister Chi, my little brothers Pei and Hao, and myself, as well as my father's translator Mr. Wong and our English-speaking nanny from Hong Kong, Auntie Yee. As a courtesy to my father, the Foreign Ministry had granted passports for an interpreter and a nanny. Relatives, friends, and servants bade us a tearful good-bye at the pier and some of them were crying. "You'll come back in two years taller, bigger, and speaking English like Americans," they told us children.

Our private cabin had six bunks made up in white sheets, three on each side separated by a narrow aisle. There was a private toilet, wash basin, and shower stall. This was the ship's second voyage as a passenger boat.

On the very first day, a Chinese ship steward came into our cabin with some fresh Sunkist oranges. He knew my father was on board and came to tell him he admired his brave deeds both as a general and a governor. He came into our cabin every day to see if we needed any special service. The oranges he brought were always wrapped inside an apron or towel, so that he would not be seen.

The journey to America across the Pacific Ocean took fourteen days on the rolling sea. The deep blue ocean was glassy under the bright sun and eerily dark in the silvery reflection of the moon, all water and sky. The liner pitched and tossed. I held onto the rail or anything else I could grab hold of, feeling the sensation of sitting in a big rocker and unable to get off, nauseated from the motion.

Many of the passengers were Chinese students embarking for their postgraduate studies abroad. There were card games, movies, and dancing on the boat, but I was too young to join the students in the card games or on the dance floor. Because of motion sickness, I spent a good part of the day in my bunk staring at the ceiling. What mitigated the boredom, when I felt good enough, was hanging around my parents' company to listen to their conversations on current affairs. In my parents' circle there were several professors and journalists. I listened to their tense discussions and began to understand the ferocity of the civil war; the fighting had begun almost as soon as the Japanese had surrendered. Between June 1946 and January 1947, more than one hundred battles and skirmishes had been fought between the Nationalist army and the Communists. I could see that my parents were very worried, along with everyone else.

In the dawn of victory, the Chinese people believed that there would be a strong and peaceful new China with abundance for all. The government would build on Sun Yatsen's Three Principles of the People to promote national recovery and better living for all. Instead, there was widespread corruption, permeating from the highest level of government down to the local villages.

Runaway inflation acutely reflected the social and economic ills of the time. Most telling was the exchange rate between Chinese yuan and U.S. dollars. At the end of the war in August 1945, the official exchange rate was 20:1. By early 1946, it was 2,020:1 on the black market, and by the end of the year it was 73,000:1. Thousands of students demonstrated in Shanghai and city after city.

In the countryside, landlords who had left the occupied territories and gone inland returned to reclaim their land and property, accusing the peasants who tilled their land during their absence of being collaborators of the enemy. The landlords demanded back payments from the peasants, leaving the peasants with little for their survival after each harvest. It intensified the hatred the peasants held for the landlords and gave the peasants reason to answer the call of the Communists.

Gen. George Marshall, who, in early 1946, was President

Truman's special envoy to China, was given the task of mediating between the Nationalists and Communists in their heightened conflict. Marshall's mission was to bring the two sides together, which hopefully would lead to a democratic coalition government. But Marshall's mission came to naught and in early January 1947, it was declared a failure. I remember looking at the tall American general coming into the room and talking with Madame Chiang Kaishek at a Christmas party at the president's palace in Nanjing, in 1946. I recognized him instantly, having seen his picture in the dailies. My mother had brought my sister and me to Nanjing to see the capital and to attend the party just before we were about to leave for America. Madame Chiang gave us children Christmas stockings with walnuts and almonds, and candies that had been flown in from America.

On the thirteenth day after we had set sail, excitement swelled as the boat neared the San Francisco harbor. At dinner, the captain came by our table to say good-bye to my parents, informing them that he had received a telegram from the San Francisco Chinese Consulate. He had given permission for two Chinese representatives to come on board to meet us. The captain had invited our family to dine at his table. He also invited us to tour the command tower, but only my parents were invited to inspect the engine room.

The next morning—sunny, crisp, cloudless, with sea gulls in flocks circulating above the dock and around the boat—we joined the other passengers on the deck to look at the skyline and get our first glimpse of San Francisco. Passengers were disembarking in a hurry, but we stayed in our cabin waiting for the representatives who would be meeting us. When the boat was nearly emptied of passengers, Mr. Wang Renjun and Mr. Albert Chow, in dark suits and coats, came into the cabin, happily greeting my parents. They told them that a big welcoming party was awaiting them that very afternoon.

As we stepped off the boat onto the pier, we were met by the Chinese consul and vice consul, and a delegation of about thirty native sons of Guangdong Province. The joy and emotions in the greetings in that moment were like in a family reunion of brothers, sisters, and cousins who hadn't seen one another for years.

My parents, the consuls, and the two representatives got into one big black limousine, while we children and the wives of the consuls and the representatives got into the other; several automobiles followed. A police car with red blinking lights and a blaring siren led the procession into Chinatown. Our newly acquainted aunties explained to us that Mr. Wang and Mr. Chow, leaders of the Chinese community, had made the arrangement with the city, possible only because China was an Allied power and a friend of the United States. When we reached Chinatown, there were over a hundred people in a big restaurant waiting to greet my parents. My five-year-old brother Hao, bright-eyed and curious, wanted to take a walk around the block immediately. We children were excused from the welcoming speeches, and two aunties took us out for a walk around the outside.

Chinatown, with its small storefronts and narrow streets, did not impress me, but it felt good to be able to stretch our legs after the boat voyage. My little brother looked somewhat disappointed and puzzled. He had heard that this was the Gold Mountain—that was what the overseas Chinese called America. He was looking around for gold and didn't see any. He thought that somebody hadn't gotten the facts straight. One of the aunties explained there wasn't a real gold mountain, but that America was given the name of Gold Mountain by the early Chinese immigrant laborers who kept their hard-earned money in gold nuggets and brought the gold nuggets back to their villages.

The overseas Chinese had a special warmth toward my father. He was their hero, who had helped fight the war and protect the Motherland. Many recalled the time when their home county Toishan had a drought, and the shortage of food was so severe that cannibalism was reported. They were especially grateful that my father had ordered the release and dispatch of grain from government storage to Toishan.

The official welcoming ceremony was held on Saturday. Nearly one thousand people packed into the high school auditorium to hear my father speak. Loudspeakers were set up outside the schoolyard for people who were unable to get inside the auditorium. Raising his voice, my father thanked the overseas community for the funds they had contributed to war relief efforts through the Emergency Commission for Relief. The contributions from the overseas Chinese had helped build emergency shelters for refugees in the counties and had promoted forestry. "Your generosity made a difference in relieving the suffering of so many," my father told them in gratitude.

He went on to describe the hardships and bravery of foot soldiers under enemy fire and the fearless heroic deeds of the fighting guerrillas. The blood and ashes of millions of brothers, sons, and daughters had been spilled and scattered all over China's soil by the time the war had finally been won after eight years of struggle. He encouraged them to be true patriots, never to deny their ethnic pride, to be mindful of the glorious history of the Chinese civilization reaching as far back as 5,000 years, and to remember the role the overseas compatriots had played in supporting the revolution led by Sun Yatsen. He told them he was especially grateful for their acceptance of him and his family during our temporary stay in America.

My mother also spoke of her relief work with the refugee children and war widows, made easier by the donations of supplies and funds by the overseas Chinese. Her stories brought tears to many in the audience.

In turn, overseas Chinese hosts told heroic stories of fighting in the European theater, and of the emergence of China as an Allied power toward the last year of the war. They were proud of China's new status, something the overseas Chinese had not been able to enjoy before as immigrant laborers. Now Chinese could buy homes in the Bay Area that had been denied to them in the past because of their ethnicity. The change was because China had joined the Allied powers and helped win the war. They were happy at being accepted as citizens of their adopted country, shedding their identities as railroad and farm laborers and houseboys and exchanging them for those of small business owners, grocers, laundry and gift shop operators, and restaurateurs.

During the rounds of countless banquets given in my parents' honor, speaker after speaker gave welcoming speeches, quoting the sayings of Confucius and ancient proverbs in their toasts. In one banquet, my ten-year-old sister and I giggled over some misquotations of the proverbs by the speakers. The way they spoke Mandarin, Toishan, and other dialects sounded funny and coarse to us. At first, we tried to maintain straight faces, then we poked each other in amusement. Eventually, we couldn't control ourselves and broke out in laughter. When we returned to our hotel room, our father scolded us. "Your attitudes and lack of appreciation of our hosts and the overseas Chinese community was arrogance," he thundered. "Your bad manners were shameful, reflecting badly on you and on our family." To my recollection, that was the first time he had ever gotten really angry at us.

Back in China, we had had a very different image of our overseas compatriots. The returning immigrants presented themselves as successful entrepreneurs who had crossed the ocean to the other side of the world. They sent large sums of money back to their villages and generously gave to worthy causes, such as financing the revolution led by Sun Yatsen and the war chest for relief. The fact that they earned the money with the sweat of their labor under degrading conditions was seldom mentioned. It was only after I came to America that I began to gain a better understanding of our early immigrant laborers. Many were illiterate and unable to speak the language of their host country. When the transcontinental railroad was built, the Chinese workers did the drilling, grading, masonry, and demolition with explosives. They met discrimination and even violence because of their race, customs and language, and because they were competing for employment. Chinese women had not been allowed to enter the United States on the assumption that they would engage in prostitution, as codified by the Chinese Exclusion Act.

We rode the train from San Francisco to New York, zigzagging our way eastward through the heartland of America. America was so rich and so beautiful, with its thousands of acres of farmland in imperial jade green stretching across the continent. We saw farms mechanized by modern technology. Farmers rode on big tractors as they seeded the soil, fertilized the land, and harvested the yields. Machines took over the backbreaking work of men, with one machine doing the work of ten able-bodied persons. My father sighed with admiration that this vast country was so blessed with natural resources and beauty. He told us that America's wealth was due to its extraordinary success in agriculture. In America, one farmer produced enough food to feed sixty people, freeing others to do other things. In China, 80 percent of the workforce was engaged in food production, still with hoes and their bare hands.

Arriving in New York City, we checked into our new quarters in a big hotel that the Chinese consulate had booked us. My parents found the hotel too expensive and, after two nights, we moved to a small midtown hotel suite on the West Side. Eager to find an apartment to save money, they enlisted the help of friends who screened the newspaper advertisements. Eventually, Gilbert Lee, who was an alumnus of my mother's alma mater Sun Yatsen University, located an apartment on 137th Street at Riverside Drive overlooking the

Hudson across from New Jersey's Palisade's Park. It had a living room and dining room, two large bedrooms and a den, a kitchen and one and a half baths. Though cramped compared to our home in Shanghai, it was adequate for our family.

We went sightseeing with friends as our guides. Standing on the very top floor of the Empire State Building, I looked out in wonder onto all of Manhattan and beyond. I marveled at the George Washington Bridge suspended above the Hudson River, which seemed to stretch for miles to New Jersey. But my father was more impressed with the cleanliness and order of the streets, and seeing the traffic directed by signal lights that were obeyed by the countless drivers and the pedestrians crossing the streets. Unlike the crowding and jostling in China, people were courteous to each other and took their place in line without pushing, whether it was the ticket window or the check-out counter. He said that such conduct reflected a people and a society that the Chinese could well emulate.

Most of all, my father appreciated how the law protected its citizens. No one could be found guilty without due process. People spoke freely and could criticize their government without fear of repercussion. Ordinary people had the right to vote by secret ballot in local elections and every four years for their president. Observing that American soldiers and policemen were handsomely dressed in pressed uniforms, wearing leather shoes, looking smart and well nourished, my father sighed in wonder. It pained him to think of the deprivation of the Chinese soldiers whose lot was cold and hunger.

We saw the Easter parade on Fifth Avenue and the Thanksgiving Day parade on Broadway in front of Macy's department store. Friends also took us sightseeing in Harlem where we saw only the faces of black people, who remained an underclass and segregated. Father thought that in comparing the deprivations of the black people with the poor peasants in the Chinese villages, black Americans still fared better under the protection of the law. He was always very sad when he spoke of Chinese peasants who for generations were unable to work themselves out of poverty or to rise above the tyranny of the landlords to whom they were indentured.

The event that marred the wonderment of our arrival in America was the illness of my youngest brother, Hao. Two days after we landed in San Francisco, Hao ran a high fever and was admitted to the hospital. He was diagnosed as having double pneumonia and remained hospitalized for our entire month-long stay in San Francisco. Crossing the Pacific Ocean, Hao had been the only member in the family who was unaffected by the motion of the sea, and he would bring saltine crackers to those of us who couldn't get up from our bunks. Upon arriving in New York, my parents were referred to Dr. Judeh Zizmor for consultation. Dr. Zizmor diagnosed Hao's illness as tuberculosis and recommended hospitalization. Daily injections and complete bed rest were required for his recovery. My parents explained that hospitalization would be a financial hardship and asked if there was any way their son could be taken care of at home. Dr. Zizmor was sympathetic and agreed to home care under conditions that included the isolation of Hao from the other children, separately boiling his eating utensils, and giving him injections of streptomycin in his buttocks three times a day. With the help of Auntie Yee, Mother carried out the prescriptions.

Hao was a quiet, gentle child, fair and alert, whose shyness endeared him to everyone. The den adjacent to the living room was his bedroom, from which my other siblings and I stayed away as we were told. Lonely and in bed by himself the greater part of the day, he would play with his drawing board and coloring books and listen to phonograph records. Longingly, he watched the rest of the family eating and doing things together while he lay on his bed. He never complained or resisted the painful injections given to him daily, except to emit a whimpering small cry when the needle stuck.

Immobile and without an appetite, his one mischief was to out-smart my mother in finding new ways of discarding the food that she insisted he eat. Chicken drumsticks, meatballs, buns, apples, and bananas could be found in the trash can or under his bed or inside the toilet bowl. Hao was eight years old before he entered school. But he made up for lost time, breezing through the primary grades and the Bronx High School of Science, growing tall and entering Columbia University at age fifteen. His teachers were always telling my mother how bright her boy was and that he could move up one grade ahead of his class.

The other disturbance in the family was that our nanny Auntie Yee became romantically involved and wanted to leave. Auntie Yee was a forty-eight-year-old widow of Eurasian stock, born and reared in Hong Kong and fluent in English. As soon as we reached New York, she acquainted herself with three Chinese laundrymen who owned little basement shops around midtown near Broadway. She bought new clothes and dressed fashionably, curled her hair, and waltzed in and out of our apartment with her romantic stories of adventures with men, singing "Jesus loves me, this I know. For the Bible tells me so. . . ." When Auntie Yee went grocery shopping, she would disappear for hours. As there were few single Chinese women in America for the columns of men who had left their wives back in the villages, there was no shortage of men for Auntie Yee. For a mature widowed woman of her age, the kind of behavior she exhibited was unknown in China, not even in fiction.

Auntie Yee's romantic involvement eventually left food in the refrigerator unprepared and dishes that piled up in the sink unwashed. Mother increasingly took on the chores of cooking and feeding the family. The first time she put her hand inside the cavity of a chicken to pull out its entrails, she jumped. Never in her life had she ever cleaned or cut up a chicken. My sister and I learned to wash the dishes and pots and pans, as well as do the laundry. Living in New York City was more costly than my parents had anticipated. My mother bought food in the wholesale market near 120th Street and Amsterdam Avenue, instead of at the A&P. We shopped at Gimbel's basement for bargains.

Then Auntie Yee told my mother that she was leaving. Mother reminded her that she had a two-year contract in coming to America and appealed to her sense of decency as well as compassion. She pleaded with Auntie Yee, telling her how much she needed her help. Mother reminded her that her little son was confined to bed and her husband was recuperating from his ear operation, and that she depended on her for English communication. Auntie Yee said that was no concern of hers; this was a free country and she had the right to do as she pleased.

Friends sympathetically explained to my parents that people change and become independent, as well as aggressive, when they come to America, explaining that in this country, even a dead salted fish could turn around and swim away. When Auntie Yee's temper tantrums became increasingly disruptive to our family, my mother had to let her go. This was what Auntie Yee wanted. While Auntie Yee created unexpected problems for our family, my parents thought that the fact that a dead fish could come alive and swim out to sea was a compliment to American society. It explained why immigrants kept coming in spite of their hardships in gaining acceptance and assimilation. Almost ten years later, we heard that Auntie Yee had hanged herself in Detroit.

"Amazing! I was fully awake," my father excitedly said about his left ear surgery, performed by Dr. Lempert at the Julius Lempert Endaural Hospital at East 74th Street shortly after our arrival in New York City. "I had no pain when I felt the vibration of the drill driving into my mastoid bones." Fitted with a hearing aid, for the first time in nearly four decades, he heard human speech without straining and asking people to repeat, and the rumbling footsteps of my brothers inside the apartment were a joy to him. During a downpour, my father was so overwhelmed and happy that he cried out, "I can hear raindrops!"

The surgery was a success, but my father was beset with dizziness as if the whole earth were churning. Dr. Lempert would not operate on the right ear until the dizziness had subsided and warned that it could be many months.

During the period of my father's convalescence, my parents realized their lifelong dream of touring Europe. Miss Ada Liu, a former schoolmate of my mother's, volunteered to take care of us while my parents were away. She was a big tall woman who was studying for her master's degree at New York University, always laughing and saying, "When in Rome, do as the Romans do." My sister and I did the laundry, washed the dishes, cleaned the bathrooms and kitchen, and she helped with the meals. On weekends, Miss Liu took us to Central Park, Radio City, and the museums. She was a fun person to be around, and we spoke Chinese with her the whole time.

In all the countries my parents visited on their trip, they were briefed and warmly entertained by the Chinese ambassadors. World War II had left deep scars in Europe. In London, my parents saw bomb-shattered neighborhoods close to Buckingham Palace, waiting to be rebuilt, and they experienced the scarcity of consumer goods. Sick with fever in an unheated hotel room, Mother was loaned a blanket by friends at the Chinese Embassy and given ration coupons for eggs to make up what was lacking in the hotel. The eggs were deposited in the hotel pantry marked with her name and served to her. They were shaken when they saw the physical effects of the war in Rotterdam, where an entire city had been flattened.

They found restaurants in Venice, Rome, and Milan that had an unlimited food supply because of black market, but beggars clustered in street corners, in front of the cathedrals, and around the squares —reminding them of Shanghai. Berlin, once the mighty fortress of Hitler's Germany, was bare to the bone. There, they caught up with their longtime friends Huang Chichiang and his attractive wife Guo Xiuyi. Huang, who had been my father's colleague in the Fourth Army, was then China's ambassador to Germany. Acting as hosts for my parents' stay in the embassy, Huang and his wife took my parents sightseeing and they chatted long past midnight. It surprised my parents when, not long afterward, the couple defected to Communist China.

The small countries of Norway, Denmark, and Sweden intrigued my parents because they were monarchies and yet welfare states at the same time. In Copenhagen they saw children playing on the palace grounds. This was so unlike China's Forbidden City, surrounded by walls and impenetrable to the eye. In the museum, they saw the exhibition of farmhouses and farming tools the Danish peasants employed. "Their tools were very much like those our Chinese peasants use," my father observed. "The difference is that what the Danes used to till the soil a century ago is what the Chinese peasants are using in their fields even today."

The postwar reconstruction had just begun under the Marshall Plan. Massive American aid was sending hope to the European countries and raising the vitality and speed of postwar recovery. My father in contrast to what little aid was provided, felt envious for China, sighing that the United States government's approaches to Europe and to China differed because of color and heritage. It didn't seem to matter that Germany had been the enemy and China had fought for the Allied cause.

During my father's convalescence from his second surgery, my parents visited countries in South America. Although the countries had not been ravished by war, they were experiencing problems with corruption, extremes of poverty and wealth, and government by the few and with the backing of the army—much like what happened in China after the republic was born. My parents were told that in Brazil, Chinese were not allowed to own property unless they were married to nationals, and there had been instances in which Chinese merchants were forced to sell their properties for less than a quarter of their worth. Harassed Chinese told their woes that, in the face of discrimination and injustice, the embassy did not intervene on their behalf—or perhaps did not have the ability to intervene on their behalf. Because China was engaged in a civil war and the government was unstable, the Chinese Embassy was held in low esteem and had no influence. Chinese in Venezuela fared the best due to the country's wealth from its oil reserves; Venezuelans were economically well-off and didn't begrudge the immigrants.

My father wrote and published two travel books on his observations in Europe and the Americas, noting, "There was a saying that the sun never sets on the British Empire. We can say that wherever the sun rose, there were Chinese people. We met Chinese people in every country and city and town we visited; they are everywhere."

Back in New York, the Chinese community invited my father to speak at the New York branch of the Nationalist Party and the Nationalist Youth League. The topic he selected for his talk was "The Three Principles of the People by Sun Yatsen as I Understand Them." He told the audience that his hope was that China would institute land redistribution to prevent the rich from becoming despotic and the poor from becoming destitute. The poor had no place to go and no roof over their heads. Hence, China was badly in need of equality and justice for all her people. He believed that land redistribution should come about by reform and not by bloody revolution, and that democratic socialism would allow the state to insure the installation of resources and capital for the communal welfare. In ensuring people's livelihood, he made the analogy of filling a cup of water. The majority of China's population was either poor or very poor. The very poor were like a cup that was nearly empty; this cup needs to be filled quickly. The poor were like a cup that was half filled; this cup could be filled a bit more slowly. The rich were like a cup that was overflowing; they should remain with a full cup, but relinquish the spillover to the state for redistribution.

After his talk there were murmurs that my father had a different stand from the Nationalist mainstream. As my father saw it, the mainstream was entirely open to interpretation, if one took Sun Yatsen's Three Principles of the People seriously. My father believed that there should be freedom of speech and an open exchange of views. Unfortunately for China, loyalty to the party or party leadership ranked above loyalty to the country, and any deviation was scorned and regarded as disloyal or insubordination. For my father, love of country came before all else.

The highlight of his visit in the United States was attending the 1948 Democratic Convention in Philadelphia. Mr. Albert Chow, who had met us on our arrival in San Francisco, had obtained tickets for my parents to go inside the convention hall. Seated in the balcony, my parents observed the activities on the convention floor. Though my father depended on Mr. Chow for translation of the speeches, the liveliness of the bands, the rallies and the waving of thousands of little flags, the handshakes and slapping shoulders in a democratic election needed no translation. The excitement of the American Democratic Convention conveyed to my parents the spirit of a people participating in a momentous event of their own making.

My father saw that the United States also had its dark corners. In Miami, Houston, and Tennessee, when friends chauffeured him around, he saw black people sitting in the back of the bus—not by choice but because of what the law dictated because of discrimination. He wondered where a Chinese would sit on the bus in those or any other southern city where discrimination was socially approved and supported by the community at large. Would a Chinese sit next to the black people or the white people? Would Chinese be told to go to the back of the bus or refused service in a white restaurant?

In the Arizona desert, he saw native American Indians on the reservations living in mud-packed villages that were completely unlike white American rural communities elsewhere. Indian reservations had no paved roads and no running water. He thought the facial features of American Indians looked very much like the Chinese, and was told it is believed that their ancestors had come from Asia, crossing the Bering Strait. It pained him to know that during early colonization, smallpox was deliberately brought to the Indians, wiping out one tribe after another. Diseases as well as guns had killed millions.

Noting the discrimination against people of color, my father thought that just as China had a long way to go to achieve democracy, the United States of America also had a way to go to achieve equality for all her citizens.

Chapter Nine

Return to China and Departure

*B*oth my parents were representatives to China's National Assembly. My mother was nominated and elected by the women's organizations of Guangdong, and my father by his home county. On March 29, 1948, the National Assembly convened in Nanjing for China's first postwar presidential election. Still convalescing from his second ear surgery, my father did not attend, but my mother returned to China to cast her vote.

The presidential nominees were Chiang Kaishek and Zhu Jun. Zhu was a contemporary of Sun Yatsen who had served as head of the Legislative Yuan, the national law-making body in the central government. No one would challenge Chiang. But Zhu's name was put forth as a second candidate for the presidency to give the election the appearance of being a democracy. My mother voted for Zhu—who received a scant three-hundred-some votes from over three thousand delegates.

The election of the vice president was by far livelier and created more excitement. In the name of democracy, Chiang threw open the vice presidency, even though he was backing Sun Fo, who was Sun Yatsen's only son. For weeks, lobbying for votes and accusations of buying votes electrified the convention floor and corridors. In the heat of the arguments, recriminations, and challenges over parliamentary rulings, an angry delegate ran up onto the stage and started to hit the presiding chairman right there on the podium. Several runoffs due to failing to achieve a clear majority delayed the election of the vice president by ten days. To Chiang's great displeasure, Li Zongren garnered the most votes and thus the vice presidency.

Vice President Li, who began his career as a warlord in Guangxi Province, had been an intermittent adversary of Chiang up to the eve of the Sino-Japan War. He supported Chiang fighting in the Northern Expedition, then his usurpation of power while serving as head of the Wuhan Political Commission brought on the Chiang-Li War. On the eve of the Sino-Japan War, while Chiang was hesitating declaring war against Japan's aggression in China, Li challenged Chiang's leadership by forming the Revolutionary Army of Resistance Against Japanese Aggression for National Salvation before acknowledging Chiang to be the national leader.

My mother made brief stops in Shanghai and Guangzhou to visit friends and to thank those who had worked hard for her election to the National Assembly. "I was shocked in what I saw compared to the time we left for America fourteen months ago," said my mother upon her return. Everywhere, beggars cried out and the destitute moaned. Businessmen preferred to hoard goods rather than produce them because that was more profitable. Merchants charged thousands more than the posted prices of goods because that would be "tomorrow's price." People carried money in sacks for shopping. As inflation skyrocketed, even those who were employed were unable to buy enough food and necessities to sustain their families. Shanghai alone reported that more than three hundred people were dying of starvation in the streets every single day.

The Nationalist government was fighting on two fronts, one against the Communists and the other against inflation. Both these struggles were beset with incompetence and corruption that resulted in debacle. The fight against the Communists escalated, leading to huge military expenditures and skyrocketing inflation. In early 1947, the government imposed price ceilings on rice, flour, cotton, fuel, salt, sugar and edible oils, which resulted in hoarding and a drop in production. By the spring of 1948, staple foods were rationed in cities. The government couldn't print money fast enough to catch up with the inflation. A standard sack of rice, weighing about eighty kilos, would sell for six million yuan in June and then be selling for over fifty million yuan just a few weeks later. That July, the government abandoned the *fabi*—paper currency—for the gold yuan at a conversion of three million *fabi* to one gold yuan.

Soon, the government prohibited price increases, strikes, and demonstrations, and ordered people to turn in their gold and silver bullion, exchanging it for the gold yuan.

Shanghai led the campaign "Striking the tigers" to carry out the emergency measures to control inflation, with Chiang Kaishek's son Chiang Chingkuo hoisting the banner. The Soviet-educated younger Chiang launched measures against hoarders and speculators, raiding homes and warehouses, ordering arrests, and even meting out death penalties to black marketers and speculators. The dailies lauded the campaign, radios publicized the government orders, which were reinforced by loudspeakers cruising the streets. "Secret-report boxes" were installed in public places to encourage people to report on those who were raising prices.

To evade the measures, businessmen as well as farmers sold goods elsewhere where the measures were less strict. Inflation continued to spiral. "Striking the tigers" fizzled to a halt when Chiang Chingkuo touched the wealth of the Soong and Kung families, and when Soong Mei Ling—Madame Chiang Kaishek—complained to her husband.

In the streets, angry students who were half-starved demonstrated, shouting slogans of "Down with the Big Four Family clans," meaning Chiang Kaishek, his Soong and Kung brothers-in-law, and two Chen brothers—Lifu and Guofu—known as the "CC" clique. Chiang was a dictator, the Soong and Kung families had controlled much of the machinery and finance of the government for two decades, and "CC" had operated the Nationalist Party apparatus including the secret police. That July in Beijing, armed police cars opened fire on student demonstrators, killing eighteen and wounding over a hundred.

In spring 1948, the Red Army, hailed as the People's Liberation Army, launched an offensive against the Nationalists' positions in the province of Shandong in the northeast. Chiang's elite army, which was equipped with American arms and headed by generals chosen for their loyalty rather than competence, had not fought the Japanese but was reserved to fight the Communists. It proved unable either on defense or offense. The Red Army recaptured the mountain city of Yanan, took towns and cities in the provinces of Chahar and Shanxi and the whole of Shandong. Armed with captured weaponry and vehicles, the Communists abandoned their guerrilla warfare tactics for more conventional battles.

In September, Chiang launched the Manchurian campaigns for exterminating the Communists. Against some of the generals' better judgement, Chiang directed the campaigns himself, issuing orders that were unworkable and at times contradictory. The Nationalist troops were defeated in three decisive battlefields in the areas of Liaoshen, Pingjun, and Huahai. The Communists captured the entire northeast and East Central China. The fighting in Huahai that began on November 6 lasted for sixty-five days. The Nationalist armies lost nearly one and a half million troops in battle or through desertion and surrender. Casualties to the Communists were nearly as many.

Confronted with nationwide student demonstrations, popular unrest in cities and the countryside, and repeated defeats of the Nationalist army, Chiang was pressured to relinquish his presidency for retirement.

In January 1949, my father went back to China alone. Because of the uncertainty of China's future, my mother and we children remained in New York. My father wrote of his departure and his sense of country and family in his diaries:

> There was never any question that I would go back to China to serve my country as a loyal Nationalist. But the thought of bearing arms and fighting my own countrymen chilled my spine. This could be my last Christmas with my family. There is no way to foretell the life and death of a soldier. Our children celebrated Christmas. The older girls were preparing Christmas stockings for their two younger brothers. They bought candies and gum and then hung the stockings by the fireplace after the boys went to bed, telling us they wanted the boys to believe that Santa Claus had come down the chimney. The boys were very excited when they found their stockings in the morning. They ran into our bedroom and climbed up onto our bed, whispering to us that they knew it was their sisters who had put the stockings under the chimney. They wanted to make their sisters happy by letting them think they believed in Santa Claus, so they pretended that it was Santa Claus who had brought them the stockings. What innocence and joy!
>
> Our little son Hao was well on his way to recovery from his bout with tuberculosis. If our visit to America had accomplished

nothing else than saving his life, it was all worth it. It hurt me to see him confined to bed for months and stuck with the needles every day. Our older son Pei is a good-natured and most delightful little fellow. Anything you ask him to do he will enthusiastically say, "It is easy, I can do it."

The girls are now on scholarship at a Catholic boarding school. On seeing them off to Chicago at the Grand Central Station, my eldest daughter said to me, "I will see you in six years." She reasoned that it would be two years of high school plus four years of college before she goes back to China. My younger daughter said it would be eight years for her. They were mature enough to know that travel crossing between the continents was a costly and unaffordable luxury and that they should expect a long separation.

On January 20, my father flew from La Guardia Airport to Hong Kong, stopping in San Francisco, Honolulu, and Manila to visit overseas Chinese communities and friends. While in San Francisco on January 21, he learned that President Chiang Kaishek and Vice President Li Zongren had jointly issued a communiqué announcing Chiang's retirement and Li's becoming acting president in his place. The next day, Fu Zuoyi, the Nationalist commander in chief who was garrisoned in Beijing, came to an agreement with representatives of the Communist Party to surrender including handing over Beijing to the People's Liberation Army.

My father arrived in Hong Kong on January 25 and left for Guangzhou by train two days later. Lunar New Year firecrackers could be heard as he visited old colleagues to catch up on the most recent moves in the central government. Top military generals and high ranking officials, but especially those from the provinces of Guangdong and Guangxi, were frustrated by the lack of preparation for the defense of South China.

On February 9, Dr. Sun Fo, head of China's top administrative body the Executive Yuan and whose position was equivalent to premier, announced my father's appointment as chief administrator of Hainan Island. My father was surprised by the announcement because he was still making up his mind and had not yet accepted the offer. Located in the South China Sea, Hainan, off the coast of and integral to Guangdong, was key to the defense of South China. My father wanted to know the overall strategic plan for Hainan in order to make an informed decision regarding the appointment. He flew to Taiwan to consult with General Chen Cheng, Chiang's trusted aide who had served as the minister of defense in the Sino-Japan War and who was now governor of Taiwan.

My father told Chen that Hainan should be fortified whether he would be its chief administrator or not.

"Hainan cannot be defended for long," Chen reported. From this meeting, my father gleaned that Chiang considered only Taiwan important to his strategic plan and that he had no intention of defending South China. Under Chen's tight control, the national treasury's gold and silver bullion and foreign exchange had been shipped to Taiwan.

In the meantime, Acting President Li Zongren announced his own selection of the Hainan administrator. Li urged my father to accept his offer to be chief military councilor in the Acting President's Office at the rank of a full general. My father accepted the appointment and took office on March 8.

Acting President Li's stand on defending the mainland, even though it was now only holding China's southern and southwestern provinces, contradicted Chiang's position to retreat to Taiwan. Nominally retired, Chiang held onto his title as Generalissimo and with it the treasury and the army, and the apparatus of secret agents. At every turn, the acting president had to seek approval from Chiang, whether he was dealing with the military or policies pertaining to personnel or finance. In all matters, Chiang insisted on absolute obedience to the Nationalist Party, which he headed.

Chiang and Li were like two tigers fighting for domain. The old tiger, king of the mountain, guarded it with all his might. The new tiger wanted his share but was chased away at every turn.

Then Sun Fo, who had become premier under Chiang—still smarting at having lost the vice presidential election to Li the year before—resigned as head of the Executive Yuan. The new head of the Executive Yuan, General Ho Yinchin, asked my father to take over the helm of the Ministry of Internal Affairs in the new cabinet. At first my father declined, knowing the enormity and difficulty of the job that lay ahead, and knowing that he would have little freedom to act on behalf of the ministry. But many of his friends, as well as the acting president, urged him to accept the post. My father had been chief military councilor for only two weeks when he handed over the office and was sworn in as head of the Ministry of Internal Affairs.

The Ministry of Internal Affairs was an enormous bureaucracy. At the time my father assumed the position as its minister, the Executive Yuan ordered the Ministry of Social Affairs, Ministry of Land Resources, and Ministry of Health to merge under the Ministry of Internal Affairs. The reorganization drastically reduced the size of the central government bureaucracy, but still nothing could be implemented without the approval of Chiang. Later, when he was an old man, my father was to tell me: "I presided over a broken machine. It was like driving an old truck that had a rusted engine with flat tires and no gasoline in the tank. I tried to push it and summoned others to help push it, but we got nowhere. There were times the ministry was so short of funds that it had no money even for the purchase of stationery."

During the next six months, my father saw the tragic drama of the Nationalists played out before his eyes. The Nationalist government crashed down the hill like a rolling boulder. Speaking from a position of strength, the Communists announced their willingness to open peace talks with the Nationalist representatives in Beijing.

On April 1, my father, along with other officials in Nanjing, went to the airport to see the Nationalist peace delegation off to Beijing. For weeks checks and balances were made on the peace delegation membership list Li offered before Chiang finally approved it. Among the terms for a peace settlement that were demanded on the Nationalist side were that the form of government should remain unchanged and land reform should be enacted without violence. As the negotiations opened, the Communists readied their forces to cross the Yangtze River. Li directed the peace negotiations, demanding an immediate cessation of hostilities and an agreement whereby the two sides would divide up the areas for control—with the Communists being instructed not to touch any land south of the Yangtze.

Zhou Enlai, representing the Communist side, put forth an ultimatum for Li to accept the eight terms that had previously been issued, plus another twenty-four subterms. The terms that were demanded amounted to the total surrender of the Nationalists. When

Li refused to accept these terms, Mao Zedong ordered the People's Liberation Army to cross the Yangtze for a countrywide advance.

Without the army and the resources of the treasury, Li Zongren went to Hangzhou to see Chiang, urging him to resume the presidency or else relinquish the control of the government. In the latter case, Chiang should then allow him to have the financial power to direct the government and personnel in keeping with the authority of his office as acting president. Chiang promised that he would not interfere in the government for five years, which was the remainder of the term of presidential office. He also proposed the creation of an Extraordinary Commission under the Standing Committee of the Central Executive Committee of the Nationalist Party. The commission would function to approve all governmental policies. Li rejected this, because it would tighten the rope around his hands. He went back to Nanjing having Chiang's promise of noninterference, but there was no change in the way that Chiang acted.

It shocked the country and the world when, in the midst of negotiations, the entire peace commission went over to the side of the Communists. As the Red Army advanced toward Nanjing, the central government evacuated and moved to Chungking, which had served as the nation's capital during the War of Resistance. On April 23, my father flew with the Acting President Li to Guilin where Li was to remain, and the plane then took my father on to Guangzhou. The next day, the Red Army entered Nanjing.

My father wrote to my mother about leaving Nanjing:

The Communists are closing in. I heard the gunfire of the artillery on our way to the airport. . . . The night before I left Nanjing, I had my hair cut in the barbershop in the government compound. When I walked back to my quarters, the night was eerily quiet. The silvery moon beamed. I saw my shadow and wished it were someone I could speak with. The loneliness I felt was more intense than during the time I retreated from Shaoguan in winter of 1944 or when I took the boat from Shantou to Hong Kong in 1936. In the retreat from Shaoguan, I had my driver and two aides with me. In the escape to Hong Kong, I had my secretary along. In Nanjing, I was alone. My personal aides had packed up and gone that afternoon. They understood that this time the change was real and that they had better find their own path for the future. I didn't try to stop them from leaving, for I had nothing to offer them. One of the men had been with me for over fifteen years and had come into my service when he was a teenager. He came into my study, saluted me, turned, and left. I was especially sad to see him go. I did not press any one of them to tell me what they would do or where they were going. They had the right to choose their future, just as I had chosen my future by remaining a faithful Nationalist follower of Sun Yatsen.

By the end of May, like an avalanche, the cities of Hankou, Hanyang, and Wuchang fell, followed by Xian and Shengxi, Nanchang and Shanghai. Whole armies of Nationalist soldiers laid down their weapons or were disarmed as Nationalist generals either surrendered or fled, or were killed by Communist fire or by their own hand. The generals who committed suicide did this for honor and for country, having failed to defend their homeland. In the city of Taiyuan, in Shanxi Province, five hundred assembled officers pointed their own pistols at their temples and pulled the triggers as the final act of allegiance to the Nationalist Party when Communist troops surrounded the city. The commander, before presiding over the group suicide, set fire to the jail filled with Communist prisoners.

In June, Ho resigned as head of the Executive Yuan and defense minister. His hands, too, were tied since Chiang controlled all matters pertaining to finance and the military. General Yan Xishan became the new head of the Executive Yuan. My father stayed on as minister of Internal Affairs at the urging of many of his colleagues. The Extraordinary Commission, which Chiang had proposed to Li in Hangzhou two months earlier, was created with branches in Taiwan and Chungking. Inflation continued its upward spiral. The new silver yuan, which had replaced the gold yuan, also became worthless. In desperation, the banks issued old silver coins bearing the head of Yuan Shikai—president of the republic in 1916 who declared himself emperor—putting them back into circulation. The operation of the ministries and the military depended on Chiang's authorization of funds. Without a fixed schedule for transmittal, the funds dribbled in from Taiwan at the equivalent of gold bullion or American notes.

Sweeping past the Yangtze River, the various Red Armies pressed onward. In August, the governor of Hunan Province surrendered to the People's Liberation Army. Shortly after, Fouzhou, the capital of

Fuzian, was caputred by the People's Liberation Army. Nationalist generals of Guangdong and Guangxi saw the urgency in shifting their forces from Central China to South China. Some tried to persuade Chiang to change his stand for a Chiang-Li cooperation for the defense of South China—building this area into a bulwark against further Communists expansion. Instead, Chiang let it be known that anyone urging him to use the resources in his possession for the defense of South China would be punished by the Nationalist Party.

The municipality of Guangzhou, rich in revenue, was under the jurisdiction of the central government; its separation from the provincial jurisdiction, at this time of great emergency, hampered the military command and any political coordination. The generals of Guangdong, my father included, advocated the unification of the two under Governor Xue Yue. To do so would involve the removal of the current mayor, who was backed by an influential provincial political faction in Guangdong close to Chiang. My father and many others believed that only with a fresh military direction and renewed popular support for the Nationalists would there be any hope of salvaging the country from losing more ground to the Communists.

The Executive Yuan directed my father to examine the question of political coordination between the province and the municipality. "This was a most delicate and difficult task that I wished I didn't have to carry out, but couldn't decline. Already, the top generals of the Guangdong had incurred Chiang's wrath in the matter," my father was to note later in his oral autobiography for Columbia University's Chinese oral history project. Speaking of his role, my father recommended to Premier Yan Xishan that it was urgent for him or the Executive Yuan to order the subordination of Guangzhou municipality to the Guangdong provincial government. My father saw the forging of political coordination between Guangdong Province and Guangzhou Municipality, along with the forging of the military commands between the provinces of Guangdong and Guangxi, as the only lifeline for the South China defense. But Yan hesitated and did not act, not wanting to incur Chiang Kaishek's wrath.

That summer of 1949 also saw Madame Sun Yatsen, the sister of Madame Chiang Kaishek, defect and join the Communist government, denouncing the Nationalist Party and her family for having betrayed the trust of her late husband.

Chiang retreated to Guangzhou. On September 29, he invited about twenty of Guangdong's Nationalist leaders to dine with him in his residence. To my father's surprise the top military commanders—Zhang Fakui, who had served as chief of the army until recently, Xue Yue, the governor of Guangdong, and Yu Hanmou, the pacification commissioner of Guangzhou—were not invited. Chen Zitang, chief administrator of Hainan, declined to attend, feigning illness. Since most of the invited were Nationalist elders or persons holding important positions in the Party, my father assumed that the reason he was invited was because he was a member of the Executive Committee of the Nationalist Party.

For thirty minutes, Chiang spoke of the strategic position of Taiwan for a third world war. He was convinced that such a war would be the inevitable outcome of the ideological conflict between the United States and the Soviet Union. In that event, the United States would have to support the Chinese Nationalists with money and arms, and Chiang himself would lead the Nationalist army based in Taiwan—launching a counterattack on the Communists to recover the mainland. He concluded by saying, "Because the United States is making a mistake by not giving us aid, we must wait for the change of the international situation in our favor. For now, we whose government is led by the Nationalist Party must follow the instructions of the Party."

Chiang then asked if anyone wished to speak. There was silence around the table.

"What is your opinion?" Chiang posed the question to my father.

My father thought he should speak frankly, confident that his colleagues present and other native Guangdong generals were anxious to defend the province and to resist the Communists for as long as possible. He stood up and said in earnest, "Most of the top generals and officials of Guangdong wish that the supreme leader of the party and the central government not only fortify Taiwan, but also defend the China mainland. Even if our cities and coastal areas fall into Communist hands, we can still lead the people up the hills and mountains to hold on in defense of our country while waiting for a change in the international situation. We are not willing to see the defense of Taiwan in isolation, separate from the defense of South China."

Chiang flew into a rage, his face turning red, his shiny bald head glittering with perspiration.

"If that is the case, I should resign!" Chiang pounded his right fist onto the table, shouting, "Who is the head of state? I am telling you the southern defense is not an option. The party governs the country. I must keep on [ruling]."

My father stood and listened in respectful silence. General Li Fulin, who had fought in the Northern Expedition and the War of Resistance, stood up and said loudly, "I would like to report to the Generalissimo that what Comrade Hanhun just said represents precisely the sentiments and wish of his colleagues in Guangdong Province. I am in total agreement with him."

But before Li Fulin went on with the next sentence, Wu Teicheng, who was sitting next to him, hushed him and told him to sit down. Wu, trusted by Chiang, had preceded my father as governor of Guangdong and had held various high positions in the central government.

Chiang was astonished with the exchanges that had taken place that evening, and so were others at the table. The banquet ended early in silence.

Many times I heard my father mourn, "My comrades failed me when I needed them to come forward and to support the stand we had all agreed upon that morning. They feared Chiang Kaishek to such an extent that they prostrated themselves without a sound. I knew then that there was neither hope nor salvation [for the Nationalists]."

Like the river current in a storm, the Red Army pushed on. By early September they had captured Xining, the capital of Qinghai in the northwest. Within weeks, Xinjiang was also in the hands of the Communists when its governor cabled his surrender and vowed his allegiance to the Chinese Communist Party. Even as south and southwest China were largely under the control of the Nationalist government in 1949, the Red Army scored victories in battles from the northeast to the central plains to Fujian in the south. The Communists were bolstered by the surrenders and defections of high-ranking Nationalist officials, generals, and soldiers. On October 1,

Mao Zedong proclaimed, "The Chinese People have stood up," establishing the People's Republic of China to thunderous applause in a packed Tiananmen Square.

Shaoguan fell into the hands of the Red Army on October 7. The next day, my father received the news that his eldest son, Ban, a brigadier general in the Nationalist Seventy-third Army, was missing in action in Fujian. The Communist force was closing in on Guangzhou. On October 12, the remaining Nationalist central government ordered all the ministries to move to Chungking.

At the same time, officials put up a façade to rally the civil servants and army officers at the Sun Yatsen Memorial Auditorium, swearing to defend South China, and government news releases on South China defense were reported by the media.

Before my father flew to Chungking to attend to the Ministry of Internal Affairs' evacuation to Guangzhou, he deeded the Dragon's Eye Cave farm to the peasants from whom he had bought the land. The Shaoxin Garden in his home village and the Yizhou Farm in Shaoguan were deeded to the Lixing Middle School as an endowment to the Lixing Institute of Learning. A parcel of land in Lingtou village was deeded to the Yici Hospital, which his mother built and he had helped support. He knew there was no longer any question that Chungking would soon fall and the Communists would overtake China. The question was what after Guangzhou?

Back at his residence in Chungking on November 7, my father was awakened at midnight and informed by an aide that Mr. Zhu Jun was in the living room waiting to see him. My father put on his robe and came into the room. He saw the elderly Zhu standing by the window, his hands locked behind his back. Years ago, Zhu had sworn my father into the Nationalist Party while he was a cadet at Wuchang.

"I had to see you tonight." Zhu, thin and dressed in the traditional long, loose *marqua*, was nervous and fidgety.

"What brings you here at this hour," asked my father, signaling him to sit down.

"Your confrontation with Chiang Kaishek was treason in his eyes. Your life is in danger." Zhu insisted on standing, his shoulders jerked as he spoke, "You must leave Chungking immediately."

Shocked, my father looked at Zhu in disbelief.

"You should know that in times such as we are in now, an

ambush with a bullet is all too easy. You must take my advice and go now. You must keep our meeting tonight in strict secrecy."

Grateful for his words, my father held Mr. Zhu's hand and saw him to the door. They bade each other farewell in silence; only their eyes met to acknowledge the parting. Of this meeting my father wrote, "When I returned to my bedroom, my hands were trembling and tears were streaming down my face." Pangs of despair and anger overcame him. He felt hurt and betrayed that his commander-in-chief should be so intolerant and harbored so much hatred for dissenters—even now, when the Communist armies were sweeping through the country from north to south, when the country was already in ruin, when unity of all the Nationalists was most necessary. Tossing and turning in bed until 4 A.M., he got up, packed his diary and a few personal belongs in his briefcase, and had himself driven to his office in the Ministry, accompanied by an aide. Father wrote his letter of resignation and then two more letters to his deputies, instructing them to take charge of his office.

At ten o'clock, my father was at the airport to see Albert Chow off to the city of Kunming, the capital of southwest Yuman Province. Chow had come from San Francisco to extend his friendship on behalf of the Chinese American community to Acting President Li. He offered to do whatever he could to rally for American aid. Because commercial flights were not available, Li had made available a military plane to take Chow from Chungking to Kunming, To everyone's surprise, my father also bid farewell to the dignitaries who were at the airport and boarded the plane with Chow.

From Kunming my father flew to Hong Kong. He was surprised that the acting president Li Zongren had come to Hong Kong and checked into a hospital. Chiang Kaishek resumed the presidency and retreated to Taiwan with what was left of his elite army and the national treasury.

On December 8, my father came back to the United States with Li Zongren and his family on a plane the U.S. government had made available to Li. Chiang and Li were each claiming to be the legitimate head of the Nationalist government, and the Nationalist Foreign Ministry in Taiwan refused to issue passports to Li and his entourage. Only when the U.S. State Department intervened, granting entry permission without passports to Li and his party, did the Foreign Ministry rescind its earlier decision and issue the passports.

My father went to bid good-bye to his old classmate and colleague Zhang Fakui, who had also retreated to Hong Kong. Zhang was against my father's going to the United States with Li Zhongren. "Is it money that you lack?" he asked. "I will buy you the ticket to the United States through London if you need the fare. Once you are on the same plane with him, you'll be identified with him forever. What if he forms a government in exile?"

My father was without money, but he didn't want to accept his friend's offer of passage. He simply said, "I need to be with my family. Nothing I do now will make any difference." In my father's heart and soul, he had decided to serve his country by leaving.

Even though many people saw my father as Li Zongren's man, his relationship with Li was a tenuous one. At the core of their disagreement was a directive by Li to Gen. Mow Pang-Tsu regarding a large sum of U.S. dollars in Mow's possession. Mow was Chiang Kaishek's relative by his first marriage, and Chiang had given Mow funds to purchase airplanes from the United States on behalf of the Nationalist government. As no purchase had been made, Chiang now ordered Mow to return the money to the central government. Li used the "Mow case" to contest his right to authority with Chiang by claiming his right as acting president, instructing Mow not to heed Chiang's order. The case was widely publicized in the daily newspapers in Taiwan, Hong Kong as well as the United States.

My father later explained: "I advised Vice President Li that he no longer had the right to the title of acting president, nor the authority to issue an executive order that now rightfully belonged to Chiang Kaishek. I thought he should make a quiet exit and not create controversy that would further split what remained of the Nationalists. I believed that we all should seal our lips and give Chiang Kaishek a last chance to do what he could to preserve the Nationalist Party."

Chapter Ten

School Days in a Strange Land

O n arrival in New York City in March 1947, my sister and I were immediately enrolled in public school. New York Public School 87 was a typical midtown Manhattan building, a multistoried building of weather-beaten brown bricks without any charm or distinction. There, in the spring of 1947, I began my initiation into American culture and American education.

I was disappointed when the principal assigned me to the eighth grade, because it was a grade lower than the one I had attended in China, while my younger sister Chi, always the top student in her class, had been put into sixth grade, but with a group of students who had failed to move on to the next grade. When I objected to the eighth grade, the principal said that all students were assigned to classes by age group and that the eighth grade was the top grade for this school. This did little to appease me. Although my English at that time was abysmal, I felt that I had been demoted. My sister, too, felt she was demoted because her class was an abnormal one.

My homeroom teacher, Mrs. Craig, looked ancient to me with her ear-length, gray-streaked, wavy brown hair, thick spectacles, big nose, thin lips, and the pouch of loose skin that hung below her chin. Whenever she tried to make a point, her forehead would crease into three deep lines. On my first day, she introduced me to the rest of the class and then asked the students what they knew about China.

"It's a big country on the other side of the Pacific Ocean," said one red-haired boy.

"Right. What else?"

"China was an ally of the United States, Britain, France, and Russia in World War II," volunteered a girl in a red polka-dot dress. I noticed that she had green eyes and brown hair, and that she spoke loudly and didn't seem shy at all. I surveyed the thirty students in the classroom and felt surprised that they remained seated not only when the teacher entered the room but also when they answered questions. In China, we always stood as a sign of respect.

Mrs. Craig assigned me to a seat next to a tall girl with shiny blond hair, blue eyes, and a pug nose who beamed whenever she talked. I thought she was pretty despite her freckles, which I had never seen before.

"Cheng," Mrs. Craig said, "this is Lorraine Falk."

Lorraine smiled at me and had me repeat her name several times. She took me along wherever she went, and I hung onto her like a shoulder bag. I followed her all over school, even to the girls' restroom. When she drank from the water fountain, I did too. From that very first day, Lorraine had me read a page out loud each day during break, while she corrected my pronunciation. I had to look up most of the words in my English-Chinese dictionary.

Mrs. Craig gave me three big books with beautiful hard covers. "They're free," she told me, "but you must return them at the end of the school year."

As I flipped through them, I was impressed by the smoothness and whiteness of the pages and by the printed pictures. The arithmetic text looked familiar, but the other two books were incomprehensible to me. I had had two years of English in middle school in China, which gave me simple word recognition but not the ability to speak with any level of fluency or confidence. I felt proud carrying the books home because they were bigger and thicker than any I had ever had before.

PS 87 had very few students who were Negroes, as they were called then. At school assemblies, they stood out like the eyes of daisies. My sister, her Chinese classmate, and I were "Orientals," as we were called then. I met only one other foreign student on the playground, a Romanian girl with a flushed pink complexion who, like me, did not like sports and whose English was only slightly better than mine.

Three weeks after I arrived, Mrs. Craig spent an entire period discussing China, talking about old "Cathay" where the compass, gunpowder, and printing had been invented. She told the class that China had hundreds of spoken dialects and that the written characters were very different from an alphabet. She then asked me to write some Chinese characters on the blackboard. I wrote *meiguo* and next to it *zhongguo*.

"*Guo* means 'country,'" I explained, "and *mei* means 'beautiful.' So the Chinese name for the United States is 'beautiful country.' *Zhong* means 'center' or 'central,' which is how the Chinese have always perceived themselves—as the center of the world."

During recess, my classmates gathered around to ask me more about China. Using sign language and my dictionary, we engaged in an animated discussion.

"Chinese people are of the yellow race," I said, "so I'm a colored person."

"No, no!" Lorraine was aghast. "You're not a colored person. You're like me, white, except that your skin is tanned."

I looked up "tan" in my dictionary, shook my head and said, "I am a yellow person."

A black boy, one of the two in our class, also protested, "No, you're not colored. I'm colored." He pointed to his coffee-brown skin and added. "You *mei*, I not *mei*."

I persisted. "I'm yellow-colored. He's colored black, and the rest of you are colored white."

Again the black boy pointed to his skin and said he was "not *mei*."

"Not same!" I told him, trying to say "different," because the different races had distinct characteristics. I thought that his rich brown color looked strong and solid.

Ever since my first school days in China, I had been taught that the Chinese were a yellow-skinned race with an advanced civilization almost 5,000 years old. I was proud of my race, of my country's history, and of its rich heritage and culture. My experience in PS 87 was the first time that I had a personal and direct confrontation with the perception that anyone who wasn't white was inferior to any white person.

Over time, I learned from my classmates that in the American South there were still segregated schools, restaurants, public restrooms, and even water fountains for Blacks. I said that did not reflect well on justice or democracy in a great country such as the United States.

That September, my younger sister Chi and my brother Pei began attending an elementary school close to our home on Riverside Drive. I started public high school in Manhattan's Washington Heights, but they assigned me to ninth grade. When I objected, I was told that my English was too limited to be in tenth grade. Again, I was unhappy because of this demotion and felt that I should have been in tenth grade.

Mrs. Ling, a family friend who was working as a librarian at Columbia University, was sympathetic to my plight and managed to get me into tenth grade at a nearby private girls' school on a partial scholarship. The Gardner School, located on Fifth Avenue around 80th Street overlooking Central Park, had fewer than a hundred students, so classes were small. I went to school by bus every day. Tenth grade was where I properly belonged, I insisted; I felt better on going to Gardner, and no longer regretted having come to America.

When school started next September in 1948, Mother took my sister and me to Chicago by train to the Sacred Heart Academy, located in Lisle about an hour from Chicago. I was fifteen and Chi was twelve. The Chinese consul in Chicago met us and drove us to the school.

During her trip back to China for the presidential election, what Mother saw in Shanghai and Guangzhou had filled her with foreboding, and she expected hard times ahead. She called on the Catholic archbishop Paul Yu of Nanjing, entreating him to help find scholarships for her daughters. Yu had given many American Catholic college scholarships for the sons and daughters of high government officials to attend school in the United States. The Chinese Catholic hierarchy believed that converting the children of the upper classes would have a healthy influence on the lower classes. The archbishop next suggested to Mother that when she returned to New York, she should go to see Fr. Joseph Mao, who was responsible for soliciting scholarships from Catholic schools in the United States.

I still can hear my mother's sigh of relief when Father Mao came to our home to inform her that he had obtained full scholarships— tuition and room and board included—for Chi and me at the Sacred Heart Academy. It meant two fewer mouths to feed for my parents.

Sacred Heart Academy was run by Benedictine nuns. The school was one huge three story rectangular red-brick building that sat on several acres of green lawns with a bed of irises on one side of the lawn, a grotto on the other, and a pond filled with water lilies in the

center. Tucked away at the back of the property was a small cemetery where nuns were buried.

On the main floor, one side housed the convent and the chapel,
and the other side the dining room and kitchen. The prioress,
Mother Josephine, and the principal, Sister Purisima, met us in a
large room decorated with life-size statues of saints and a large cru-
cifix on the wall. I liked Mother Josephine, a chubby, soft-spoken
woman who assured Mother that we would be well taken care of. I
did not warm to Sister Purisima, a tall woman who would flash us a
big ingratiating smile from time to time. To me, Sister Josephine
appeared more sincere. Then, Sister Purisima gave us a tour of the
classrooms on the second floor and the dormitory for about a hundred and sixty girls on the third floor. Chi and I both cried when our
mother left, and she was in tears as well.

The statues of Christ the King, the Virgin Mary holding the
Infant Jesus, and the saints looked much friendlier to me than the
fierce protector deities in Chinese Buddhist temples. Those gods,
with their bulging eyes, red-painted faces, and long spears, were supposed to chase away demons, but they used to frighten me so much
that I would enter a temple only if I were with an adult whom I
could cling to. Later on, when Chi and I talked after attending our
first Catholic Mass, she asked me if the nuns' singing reminded me
of the Buddhist monks' chanting.

"Yes," I told her. "It did."

I was in the junior class and my sister the freshman class. Students at Sacred Heart wore white blouses and navy-blue skirts. We
had to put on light-blue veils whenever we entered the chapel. Our
daily schedule was totally regimented. When the bell rang at six
o'clock every morning, we got up in silence, made our beds, washed,
and lined up in formation to go to the chapel for Mass. Evening ves-
pers were at five, and we recited the rosary every night after supper.
We had two study periods in addition to our classes. The lights were
turned off at ten. We walked in formation everywhere—to the
chapel, to our classrooms, and to the dining room.

I hated hearing the nuns and other students speak of China as a
"pagan" country and referring to nonbelievers as "heathens."
Carmen and Rosa, two other Chinese students, were from Lima,
Peru. We were the "special students." I detested the term because it
told me that we were not like the other students.

In the dining room, we ate four to a table. All the girls took their turn serving the tables, rotating each week. During the second week of school, Sister Purisima called the four of us Chinese students out of line after supper and led us into the kitchen. "You girls will dry the dishes as they come out of the dishwasher," she told us. "That will be your job before study period from now on." Sister Francine, who supervised the kitchen, gave each of us a towel.

I stood there stunned. Father Mao had never told us that we would have to work in the kitchen, and neither the principal nor the prioress had mentioned anything about kitchen duty to my mother—or any other duty, for that matter. Chi and the girls from Peru were quiet. There was nothing any of us could do to protest, but to make my displeasure known, after wiping each dish, I slammed it onto the table hard enough to make a cracking noise but not hard enough to break it. I pretended it was just my clumsiness.

Sister Francine watched me for a while, then left the kitchen and returned with Sister Purisima. The two stood behind me watching me in silence. I ignored them and kept slamming the dishes onto the table. Every night for the next several weeks, Sister Purisima came and stood there watching me. Sometimes other nuns would join her. I didn't care. I kept slamming the dishes around whenever I felt like it, which was most of the time.

I didn't mind the religious atmosphere and regimen since I had studied one semester at the Aurora Middle School as a day student in Shanghai before coming to the United States. Aurora was a Catholic school, but students were not required to attend chapel and religious functions. What kept me sane at Sacred Heart were the Gregorian Chants, which I loved, which I learned to sing along with the nuns and the girls at Mass and Vesper. The chants gave me much peace in my personal anguish and solitude. The soft crescendos with their repetitive rhythms soothed my troubled spirit, and the supplication, "*Kyrie eleison, Christe eleison*" ("Lord have mercy, Christ have mercy"), eased the pain that I felt as yet another civil war, now between the Communists and the Nationalists, racked my country. We Chinese have endured so much, I thought. In the last century we were forced to give up Hong Kong to the British, Macao to the Portuguese, and ports and concession territories to foreign powers. In this century we have endured relentless civil war after the birth of the republic, then the ravages of the warlords, then the Japanese invasion, and now the Communist threat.

"If there is a God, why?" I asked a thousand times. "Why?"

One day, I picked up a newspaper and saw a photograph of a bony, sunken-eyed Chinese woman dressed in the traditional pajama-like garb, her hair pulled back in a disheveled bun. She was cradling an equally bony child, eyes closed, in her arms. The caption read, "Madonna and Child."

My tears rolled down and splashed onto the page. I took a pair of scissors, cut out the picture and put it in my scrapbook next to the holy pictures I had collected. In God's eyes, I told myself, that mother and her dying child were no less holy than the men and women who chose to live lives of penance in the hope of attaining eternal salvation. That poor Chinese woman loved her child no less than any auburn-haired American woman feeding baby food to her blue-eyed infant. Nor was her love any less than the love my mother felt for me. But that Chinese child had never stood a chance.

Sister Purisima's revenge came several months later on the night of the junior-senior social, an evening of dancing with the boys from St. Procopius College. This was the school's big event of the year. For weeks, the other girls talked about nothing else except the social and what they would wear. They tried on each other's frilly dresses, showed off their party shoes, and experimented with hairstyles. I watched in bemusement my classmates' excitement. Friday afternoon before the social and all day Saturday, under the watchful eyes of the nuns, we decorated the gym with flowers and leaves cut out of pink and green paper.

I wore a fitted, high-collared, lavender silk brocade *cheongsam* with side slits to above the knee, which had been tailor-made in Shanghai. As we were assembling to walk to the gym—in formation, of course—Sister Purisima told me to step out of line. "Cheng, you're looking so tired," she said with her sweetest smile. "Instead of going to the dance, you need a good night's rest."

I stepped outside the line and stood there watching the girls walk down the stairs. Meeting boys was not important to me, and I had not shared my classmates' excitement about the dance. But I resented the game Sister Purisima was playing with me. Feeling more lonely than humiliated, I went to my room, got into my night-clothes, crawled into bed, and took out my book of Tang poetry, which contained all the poems that I had memorized as a child. That night my heart ached with homesickness for my family in New York and for my homeland as I read and recited:

Thoughts of my brothers swell on mountain climbing,
Alone, a lonely stranger in a foreign land,
I doubly pine for my kin folks on holiday,
I know my brothers would, each with a dogwood spray in hand.

Our dormitory room slept twenty girls. Carmen's bed was next to mine. She was the gentlest girl I had ever known. Her broad forehead dominated her face, and she was in the habit of folding her arms in front of her chest, tilting her head to the right, and saying *"sí"* whenever anyone spoke to her. After class each day, we all changed out of our uniforms and into casual clothes. Carmen always changed into the same thing, a short-sleeved blue cotton dress and a heather-gray sweater. She had a suitcase full of beautiful new clothes, but she never wore them.

My stories of China in wartime were news to her. "Why are you always talking about oil, salt, firewood, and grain?" she asked. "Were these the things you worried about?" I told her that next to survival and safety, these were everybody's worries. It surprised me that she, a Chinese person, did not know anything about the war conditions of China.

Carmen was my closest friend. In my class, there were two girls, twins, from Costa Rica, and we bonded because we were foreigners and on the periphery of things. On weekends all the students went home except for us foreign students and the three girls from the orphanage.

At Christmas recess, my sister and I took the train home for the holiday for the first time since we had left home in September. Carmen and the other girls from South American did not go home and stayed in the dorm. When we returned after the New Year, Carmen had been moved out of the dormitory and into a private room. Sister Rose, our class advisor, told us that Carmen had a lung ailment and would eat her meals in the infirmary by herself, and she would be excused from gym. As she would need plenty of rest, Carmen was also excused from drying the dishes. But she still sat next to me in classes and in the study hall, and I was glad we were able to spend time together on weekends.

One afternoon in March coming back from the gym, we saw Carmen scrubbing the staircase on her hands and knees. Startled, we froze at the stairwell. "What are you doing?" we asked. "You're sick. You should be resting!" Carmen looked up, her eyes red from crying. "Sister Purisima told me that it's my job from now on to scrub the floors once a week."

After Sister Purisima singled her out to scrub the stairs, the twins from Costa Rica thought that Carmen should change her image and start dressing up in her tailor-made clothes. We all suspected Sister Purisima looked down on her because she thought that Carmen's family was poor. Every Sunday, we would help her pick out a different outfit to wear to Mass. We hoped that this would impress Sister Purisima. Our scheme didn't change anything, but we felt better just seeing Carmen looking so pretty.

Enraged by the way Carmen was treated, I slammed the dishes in the kitchen even more fiercely. "You should ask your parents to protest to Sister Purisima and to the prioress," I repeatedly urged her. But Carmen always said "no." Her parents were already worried about her health, and she didn't want them to worry even more. She had been thinking of entering the convent, and she believed that this was God's way of testing her humility.

Carmen entered a tuberculosis sanitarium in Springfield after school recess.

Sacred Heart had no public telephones, and students never received calls except for emergencies. One evening shortly after we returned to school in the fall of 1949, as Chi and I were getting ready for bed, we were summoned to the phone.

"China is in the Communists' hands," our mother told us, her voice soft. "We're refugees now."

"Where is Papa?" I asked.

"In Hong Kong. Papa will find a way to come back to us."

As she hung up, I went limp. I turned to my sister and told her, "China is in the Communists' hands," but I didn't tell her about our being refugees. She and I looked at each other in silence, and I knew that she already understood what had happened. Her lips were tight, and her big, bright eyes looked bigger than ever, and very sad.

I said nothing when I went back to the dorm. The other girls were chatting and laughing, trying on each other's clothes, running in and out of the shower. Amid all that sound and motion, I felt as if I were alone in a boat on the Atlantic Ocean. I was frightened, looking for the shore, hoping that I would see something, anything. That night I hid my head under the bedcovers and cried.

I was sixteen, but I felt ancient, uprooted, with no place to call home. I was no longer a temporary visitor to America, but a refugee. I was a citizen of China, but I belonged neither to Communist China nor to Taiwan, nor did I belong to the community of overseas Chinese.

Lonely, homesick, and worried about my father who had returned to China and about what would happen to China, I found solace in the quietness of the chapel, in the soothing Gregorian chants, and in the anchoring of the belief in the Holy Trinity and life everlasting. In November 1949 I wrote to my mother for permission to be baptized into Catholicism, since my father was still in Hong Kong at the time. My mother wrote back and said that I was too young to make that decision and that I should wait. But since she did not explicitly say "no," I decided to go ahead with my conversion anyway. On December 8, on the Feast of the Immaculate Conception of the Blessed Virgin Mary, I was baptized into the Catholic Church. My conversion to Catholicism only mildly mitigated my defiance in the kitchen.

My parents did not make an issue of it, for what was done was done. That following spring, when my sister asked for permission to be baptized as Catholic, they emphatically told her that there would be plenty of time to make the decision when she was older. My sister waited and was baptized just before her graduation from Marymount Academy in Purchase, New York, where she had transferred in her junior year.

The academy had admitted Anita Brown, a black girl from Louisiana, to the freshman class. One weekend afternoon, several of us who remained in school were chatting outside the principal's office when we heard Sister Purisima scream, "You're disobedient! You're unworthy . . ."

We looked at each other wondering who could have made her so angry? Moments later, her office door opened and Anita came out, her face expressionless. She ran outside past the grotto and into the open cornfield. A few days later, her mother came and took her away.

To me, this incident was one more proof that in America, one's worth as a person was in too many instances judged by the color of one's skin. I thought of the Chinese madonna and her child. Anita had no better chance of surviving at the academy than that Chinese child had. I also thought of Carmen. Why had she been made to wash the stairs when everyone knew she had tuberculosis? Because she was yellow, and she was meek, and because Sister Purisima had thought she was poor.

One Sunday morning, I finally lost control of myself. Only we the special students and the orphan girls were around. Sister Purisima was talking with us in the corridor.

"It was pride," she said, "that caused the archangel Lucifer to listen to the devil and to turn against God so that he was damned to hell for all eternity." She turned to me, flashing that smile of hers. "And what do you think about pride and Lucifer?"

I knew that she was referring to my defiance in the kitchen, and I could no longer control my fury.

"You're a hypocrite!" I shouted at her.

I left her and my classmates standing in stunned silence and rushed outside to the grotto. It was a sunny but cold day in February and I had gone outside without my coat. But I didn't care. I went to the grotto seeking refuge as much as solace. After a while, my anger and pain turned into reflections on the nature of religion.

I began thinking that, at its best, religion could be a way of living life for the better, as with St. Francis of Assisi, who, in his consuming love for God, treated all creatures, great or small, with equal tenderness and devotion. Yet religion can also beget suffering and inertia, as when blind faith breeds hope founded in passive acquiescence. And I knew only too well from my experience at the convent school that religion can easily take the form of intolerance embedded in righteous arrogance and even cruelty.

I thought then of faith, hope, and charity. The last of these is most difficult to live by, even for the most virtuous. We can have faith through grace or through blind trust, and hope can stem from external stimuli and our internal perceptions of what the future may hold. To love one's neighbor as oneself is easy when the neighbor has something to give, or is perceived as someone one desires to emulate. But true love requires a moral fortitude beyond faith and hope. It requires an unconditional willingness to reach out and embrace those who are different or less fortunate. Charity connotes generosity—not self-imposed poverty, or even giving alms, or performing services to the sick and the needy in the hope of gaining salvation. Charity is the opposite of indulgent self-love. I felt the suffering of God's little ones, the weak and the orphaned, and in my new faith I felt redemption in Christ's suffering, in the forgiveness of sins, and in the resurrection to come.

Of all the stories about the saints I had learned in the academy, I was most captivated by St. Francis of Assisi and his famous prayer. I memorized the prayer as I had the Tang poems my father taught me:

> Lord, make me an instrument of Thy peace.
> Where there is hatred, let me sow love;
> Where there is injury, pardon;
> Where there is doubt, faith;
> Where there is despair, hope;
> Where there is darkness, light;
> Where there is sadness, joy.
> Let me not so much seek to be consoled as to console;
> To be loved as to love;
> To be understood as to understand.
> For it is in giving that we receive.
> And it is in dying that we are born to eternal life.

While Catholicism gave me an anchor, it had not lessened the pain and loneliness I felt. Soon we began hearing terrible stories of the revenge that the peasants were wreaking for the wrongs and exploitation they had suffered over generations. These stories were told in newspapers, in letters from Hong Kong, and by people we knew who had firsthand information from their families and friends. Landowners who were not killed outright were beaten or tortured. They would be stuffed into the bamboo cages used for transporting hogs and then submerged in rivers, pulled up and then submerged again and again, like the dunking inflicted on those accused of sorcery in America's Plymouth Colony. Neighbors, friends, and even family members were encouraged to report on each other and on anyone who might be an enemy in the class struggle—based on their connections or comments they made. Children who reported on their parents were hailed as patriotic revolutionaries.

Adding to the incessant stream of bad news was the clamor in the U.S. Congress and media that America had "lost China." Whenever I heard those words, I could feel my guts sizzling like burning coals.

"You haven't lost China!" I wanted to shout to the world "The United States hasn't lost China because China was never yours!" I wanted to shout at Chiang Kaishek, whose dictatorship and corruption had fueled the Communist revolution.

I wanted to shout because of the suffering my countrymen had endured for so long and were still enduring. Instead, I slammed the dishes even harder at school and I shouted at my two little brothers over trivia at home.

At graduation, I received a scholarship from Salve Regina College, a Catholic women's college in Newport, Rhode Island, again with the help of Father Joseph Mao. The college-by-the-sea was housed in a castle-like estate, Ochre Court. Before the 1929 stock market crash that had thrown the country into the Great Depression, Newport was the summer playland of the rich and powerful. Ochre Court was edged with gold ceilings painted with cherubs and mythological figures above marble pillars; crystal chandeliers glittered in rooms and the walls were lined with silk brocade and tapestry. The building that housed the main dormitory, the Chemistry and Home Economics laboratories, and the gymnasium had once been its horse stable. The heirs of Ochre Court donated the estate to the Archdiocese of Rhode Island. It was then given to the Sisters of Mercy to open a college for women.

My freshman class of fifty-one students had the distinction of being its fourth class, thus making Salve Regina a four-year college.

Except for the two priests who taught theology and a woman who taught French, all our teachers were Sisters of Mercy. The Sisters lectured by outlining the chapters from the text assigned for reading. Students wrote down what the nuns and the priests said, to be regurgitated verbatim at test time. By the end of my freshman year, I realized that I would be way behind other college graduates at the end of four years in Salve. I tried to transfer, but no reputable university or college would accept my credits in spite of my good grades. One Catholic college accepted half of the credits, those in theology and English. Unwilling to lose a whole year in the transfer and to face the problem of losing the scholarship, I remained at Salve.

I was not good in mathematics and science, and that narrowed the choice of a major. I liked history and the social sciences, but I knew that a Chinese person had no future in social sciences, the humanities, or the arts. I had seen too many Chinese students with advanced degrees waiting on tables or serving as restaurant hostesses. I needed something practical that could get me a job when I graduated, so I chose food and nutrition, a sub-specialty of home economics. But I was embarrassed to be in home economics and used to hide the fact. "I major in food and nutrition," I would say when asked what I was studying.

Throughout my college years, I wore Chinese *cheongsam* I made from store-bought remnants. Even though I had worn Western-style dresses, blouses and skirts all my life, my mother thought I should wear Chinese dresses in college to avoid comparison with my schoolmates since we couldn't afford to buy nice Western clothes. One-and-a-quarter yards of material was sufficient for my petite frame, and it only cost from five to ten dollars. My mother taught me how to cut a pattern with brown wrapping paper, stitch it with an old sewing machine bought from a neighbor, and then finish it by hand.

My *cheongsam* set me apart from the preppy look of white woolen flannel blazers with the pale blue Salve emblem, solid-color blouses and plaid skirts, and argyle socks. I was definitely out of tune, like a flat note in a chorus. Several of my classmates spoke to me about my quaint look and encouraged me to give up my Chinese *cheongsam* for skirts and blouses, but I stuck to them like a stamp to an envelope. It was not only out of my family's tight budget situation. It was pride. I was proud that I could make my own clothes, proud of my heritage, and proud of my ethnic identity.

Dormitory talk was all about boys, going steady, what dresses and shoes to wear, and the steamy accounts of making out in the backseats of cars. There was one telephone in the dormitory, which was on the first floor. If a girl was expecting a call from a date, she would have another girl pick up the phone. The girl who answered would tell the caller to wait. The girl who had been waiting for hours or days for that call would hold the receiver for a minute or so before saying "Hi, who is this?" in a nonchalant tone. On weekends the ones who did not have dates dressed up and went to the bars frequented by officer candidates from the nearby naval officer school. Having grown up in war-torn China and in a culture in which a student was expected to learn and achieve and, later, contribute to society, I had a hard time understanding my classmates' total absorption with boys and their frivolous and strange activities.

For girls, taking up cigarette smoking was like joining a sorority. There were designated smoking rooms where the girls congregated between classes and in the dormitory. I was further alienated because I was a nonsmoker and was repulsed by the smell of cigarette smoke.

I had no dates, so I stayed in my dorm room and stuck to my books. The books kept me occupied and also gave me hope that I would make it in my adopted country one day. When I was very lonely and struggling with myself, feeling as though I were climbing over the mountains and the hills under a hot sun, I told myself that this was a passage, that America was a land of opportunity, and that there was a place for me if I was determined enough. I just had to keep going to get there.

Chapter Eleven

Cooking Up the Future with the Good Will Wok

As the governor's wife, my mother was the First Lady of Guangdong Province in China. In America, she became a restaurateur to support the family. We were no longer visitors in America, but rather aliens searching for a livelihood in a new world. Even though my father was a high-ranking official, he had little accumulated wealth. In their displacement to the United States, my parents were handicapped by language and had little capital. The only viable option open to them was to open a grocery store, or a *chop suey* restaurant, like other immigrant laborers before them.

Their first attempt at business was an investment of U.S. $3,000 in a small company to make shrimp chips for Chinese restaurants and grocery stores. An enterprising acquaintance convinced them that he had successfully developed the techniques for manufacturing shrimp chips. There was a market for the product in the thousands of flourishing Chinese restaurants. This venture turned out to be a hoax. In no time my parents' money had been spent, mostly for the salary of the developer who sold them on the idea. The company was a complete bust.

Their second try at a business favored a restaurant, because an eating place would eliminate the necessity of cooking at home, thus freeing time and energy for making a living.

For months my parents and their good friend Gilbert Lee frequented as many as two hundred Chinese restaurants in the five boroughs. They decided they would become partners in the restaurant business. My parents talked with the restaurant owners and managers to get ideas on how to make a successful business, but they dared not reveal that they had a restaurant business in mind. In Chinatown, people were already saying that high officials like my parents should not be competing with the immigrant laborers for the same bowl of rice.

My parents relied on another friend, Mr. Won, for advice in learning the trade. "Location, location, location," he told them. "That's what's so important in this business." Mr. Won was the owner of the Golden Phoenix in Brooklyn, always looking smart in his dark suit and bow tie. The Golden Phoenix had a full house for lunch during the week and a line waiting for dinner on the weekends. "I give my customers their money's worth. Good food, good portions, good service, and cheap," said Mr. Won. He greeted the customers like old friends, grinning boyishly as he told them, "So good to see you! How have you been? How's the family?" He would go to their tables and make sure everything was all right.

Mr. Won taught my parents about catering to the customers, about credit and bookkeeping, and my parents spent many hours at the Golden Phoenix observing the cooks in the kitchen and the waiters in the dining room and bar. Every week my mother would spend an afternoon observing in the Golden Phoenix. Mr. Won would reserve a table for her, usually in the rear, so that she could see what was going on in the dining room and easily slip into the kitchen to watch the cooks. "Pork *chop suey*, charcoal!" my mother heard the waiter shouting to the cooks. "What is that?" asked my mother. "That is to alert the cooks to leave out the seasoning for the black customers." Mr. Won told mother to turn around and look. "My regular customers do not like the black folks. We put them in the back near the restroom."

"That's terrible! That is injustice and discrimination. It's like slapping yourself," my mother scolded him, stunned. Mr. Won admitted that it *was* terrible, but it was either survive or go out of business. He explained that just about all the New York eating establishments covertly discriminated against "colored" people. Chinese restaurants were no exception, if they were located in white areas. Mr. Won told my mother that white customers complained and warned him that they would go elsewhere if they saw black people around. His waiters signaled the cooks when placing orders for the black customers except for takeout. The cooks then left out the seasoning ingredients for the dishes, to make the food less tasty to discourage their return. But he didn't mind if black customers came for takeout. "You'll beware of neighborhoods that black people are moving into. White people will move out and the business will collapse before you know it. That's happened to me twice before."

My mother felt bad hearing what Mr. Won said. In telling me the story, she recalled, "White people see Chinese as colored people. I became more attentive when I went into a Western restaurant, making sure that I was not put in the back, out of sight."

Opening a restaurant not only required capital but also American citizenship for acquiring a liquor license for business. After World War II, the immigration quota for Chinese was only 150 a year and citizenship applications went to long-time residents who were already established in the country. The Chinese consul in New York, who was a good friend, advised my parents that the best course of action for exchanging their temporary visa status for American citizenship for themselves and for their four children was to have an American-born child.

Our youngest sister, Christina Mae, was born in December 1950. My sister and I suggested the name "Christina" for our newborn sister, as she was a Christmas baby. My parents gave her the name Mae in honor of *Meiguo*, the "Beautiful Country" where she was born. We called her Tina. At that time, we children all adopted English names: Cheng (Zhen), Chi, Pei, and Hao became Virginia, Angela, Frederick, and Victor. Both "Virginia" and "Angela" had their origin in our Chinese names and were given to us by Father Joseph Mao, but my sister and I chose to retain our Chinese names at the Sacred Heart Academy and throughout our college years, not willing to detract from our heritage. Pei selected his own because he liked the name "Frederick." The name "Victor" was given to Hao by the obstetrician in Hong Kong who delivered him.

My parents were counting on U.S. $30,000, their life savings, to open a restaurant for their livelihood so they could support the family. At the time my mother returned to China as a representative of the National Assembly for the country's presidential election, in fall of 1948, she sensed that a hurricane of Herculean proportions would hit China and that we might end up staying in America for a long time waiting for the storm to pass. Her cousin's husband, who was an official in an aid agency that dealt with international organizations, had access to U.S. dollars at the official rate of one U.S. dollar to thirty yuan instead of several thousands at the black market rate. He was able to exchange my parents' assets into U.S. dollars at the official rate.

My mother contacted her cousin's husband to ask him to help transfer the sum to New York. After many months of waiting and some alibis from my cousin's husband about the delay, my mother asked the Bank of China to trace the transmittal. The bank showed my mother a memo that had my mother's signature directing the money to Singapore, but the bank official pointed out her name and the words, "Sincerely yours, Chufang Wu Li," that were typed clearly above her signature. The typed words, however, were distinctly from a different typewriter than the one that had typed the memo. The investigation concluded that fraud was involved in the transfer to Singapore. My mother was both shocked and hurt.

With the bank's evidence, my mother confronted her cousin who, by then, was in New York. The cousin pleaded with my mother not to push the investigation any further. She confessed that her husband had cut off the top of the page that had my mother's original instructions, which she had helped type, admitting that she had typed a new statement in the blank space above my mother's signature to instruct the transfer of the U.S. $30,000 to Singapore. She said the forgery was her husband's idea, but that he was not a bad person. They had only meant to borrow the money temporarily to make a quick profit in a business investment in Vietnam that a friend of theirs had offered. But they, too, were swindled by their friend. She gave my mother several pieces of her jade jewelry to compensate for the loss, calculating what she and her husband owed in yuan by using the substantially higher black market rate, rather than the official exchange rate. When I was sorting my mother's papers after her death, I found the letter her cousin's husband wrote to her, expressing his regret about his role in the fraud.

Our baby sister became our meal ticket in America. Good Will Restaurant opened for business in spring of 1951. Its liquor license and my parents' share of the Good Will restaurant were recorded in our baby sister's name. There were seven partners, including Gilbert and three cooks. My parents' share was $12,000. They put up the row house they had just purchased as collateral to borrow $4,000 from the Chase Manhattan Bank for their share. The red-brick house we lived in on 183rd Street behind the restaurant was bought for $15,000 with a thirty-year loan and 10 percent down. The house was only four blocks from the Good Will Restaurant and functionally met our family's needs.

The Good Will Restaurant was located at 181st Street and Broadway. The Washington Heights neighborhood in New York City had a large Jewish clientele, and they were good consumers of chop suey and chow mein. Gilbert Lee managed much of the purchasing, my father kept the books, and my mother was assistant manager, receptionist, cashier, and occasionally bartender all rolled into one. She had given up her dream of an advanced degree and took courses in food management at the Columbia University Teachers College instead. She also attended a bartender school and became quite an expert in concocting and shaking cocktails. She learned that even a few drops of alcohol too many in each drink would make a difference in the amount of profit earned.

At ten each morning, my mother left the house to go to the restaurant. From the time my father came back to New York in late 1949, he always squeezed a glass of fresh orange juice and had it on the table for my mother each morning. At closing, my father went to the restaurant to walk her home. During the first four months, my mother would not take a single day off and worked on holidays and weekends. She nervously watched the cash register ring, adding up the receipts nightly to see if the money would cover the payments for the grocers, the rent, the electricity and water, and salaries for the waiters and the cooks.

"The first paycheck I got from the restaurant was three hundred dollars. I held the check in my shaking hand, tears rolling down my cheeks. We had made it." My mother said this slowly in one of my talks with her in winter of 1997.

> That night Papa and I looked at the five of you sleeping soundly. We knew that you, too, would make it. . . . At the time Good Will opened for business, we only had seven hundred dollars left to our name. Papa and I weren't sure what would happen next. The grocers didn't want payment on credit and insisted on cash on delivery. If we asked a grocer for a credit extension, he became rude and threatened to put back into the truck what he had just

delivered. If we had failed, Papa and I weren't sure about what would happen next.

We were so afraid of losing our credit. The fact that we had no money was something we used to hide from the meat man, the liquor man and the vegetable men—as well as from everyone else. Tongues would have wagged if people had known and they would have made things more difficult for us.

My parents had always been good partners. My father supported my mother's university education when she was already a mother of three children, something unheard of in China in those days. Then he encouraged her to become involved with the women's movement in Guangdong and the relief work during the war years. While he was governor, she introduced him to reading famous biographies and about Western thought and government. She used to select important paragraphs from a book, pretending she didn't quite understand the meaning and ask him to explain them to her. This was her way of protecting both his time and pride. My father recognized that there was always much to be learned.

Now that she had a command of the English language, albeit an imperfect one, whereas my father did not, my mother was better suited for the restaurant business. He took care of Tina, or Muimui —younger sister, as she was called—and looked after my two younger brothers. Every day he brought food in stacked containers home from the restaurant to feed them. When Tina was a toddler, he took her to the restaurant with him and she sat next to him with her coloring books while he did the bookkeeping.

Cooks had to be coddled with humor and deference, since the success of the restaurant depended on them—the flavor of the food and the amount of ingredients used or wasted. Their tempers rose with the temperature in the kitchen, and they burst into tantrums when they felt the waiters or customers had complained too much. In one episode shortly after the restaurant opened, the head cook and the number two cook each held a cleaver in hand, ready to swing at the other. Two waiters and the dishwasher shouted, "Stop! Stop!" They jumped at the cooks, trying to hold them down. In the ensuing melee, dishes crashed all over. Gilbert tried to talk some sense back into the cooks, but they peeled off their aprons, flung them on the floor and walked out the back door. Number three cook couldn't manage the kitchen alone for the full house. So Gilbert put on an apron, tossing meats, onions, and garlic into the sizzling wok, while my stunned mother tried to calm the hungry customers waiting for their food.

Good Will could not afford tablecloths. The dining room had virtually no decorations, but was immaculately clean. All the waiters had master's degrees, and one a doctoral degree. After the Communists took over the mainland, students who were here for their graduate studies lost the source of support that had previously been provided by their families. Those who were engineers and scientists found jobs without difficulty, but sociologists, political scientists, and students in the humanities and education had a hard time. They worked as busboys or dishwashers before waiting tables because they could not communicate with the cooks in Cantonese. Until the 1960s, when the United States relaxed its regulations to allow "essential personnel" to enter the United States, cooks were all immigrant laborers from Guangdong.

Like other restaurants at the time, Good Will served mostly chop suey, chow mein, egg rolls, and spare ribs. The cooks called chop suey "hog feed"! Chopped bamboo shoots, celery, carrots and onions, and soy sprouts were thrown together cooked with garlic, pepper, salt and cornstarch made into a thin gruel, with MSG added for flavor. Chicken chop suey, beef chop suey and pork chop suey were all from the same pot mixed with thin slices of the meat. Customers loved egg rolls and spare ribs with plum sauce and mustard.

The immigration officers used to come looking for illegal immigrants at Chinese restaurants. Most illegal workers were deserters from ships who came into port. Unskilled, the majority worked as cooks and dishwashers. Restaurants dreaded such a search, especially during the lunch time, since it created havoc in the kitchen during a peak hour. Customers complained when they had to wait.

The immigration officers usually came into the restaurant in twos or threes and blocked both the front and rear entrances. One officer would identify himself to the manager, while the other headed straight to the kitchen demanding that everyone show his passport or other immigration document. The third officer would look inside the bathrooms and search the basement. Such searches instilled fear in the Chinese community. The penalty for the illegal workers who were caught was deportation. But where would they go? The home to which they had once longed return to was gone.

At Good Will, Gilbert and my mother tried to deter the immigration officers at the entrance if it happened that an illegal worker was on the premises. They talked to gain time for the worker to escape out the back door or go into hiding in the storage area behind the stacked groceries if the back exit happened to be blocked. Often the immigration officers sat in the dining room for hours watching.

The practice of a search without warrant was finally put to a stop in 1971, when my brother Victor was a young law professor at Columbia University. He mobilized the support of his colleagues, as well as the American Civil Liberties Union, the Chinese Student Council, the Chinatown Advisory Council, and the Chinese dailies to put a stop to the searches without warrants on the grounds that they were illegal. Eventually the Immigration and Naturalization Service acknowledged that restaurant owners had the right not to permit the search during business hours.

Restaurants like Good Will also dreaded the sanitation inspectors. The inspectors picked and poked, throwing their weight around, threatening the restaurants with citations and shutdowns. Gilbert learned to take care of them with his hundred-dollar handshakes, inviting them to come back after duty for some delicious chop suey on the house. "Bring your wife, too," Gilbert would tell them.

My mother's aching feet kept going from one end of the dining room to the other many times each day. For some ten to twelve hours a day, she attended to the customers, stood in the bar shaking and concocting cocktails, and worked behind the front counter for the take-out orders and to ring the cash register. My father, siblings and I used to watch her pulling her shoes off at night. They were so swollen that they looked like pigs' feet.

Ironically, the overseas compatriots who had welcomed my parents so warmly before, now met my parents' venture into the restaurant business to earn a living with misgivings, derision, and resentment. Culturally and traditionally, the Chinese were disdainful of merchants. Academics, scholars, and government officials have always been the most revered in Chinese society, whereas the merchant class was looked down upon as the lowest in the Chinese social strata—in spite of their wealth—and theoretically they were considered to be even below the peasant and worker classes. As restaurateurs now, my parents were lumped by many into this lowest class.

Tongues wagged about the fact that the former governor and his lady had sunk so low as to open a chop suey house for profit. After all, the chop suey business was a livelihood for the immigrant laborers; the former governor and his lady should not compete with these immigrant laborers for the same pot. Some said the restaurant was just a façade for hiding their wealth; it was not possible for my parents not to have money because so many Nationalist government officials were well known to be corrupt. But the cruelest criticism of all came from my parents' former colleagues who had held high positions in the Nationalist government, some of whom were living in Long Island mansions and mid-Manhattan East Side apartments. They asked in outraged candor why the governor and his lady would cheapen themselves to the level of restaurant service, engaging in work that was so distasteful.

"Friends as well as the entire Chinatown community gasped and shuddered when they saw me serving customers," my mother would recall. "When Madame Yu Hanmou came to visit from Taiwan, she asked me if I had to do what I did. I said that the restaurant provided a livelihood for me and my husband to feed our five children. But when Madame Zhang Fakui came to visit from Hong Kong, the first thing she said to me was 'Madame Li, why do you take on such low-class work and cheapen yourself to this degree?' I felt the sting of her remark and told her, 'Madame Zhang, if I didn't do this, I would have to borrow money from you. The first time you might be willing to give me a loan for old time's sake. If I asked again, you would tell me that I should be self-reliant. The third time I came, you would have your maid tell me you were out and refuse to see me.' Sneers and gossip could be ignored, but not the customers. That was why I worked long hours, six days a week. What was important to me was for the restaurant to succeed and to be able to give you children a good education. My only fear was not to make it and fail."

After school, my brothers, ages ten and nine, helped with polishing the knives and forks at Good Will. My mother was protective of my sister Chi and me and never had us do more than serving as hostesses in the dining room or tending the cash register. "All my children had experienced a privileged upbringing in China. I knew the change in America was especially hard on the two older girls," she acknowledged to others.

Good Will's business was profitable, but the neighborhood deteriorated with the appearance of delinquent teens. My parents wanted to protect my brothers and decided to leave New York City for suburbia. After five years of running the Good Will Restaurant, they decided to strike out on their own, and sold their shares to the other partners. Mother's glee could not be contained when handing Mr. Won a check for more than triple his investment. At the time Mr. Won invested a $2,000 share in the Good Will, he had told my mother he considered it a gambling bet just like at a horse race. "What he really meant was that he had little confidence that I could ever succeed in the restaurant business. That remark stabbed me hard. I was determined to show him he was wrong," my mother explained.

In 1955, my mother, my siblings and I became naturalized American citizens. My father chose to hold onto his Chinese citizenship. "American citizenship for me would mean that I was taking up a slot that could benefit someone younger. To be an American means a new lease on life," my father explained. "A younger person should have that opportunity." I watched my mother choke with emotion when the immigration officer took her fingerprints. In November we went to Yankee Stadium for the naturalization ceremony. The stadium was filled with thousands of jubilant people, and some women wore corsages. But our mood was somber, mindful that we were refugees in an alien land.

The year 1956 began auspiciously and upbeat. With the money from the sale of their share in Good Will restaurant and a bank loan, my parents opened China Garden Restaurant in White Plains, diagonally across from the county center. I had earned my master's degree from New York University and was a chief nutritionist in the metabolic ward at Montefiore Hospital in the Bronx. My sister Angela was in Manhattanville College on a work-study scholarship, and my two younger brothers, who had attend the Bronx High School of Science, both skipped a grade when transferring to White Plains High School. Our family was living in a new home, a white-frame house on Kensico Road in White Plains, which was within walking distance of the restaurant.

It was a bright March morning when I got the call from my mother saying that Papa had suffered a head injury falling down the basement stairs. He had just washed the bathroom floor and was carrying a pail in his hand when he fell.

I immediately left work and took a bus to the White Plains County Hospital. My mother, still elegant in her fitted high-collared Chinese *cheongsam*, her lustrous black hair slightly disheveled in a French twist, was standing outside the hospital room waiting for me. She was very distraught and upset. "I went to the emergency room. They told me Papa was having some X-rays taken. I waited two hours and didn't see him. I went to the X-ray place, but they told me he hadn't been there. I went back to the emergency room and asked again. They finally located Papa in the ward. . . ." My mother was rambling. "I just had Papa moved to this private room. I had told the ambulance attendants and telephoned the hospital to put Papa in a private room . . . but they treated him so badly, like he was a laundryman."

When I entered his room, I saw my father's left hand and leg shaking uncontrollably, his eyes were shut tight and his face white, blood oozing from his left ear. I touched his hand and it felt cold. At the nursing station the young attending doctor was flirting with a student nurse. I asked him what was being done for my father. Shuffling some papers in front of him, he said that he was sleeping comfortably and was under observation.

Wanting some assurance, I telephoned my boss Dr. Raymond Weston at Montefiore and described Father's condition to him. "You need a neurosurgeon to look at your father," Dr. Weston said with urgency. He gave me the telephone number of Dr. Kenneth Gang. Dr. Gang was in his office when I called. He said that he would come to the hospital at once if the situation warranted. Dr. Gang rang the nursing station and spoke with the attending doctor whom I had spoken with earlier—who was still at the station chatting with the young nurse. I heard him assure Dr. Gang, as he had assured me, that my father was resting.

An hour later—three hours after the fall—Dr. Gang arrived in my father's room, He took one look at Father's eyes before turning to the nurse and calling out, "Coma! We'll need an operating room right away." The nurse who came into the room with Dr. Gang pricked my father's feet with a needle and got no response. "He is in deep shock," she announced.

Dr. Gang, hair thin and fortyish, took charge from then on. He explained to us that my father was in very critical condition; he would need to open up his skull to release the pressure in the cranium. "I can't promise a successful operation, but that's the only chance he has." Dr. Gang first looked at my mother, and then to me. "What are we going to do?" my mother mumbled. I knew we had no choice but to allow Dr. Gang to operate, but I couldn't bring myself to utter the words.

My mother went to the phone and dialed a family friend, who was a physician, for advice. Unable to accept her friend's advice to heed Dr. Gang's recommendation to operate, she put in a call to her internist. When she hung up, she stood very still saying nothing.

"We have no time to lose. Every minute counts," implored Dr. Gang, who had been waiting while Mother made these calls. "I want you to do everything you can to save him," my mother whispered, her voice breaking. My mother stared at the consent form the nurse held out to her. I took the form from the nurse and signed, giving consent for the operation. My mother broke down and kissed my father on his cheek in a display of emotion I had not seen before. I held her hand as my father was wheeled away on the gurney.

We waited anxiously outside the operating room. Mother spoke incoherently about the restaurant, opened only three months, and of my brothers and sisters—three teens and a five-year-old. "What are we going to do?" she repeated to herself as much as to me. Five hours later Dr. Gang, clad in his green surgical garb, a white gauze mask hung around his neck, came into the waiting room. He told us that the operation had been a success, but he could not predict the outcome. My father was in very critical condition and could remain comatose for days. To make sure that Father was properly attended, my mother arranged for twenty-four-hour private nursing care. It was midnight before my father was wheeled to his room, his head bundled in white gauze, his face swollen and eyes closed.

We tried to assure Tina that Papa would be all right, but she had picked up enough from the tone of our conversations and from our worried expressions to know something grave had happened to her Papa. A special bond existed between my father and my youngest sister. While the rest of us children had little access to our father while we lived in China, ever since she was an infant, Papa had fed her, washed and combed her hair, held her hand when they crossed the street, and tucked her in bed at night. She looked to her Papa for company and comfort. When my mother found Papa in a puddle of water on the basement pavement, he opened his eyes for a few seconds asking, "Where is Muimui?" before he lapsed into unconsciousness.

The days following the accident, Tina, home from kindergarten every afternoon, would sit by the window in the living room watching the cars go by, making up songs to the tune of the cowboys in the Western movies that featured Roy Rogers and Dale Evans, singing to herself, ". . . riding my horse to the mountains and far, far away, I buried my father. . . . I loved him until I died." She sang on and on until the sun set, then she started to whine, softly crying, "I want my Papa, I want my Papa." To the end of her days, my mother said she felt sad at sunset, remembering how her little girl had wept at what happened to our father.

My parents had no medical insurance. Dr. Gang, a kind man and a caring physician, advised us that we would have to pay the three private-duty nurses promptly; payment for the hospital could be arranged on installment. He told us not to worry about his fee for now.

When Aline, who had been our housekeeper for three months before she was diagnosed with tuberculosis and hospitalized in a sanitarium, heard about my father's accident and that we needed money to pay the nurses, she offered Mother her savings of three thousand dollars to help out. My mother was touched by her generosity, but couldn't possibly take her life savings. My mother borrowed money to pay for the private duty nurses as we kept vigil while our father lingered in a coma for eight days before waking up. He stayed in the hospital for twelve more days. A friend volunteered to sleep in a cot in my father's hospital room at night so that we could eliminate the eleven to seven shift of the private duty nurse to help reduce the cost of care.

I spoke with Dr. Gang about the care—or lack of care—my father had received in the emergency room and from the young doctor on the floor. Dr. Gang acknowledged that the hospital had made a mistake in the care of my father. Neither my mother nor I had any knowledge of what actions a patient or his family might take in confronting negligence and malpractice. This was in spite of the fact that I worked in a hospital. My physician associates were solicitous about my father's condition, but none ever suggested that we file a complaint with the hospital or possibly with the court for gross negligence.

My father made a remarkable physical recovery and regained the use of his limbs, but his memory would never be the same again. He forgot all the English he had so painstakingly learned, and it was hard for him to recall names and events associated with the past. He was tormented at his inability to help my mother manage the restaurant, and he lamented that he had become a burden to the family. A stoic man, he now spoke of his anguish at being a refugee in a foreign land and unleashed his frustration and fury at the events over which he had no control. His outbursts were unpredictable and sudden, and then they subsided just as abruptly. Once calmed, he retreated into his usual quiet self. But he never forgot that he was a displaced person, a man without a country.

Only two weeks before he fell, my father had written a poem in which he commemorated old comrades, meditated on life and his love for his homeland. The poem, reflecting his mental state, had four quatrains of seven characters each.

Mourning Mankind

Tear-stained pillow dreaming of days gone,
Pity those killed one another in war,
Chosen destruction over coexistence,
God of war won over god of freedom.

Crying for My Homeland

Angry torrents racked the land;
Tear-stained pillow dreaming of days gone,
Sweet home remained, divided country remains,
My heart aches, deep in pain.

Remember Old Comrades

A hundred thousand combatants and five hundred brave men,*
Once shared the will for justice regained;
Tear-stained pillow dreaming of days gone;
Farewell forever, my brave, royal men.

---

*"A hundred thousand combatants and five hundred brave men" refers to the elite army equipped with the best weaponry in the War of Resistance and the five hundred officers who committed suicide when Taiyuan was surrounded by Communist troops.

Reflection on Life

Sixty years of living and many more,
The heart yearns to serve though far from home;
Tumultuous calamity unyielding, senescence descends;
Tear-stained pillow dreaming of days gone.

"Think of yourself as a big tree that gives shade to the house and gives us comfort," my mother told him, assuring him of the important place he occupied in our hearts and in the family. She now assumed the dual responsibility of sustaining the restaurant and providing for the family. Thereafter over the next several years, we had a series of housekeepers taking care of Father and Tina.

My brothers Fred and Victor helped out in the restaurant dining room as maître d's on weekends and holidays. But my mother never allowed them to work as waiters, not wanting them to judge people by money and the tips they left on the table. While still in grade school Fred once commented that waiters were making more money than some people with their Ph.D. degrees, which he had observed at the Good Will restaurant. His remark alerted our mother to be cautious so that her boys would not be misled into making seemingly easy money and losing interest in pursuing higher education. Through college and graduate school, Angela came home on weekends and helped in the dining room. My help in the restaurant was negligible. I had married in November 1956 and was living in upstate New York with my husband, who taught at Clarkson College.

China Garden thrived. Several years later, my mother was able to double its capacity to 300 seats by acquiring the space of the shoe store next door when it went out of business. The architect designed and remodeled a four-thousand-square-feet space into a main dining room, a private gourmet room, a bar, and an office. The main dining room had a huge wall-to-wall mural painted by the famous Chinese artist Wang Yachen. The mural pictured graceful bamboo, floating lotuses, and frolicking goldfish against an aqua-blue background. Some goldfish were typically of Chinese stock and others more Western, symbolically suggesting friendship between the Chinese and American people. My father wrote a poem to the effect, "Goldfish make no distinction between China and America." The smaller mural in the bar depicted a Chinese pavilion with rocks and trees. Near the entrance was a small pond filled with carp. Sitting in the dining room, one had the aura of a classic Chinese garden.

China Garden was a departure from the chop suey and chow mein houses of the time. Its glossy pink menus were beautifully designed, featuring lichee duck, roast pig and squab, shark fin soup, seafood clay pot, as well as crab meat roll and crêpe Mandarin to tease the palate. One of the first restaurants in the United States to feature and serve authentic Chinese cuisine, it introduced the chafing dish "Ho Go" to New York gourmets.

Lee Wagner, the originator of *TV Guide*, and Milton Bordin, a successful importer, were China Garden customers and became good friends of my mother's. Lee was a gourmet who knew a great deal about food and restaurant service. Milton, who often traveled to Hong Kong, was a connoisseur of Chinese cuisine. They helped my mother with ideas for advertisements, including in the *New Yorker*. Lee got my mother on television shows for cooking demonstrations and interviews on the local channels. Her years as the first lady of Guangdong had allowed my mother to develop a genuine talent for being entertaining. On camera, she had a charismatic presence and was charming. She had a flare for showmanship and was a great storyteller. Besides TV appearances, the Yonkers Raceway featured a China Garden night. The *New York Times*, the *New York Telegraph*, and the *New York Herald Tribune*, as well as local Westchester papers, featured China Garden's festivities of the August Moon and Go Ho-Go.

Whenever the chefs came up with a new dish, my mother would invite Lee, Milton, and their wives as tasters. If the two gentlemen gave the thumbs up on what they sampled and their wives cheered, she put the item on the menu. If they thumbed down, the dish would be eliminated right then and there.

On Saturday nights, my mother staged a banquet to invited friends and her most valued customers. Special dishes like Peking duck and roast piglet were brought to the large round table in the center of the dining room with the sounding of a gong—Bong! Bong! "In my grandfather's house, we used to sound the gong whenever a distinguished guest came to call," my mother explained. "I want to give our customers a touch of class. It's good public relations and good advertising at the same time." Upon hearing the gong, heads throughout the restaurant would turn and crane for a look curious as to what was coming out of the kitchen next.

My mother wore the finest silk *cheongsam* embroidered with floral designs tailored in Hong Kong. Until Good Will became profitable, many of the *cheongsam* she wore were do-it-yourself. Some of the customers came to China Garden not only for the cuisine but also to see the costumes that the dining room hostess Deana Hong and my mother wore. On weekends and holidays, my mother and Deana changed their clothes two or three times an evening, like Chinese brides changing their costumes on their wedding days. Deana was the wife of a former diplomat of Nationalist China who spoke fluent English. She had a pretty oval face, long eyelashes and a girlish waistline. Vivacious and aggressive, Deana would laugh and wink and could talk customers into trying any dish. But it was my mother who was the reason why so many customers came back as regulars. Generous, friendly, attentive, she was the consummate hostess.

For Chinese Lunar New Year celebrations, China Garden hired musical troupes from Chinatown to sing Chinese operetta and to entertain. Gongs and drums sounded and firecrackers sparked the air as the golden silk lion wriggled and wound all around the dining room. China Garden attracted the famous and the not so famous from Manhattan, Connecticut, Long Island, and the whole of Westchester County. On weekends, customers would line up outside the entrance.

In 1961, my father was one of four individuals selected for an oral project sponsored by the East Asian Institute at Columbia University. For eight months, Dr. Minda Wong, a researcher from the Institute, came to our home to interview Father twice a week. While it was agonizing for my father to try to recall events and names, nevertheless the prodding and the attention he received was therapeutic, and helped him regain some measure of confidence.

Still, my father would not leave the house unless my mother chauffeured him. Dr. Gang told my mother that she was spoiling her husband with her attention. "Take a vacation and start taking care of yourself." The good doctor advised her.

Heeding the doctor's advise, Mother, in a state of exhaustion, took a two-week trip to Hong Kong and Taiwan with my sister Angela, who was then a postdoctoral fellow in physics at Yale University. Mother explored the possibility of our father's living in Taiwan or possibly Hong Kong, where he had many friends and no language barrier. The trip only confirmed to my mother that neither Taiwan nor Hong Kong was an option. In Hong Kong, position and social status conditioned one's actions, and they couldn't possibly seek the kind of livelihood they did in America. Ever since my father had flown to New York with Li Zongren, my parents were persona non grata to Chiang Kaishek in Taiwan. During my mother's brief visit with my sister, intelligence agents trailed her every movement.

By the time my mother and my sister returned from their three week-vacation, Father had ventured out to visit friends in Chinatown, first in the company of a friend and later alone. A year later, in 1966, my father went to Hong Kong and stayed six months. There he organized and published four volumes of his diaries with the help of friends.

My father's one hobby in life was the collection of rare books. Returning to New York, he brought back a gift of 6,000 of these rare books to Columbia University. The books were the treasures he had collected in the course of forty years and had been kept in Hong Kong for nineteen years for safety. The collection included the 1871 edition of *The Thirteen Classics* with annotations and commentaries, based on a 1739 version, and the 1865 edition of the collected works of Wang Fu-Cjic, a Chinese philosopher who expounded democratic principles in the Ming dynasty in the sixteenth century, as well as military science and belles-lettres. A number of these books had been inherited from my father's grandfather.

Many of the books were fragile pamphlet-like, paperbound volumes printed on rice paper from hand-carved wood blocks. Some were grouped in "collectanea"—individual small collections—a traditional Chinese form of publishing. The books were valuable for the famous publishers who artistically cut the wood blocks from which they were printed, as well as for their contents. In offering his books to the East Asian Institute, my father hoped that the collection would help to increase the West's knowledge and understanding of China and that this would be followed by cooperation and friendship and, in time, by a just and lasting solution to problems that existed between China and the West. He gave permission to Columbia to microfilm his diaries of forty years with the instruction that the diaries covering the period 1949–1952 not be released until after his death. It was a precaution he took because he didn't wish to add controversy or recrimination to the tragedy that already beset the Nationalist Party.

We celebrated our father's eightieth birthday with a big party in 1975, in a midtown Manhattan hotel. The joyful occasion was enlivened by the presence of a third generation, joined by some three hundred friends, including Dr. Gang, who had retired to North Carolina but had come for the occasion. Friends in Hong Kong sent their good wishes, writing poems and calligraphy, and some mounted their brush paintings in scrolls.

My father was happy and reflective, feeling good that his friends on both sides of the Pacific Ocean had remembered him on this occasion. "If I were to live my life over, I would live it in exactly the same way," said my father. I thought that I would like to be able to say the same thing when it was my turn. It was quite an accomplishment for one to say, nearing the end of life's journey—that one would live life in exactly same way.

Our parents had encouraged us to study science for both the potential contributions it makes to human progress and for its ability to sustain a living in the competitive job market. They had expected us to get on with our education and to find our own callings in our adopted country. By then, my sister Angela was a professor at SUNY–Empire State College. Fred took his medical degree at the University of Rochester and was a researcher at the National Cancer Institute, and Victor received his Doctor of Juridicial Science from Harvard and was a professor at Columbia University Law School. Tina, our little sister, graduated from college and, later, Cornell Business School. I was a professor at the Johns Hopkins School of Hygiene and Public Health. Among my five half-siblings, Huon received his doctorate in hydraulic engineering from the University of California at Berkeley, Kam received his doctorate in electrical engineering from the University of Pennsylvania, and Lanfun her doctorate in biochemistry from Cornell University. They were highly successful professionals in the public and private sectors.

Yung was working for a publisher in Los Angeles. My eldest half brother Ban had retired and was living in Los Angeles.

The construction of the new Interstate 287 in front of China Garden was the beginning of the end of the restaurant business. For months, the parking lot and entrance to the restaurant were barricaded and filled with debris. My mother was unwilling to give up. "Eisenhower has enough energy to be president at seventy, I should have enough energy for a new restaurant at sixty-two," said my mother. Acting on an impulse and encouraged by past success, she ventured out once more and opened a new China Garden in Eastchester, a mile from the White Plains Mall. The largest share in the corporation belonged to my parents, and each of us siblings had a small share, as did the head chef and the manager. But the business was a struggle from the start. By then, there were several Chinese restaurants in the area, and the two China Gardens competed with these restaurants and each other for the same customers.

No longer economically viable, the old China Garden was sold first, bringing very little profit. Exhausted from commuting from their new home in Confucius Plaza in lower Manhattan, my mother tried to sell the new China Garden. Buyers were scared off by its high rent and were superstitious of the fact that the location had a history of failure. She struggled for two more years before China Garden Eastchester was sold at a loss.

"The restaurant business made it possible for our three younger children to pursue their education as they would like to," my mother summed up her thirty years as a restaurateur. "The restaurants also provided sponsorship for nearly fifty individuals, some with families, to come to America to make their living and to start anew." In all, I would say that my parents had not failed in the least bit in their goal of providing for us children.

Chapter Twelve
Finding My Path

Moving to the Tarheel State of North Carolina in 1960 was not my choice. I supported my husband Douglas Wang's decision to come South when he accepted an offer of an associate professorship from North Carolina State University. He had taught at the University of Missouri. Each year, his annual salary increase turned out to be much less than that of the other faculty members. When this happened for three consecutive years, he spoke with his chairman about the inequity and asked for an explanation. The chairman, who had always been cordial to Douglas, looked him in the eye and asked, "Do you compare yourself to Americans?"

I worried about living in the South, with its reputation for Jim Crow racism at the time. I remembered the press report of the mutilated body of Emmett Till, a fourteen-year-old black boy from Chicago in 1955, who had been pulled from Mississippi's Tallahatchie River. He was abducted, severely beaten, and finally thrown into the river with a cotton-gin fan that had been fastened around his neck with barbed wire. Till had been murdered for whistling at a white Mississippi woman. His murderers—the woman's husband and his half brother—were quickly acquitted by an all-white jury.

At the time of our arrival in Raleigh, there were already three other Chinese professors at the university; two of them were engineers, as was Douglas. Jack Shen was in the economics department. He and his wife Susan and their two children were the first Chinese faculty family to settle in Raleigh. At our first get-together at the

Shen's home, I asked Jack if there had been any incident of discrimination toward Chinese. Jack said that the South had been hospitable to them, and they had not experienced overt discrimination. But Susan told us that a Chinese student had been drowned in a stream on the edge of town. The student had dated a white woman. It was not clear whether the death was an accident or a homicide. Jack and Susan believed that it had something to do with the fact that he had crossed the forbidden path.

Our ranch house, the first home we owned, was on a half-acre slope shaded by tall pines, seven miles from the university campus. The kitchen, located in the front part of the house, was by a pink dogwood grove, home ground for squirrels, red robins, blue jays, and hummingbirds.

Southern hospitality was gracious. The welcome-wagon lady brought gifts and coupons from local merchants, and the dean's wife called to see if there was anything she could do to help me get settled in my new home. I met other faculty wives at teas, and neighbors dropped by to say hello.

The Civil Rights movement was already spreading throughout the Deep South. My body tensed as I watched on television the memorial service for the four little girls who died in the bombing of the black church in Birmingham and the bus boycotts in Memphis— with the police turning on hydrants to hose down and disperse the boycotters and unleashing German shepherds on the black marchers. Black marchers carried the sign "I am Man" to remind us of men's cruelty to men. I cringed each time I heard on the radio or saw in the newspapers or on the television screen pictures of the crosses burned in front of black churches and homes of the civil rights leaders by the ghostly hooded Ku Klux Klan. Alone after the children went to bed, there were many nights when I looked out on the lawn and conjured up images of the burning cross in front of the yard. The fear that gripped me was one that I could not easily shake.

Every evening, I turned on the television in the living room for the nightly news, though I might be buzzing around in the kitchen. Chet Huntly and David Brinkley were reproting the threat of the Vietnam War spreading to China. It reminded me of the Korean War in which the Chinese Red Army fought the American forces and of the United States' possibly using a nuclear weapon on China to curtail the Yellow Peril.

Douglas was tall, slim, and his angular face handsome. He, too, had come to the United States on the *General Gordon*, although we didn't meet until almost ten years later at a Chinese student party in New York City. He was fresh with a new doctoral degree in engineering and earning a good salary in an engineering firm in Manhattan. I was finishing my master's degree in nutrition education at New York University. Shortly after we met, he left for a teaching post at Clarkson College in upstate New York. To a large extent, our courtship was carried out by courtesy of the U.S. Postal Service, and we saw each other only on long weekends and holidays.

Our marriage on Thanksgiving Day 1956 was celebrated by both families and friends as being an ideal match. I gave up my professional work to be a full-time housewife and to raise a family. But even on our honeymoon in Miami, Douglas was moody and his temper flared. I suffered from his silence days at a time and sometimes, even weeks. While his mother was dying of cancer, he had obeyed his father's order for him to leave home and attend graduate school in America, even though this was against his own will. That anger never left him. He loved his mother, who never complained in all her adversities. "My mother was perfect. You should be perfect," he told me early on. I was stunned with his statement, but did not argue, comforting myself that "Blessed are the meek."

Douglas's consuming passion was bridge, both playing and reading about it. A life master, he was an equal at the bridge table and he retreated to bridge for friendship and company, playing at local clubs or friends' houses in the evening during the week and on weekends, often in tournaments out of town.

Except for gatherings with other Chinese families and occasionally entertaining the Chinese students, my days were occupied with the children, the kitchen, and the washing. I'd joined the church choir to sing, both as a chance to get away from the ruckus of the children and out of loneliness. For choir practice on Monday nights, I had a baby sitter for the children, and a friend picked me up so we could go together. But if the baby sitter happened to be sick, I would stay home with the children while Douglas kept his engagement. "My game is more important," he would say. Many a night I sat in the kitchen, listened to the children playing noisily in the basement den or in the living room, struggling to control myself from breaking, from making a scene. Six years of Catholic schooling had drummed into me that sacrifice and self-denial of earthly pleasure was the way to salvation. It was my duty to procreate, to love and support my husband, who was the head of the family. Our three children, Michael, Lawrence, and Caroline, were born in the first four years of our marriage. I prayed that God would lead me kindly, for "I do not ask to see the distant shore. One step is enough for me." Whenever my friends caught me blinking back my tears at Sunday mass or during choir practice, I would say that I had a terrible case of hay fever.

Loneliness overwhelmed me, even though I had three little ones to keep me occupied and alert to their mischief. I would hear no adult voice for days, as Douglas would read his Bridge bulletins as soon as he came to the door and bring it to the dining table. The neighborhood was quiet, graced by blooming azaleas in pink, red and lavender and white. Nostalgic for my childhood home in Huang-gong where azaleas were everywhere, I loaded the children into the station wagon and drove to the nursery. I selected eight shrubs with red buds. When we got home, the two boys helped plant the azaleas by the carport, scooped the dirt with plastic spades, and sprinkled the azaleas with little buckets of water. "The azaleas are so pretty, Momma should wear one in her hair," five-year-old Mike glowed.

I went inside the house to give my one-year-old daughter, Caroline, her bottle and put her in her crib for her afternoon nap. When I came back to the kitchen, Larry was standing there holding a bundle of the azalea branches, happily offering them to me.

"You killed the azaleas!" I thundered at my two-and-half-year-old child, pulling him toward me by his hair.

"I brought you flowers," my little son yelped in pain.

Releasing my hand, I saw blood oozing from the spot on my little son's scalp. Horrified at what I had done, I knelt down and wrapped both arms around him. "Momma is so sorry," I whispered, my forehead against his. I took the azalea flowers from his hand and touched his face with my trembling hands.

I knew I was dangerously close to having a breakdown. Desperately wanting to hang on, to remain sane, I decided to go back to school or work in a professional role. It took me months to convince myself of the thought and to resolve such an act in my mind. In the context of my upbringing, it was rebellion under the constraints of my faith and of being a wife and mother. Douglas did not object to my going back to school or getting a job on the condition that I could pay for a maid to take care of the children and do the housekeeping.

Neither the University of North Carolina at Chapel Hill nor North Carolina State University offered doctoral studies in nutrition. But I did find out that the University of North Carolina had a fine School of Public Health and my two degrees in nutrition could easily be applied. Even in college, my dream had always been to work in the World Health Organization (WHO), lending technical assistance to developing countries. Two decades later, that opportunity was to come my way twice. But because of my family, which came before a career, I had to turn them down. Instead, I took on numerous short-term consultancies as a temporary advisor to WHO.

I was admitted to the program in the School of Public Health, but failed to receive the Public Health Service traineeship from the federal bureau in charge of the award. Despite a master's degree and two years of work experience, I was a woman of reproductive age, and a mother of three preschool children and was perceived to be a "high risk."

Several interviews led me to teaching nutrition part time at the UNC School of Nursing. It was a satisfactory solution, at least temporarily. Working three days a week was a good way to ease myself back into the professional world.

My older colleagues in nursing were all single women who had either never married or were widowed or divorced. I sensed their lives were even lonelier than mine. On long weekends or holidays like Thanksgiving or Christmas, they had no place to go, unless they attached themselves to the family of a brother, a sister, or some other relatives. At lunch hours, the nurses talked about the frustrations of their profession, of being little more than handmaids to doctors, who were almost all males. The nurses were searching for a new role identity that would give them greater professional autonomy. Germaine Greer's *The Female Eunuch* and *The Feminine Mystique*, by Betty Friedan, were popular readings among the nurses. It surprised my colleagues that I had not read these books and was not more interested in women's liberation. I defended myself saying that I was a working mother of three young children, and that alone attested to my commitment to women's liberation. While fighting for my rights as a woman, I had a deeper concern with racial equality.

Stella, our babysitter, worked three days a week while I commuted between Raleigh and Chapel Hill. Near the end of my second year of teaching in the nursing school, I went to see the head of the health education department, hoping to find my way back to graduate school. Dr. Ralph Boatman, a soft-spoken man with a cherubic face, told me that the awarding of traineeships had been transferred from the federal bureau to the university and suggested that I apply again. I did receive the Public Health Traineeship award, in 1964. It covered my tuition, and I used the stipend to hire Stella full-time.

Each morning, I watched the pale blue Chevy sedan drop Stella off at the curb at seven almost on the dot. Stella was a twenty-eight-year-old black woman who had graduated from college. Stella did not have children herself, but she was good with mine, playing and singing with them "Ring around the rosie" and "Row, row, row your boat." She also cooked and cleaned. When Stella first presented herself as a maid, I asked why she would want the job with her college education. She said that there was no office work available to her. While I was lucky to have Stella taking care of my children, my heart went out to this young black woman who could do no better than find work as a maid with her bachelor's degree.

Many a morning I turned the car around. It was not for the Thermos bottle of coffee left behind that I turned around and drove home. Rather, I wanted to linger a little longer with the children. The hardest thing about going back to graduate school was leaving home in the morning.

The children were fresh in their cotton shirts and shorts. "Momma forgot her Thermos bottle again!" they would yell as they gleefully ran to the carport. I gave each one a kiss and a hug with a pang of guilt in my chest. Stella handed me the Thermos bottle laughing, "Missus always forgets." Waving as I backed my station wagon down the driveway and looking at the healthy and rambunctious children, I was happy they were my babies.

At eight-thirty, my neighbor Mrs. Gayland would be picking up the boys to take them to kindergarten.

After class, I would rush home without stopping to socialize with my classmates. The children ran from the backyard or swung through the kitchen door and out to the carport as my car pulled up in the driveway.

Before sitting down to study in the kitchen, I would open all the doors and windows. Noise did not bother me, but silence did. I knew just where my children were and what they were doing by the sounds they made. The children horsed around and played in the yard, sometimes joined by the Gayland boys. The boys laughed, sang, howled, and ran around the house with little Caroline trying to keep up after them. The four boys played war games, the Americans against the Germans. I could hear my sons protesting that they shouldn't have to be the Germans every time, they wanted to be the Americans and win.

I spoke to several of the faculty about my interest in doctoral studies, but because of my ambivalence about the long years required to pursue a doctorate, hadn't completed my application. So it was a surprise when Dr. Boatman stopped me in the hall to say, "We've already made two traineeship awards for the coming year. The third one is yours, if you decide to go on for your Ph.D." He added that in the eyes of the faculty my bicultural background and the fact that I had a clear sense of purpose had made me a strong candidate.

Douglas saw the doctorate as insurance for the family. When I mentioned to one of the professors the gratitude I felt about my adoptive country's generosity in awarding me, an alien, three years of financial support toward my doctoral study, he reminded me that the United States is a nation of immigrants. "One reason it's a great power in the world today," he said, "is its ability to absorb talent from other countries. You're an investment to us. Someday you'll pay us back tenfold and more." It was a prediction that I knew I would make true.

That summer before I began my doctoral study, I was in the kitchen baking Toll House cookies when a red Volkswagen came up the driveway. Seeing my sons' kindergarten teachers getting out of the car, I ran to the bedroom, quickly brushed my hair and put on some lipstick.

I showed the two women into the living room, wondering what this was about, glad that the place was tidy except for the plastic tractors and the GI Joes on the floor.

"We don't mean to barge in, but we do want to speak to you," said Mrs. Cummings, Larry's teacher. A dainty Southern belle dressed in floral Sunday attire complete with a white straw hat adorned with red silk carnations, she sat very straight on the Danish sofa chair. "We're very concerned! Larry told us that you're going to study for your Ph.D. Both Mrs. Perkins and I have vicariously gone through the whole experience of a Ph.D. program while our husbands were graduate students studying for their degrees. It was one hurdle after the next. It will be so demanding that you'll have neither time nor energy for your children."

"A wife and mother's place is in the home," Mrs. Perkins jumped in, glacing at Mrs. Cummings for acknowledgment as she spoke. "You have three darling children and they should be first in your life. You're placing your own self-interest above your family. You won't have time for your children, and they do need you."

Mrs. Cummings nodded. "We would be less than Christian if we failed to tell you that you're making a dreadful mistake."

"Please, please do not neglect your children." Mrs. Perkins folded her hands as if in prayer.

I was speechless facing the two women across the coffee table. When I recovered, I thanked them for their kindness and for taking the time to counsel me on a Sunday afternoon. I said that I appreciated their interest in my children and assured them that I did have my family's well-being uppermost in my mind. But I didn't feel that I owed any explanation to these women or to anyone else. I knew the hazards of benign neglect when pressure mounts, but I also knew the benefits of a doctoral degree and what it would mean to me and to my family. I was striving to find a way for co-existence with my husband, to survive with dignity so as to provide a reasonably normal family life for the children. This was something I had to do. I chose to think it was purely good will that prompted their visit.

I was lucky to have Stella's service for four years. But then one day she quit. She had found a job plucking chickens in a newly opened packing house within walking distance of her home. "My husband won't have to drop me off every morning," she explained.

I put an ad in the local newspaper for a new sitter. In the span of three months, I tried four different ones, black women with small children of their own, but none of them worked out. Many a morning I stood by the carport waiting in vain for the sitter to come. Then came Annie. She was fiftyish, a big white woman with short straight sandy hair, large hands, and fleshy arms. In our interview Annie said she was a cook, but that she would like to change jobs so not to have to suffer the heat in the kitchen; she had brought up five children of her own.

I started Annie that very Saturday, in order to show her what needed to be done in the house and to help the children get used to their new sitter. From the kitchen window I saw a black pickup truck dropping Annie off by the curb. I was glad that she was on time.

I showed Annie around the kitchen, explaining the master menu that was tacked inside the broom-closet door. Again, Annie said she was a cook and "beef stew, Southern fried chicken, and mashed potatoes are easy."

At ten, Annie started cooking lunch. I thought it was too early, but she said she wanted to do things right and should get going. She put the string beans into a pot of water, boiled them for almost thirty minutes and turned them down to simmer. "I'll be just right at noon," said Annie. I realized that she wasn't a cook at all.

I had hired Annie before I received the callback on her reference. The telephone rang while we were eating lunch. On the line was the woman whom Annie had given as her reference. She told me Annie was an ex-convict recently released from a six-month jail term for robbery and physical assault. "I wouldn't have Annie in my house," she said emphatically.

Frightened that I was alone with the children, I decided to keep Annie in the kitchen until her ride arrived. When Mike helpfully told Annie, "Momma keeps her silver in the bottom cabinet," every muscle in my body tightened. All I could think of was robbery and the black pickup truck that had dropped Annie off that morning.

I sent the children outside to play and asked Annie to sit down to have a cup of coffee and a donut with me. Gently, I told her that her reference did not recommend her for the job, thanked her, paid her for the day, and said that I couldn't employ her.

Annie looked a little sad. All she said was, "What could anyone have said that was so awful?" When I told Mrs. Gayland about Annie, she said that in the South only black women worked as nannies. "You should be cautious if a white woman wants to be a maid or a nanny," Mrs. Gayland told me. I did finally hire a sitter for my children, but she was not nearly as good as Stella had been.

At the university, my mentor was Dr. Lucy Morgan, a stately Southern lady whose eyes were steely. She had started the health education department at the School of Public Health in 1943, and for the next twenty-five years she had trained a generation of health educators. Dr. Morgan also started an identical program at North Carolina Central College in 1945, teaching the same courses to two separate student bodies, one white and the other black. She tried to persuade the authorities at UNC to allow her black students to sit in the same classroom with her white students. When the university refused her, she integrated the two classes in the living room of her home. I admired Dr. Morgan's tenacity, compassion, and sense of purpose. She once told me, "Your childbearing years are behind you. The years ahead will be the best years of life." Those words gave me comfort and confidence.

I came to know the black experience during my field work in Durham. Because all my work experience was based in a hospital or a classroom, my professors had made field work in a community agency a requirement for my doctoral course of study. President Johnson was waging his War on Poverty to help the poor help themselves. I was assigned to the Office of Equal Opportunity (OEO) in Durham for six months to gain firsthand real-world experience.

I discovered black neighborhoods had unpaved streets and no indoor plumbing. I visited homes and neighborhoods with the OEO community organizers, spoke with teachers and aides in Head Start for preschool children, adult-literacy classes, and job-training programs sponsored by the antipoverty program. I heard church ministers and community leaders speak of the failure and rejections that black people suffered from their childhood and continuing throughout their adult lives because of society's prejudice and discrimination. I also discovered that people living in extremely poor homes had a sense of aesthetics with their plastic flowers in bottles or a little goldfish or two in a glass jar. I saw mothers feed their children Coca-Cola and jelly sandwiches for lunch, believing Coca-Cola would give them energy because of Anita Bryant on TV commercials singing "Zing! Coca-Cola gives you energy." A black man who had marched in Selma proudly told me, "I was there." Having been "there" was a badge of courage lauded by the onlookers, whose black faces were wet with tears.

What concerned black people most was getting a job. The OEO radio announcement that there were four openings for custodians in the IBM quarters at the Research Triangle brought in more than two hundred applications. Convinced that this kind of announcement did more harm than good, I went to the OEO director and told him that I thought it was wrong to mislead so many people to believe that there were jobs for them. I thought the rejection of so many would only reinforce for them their life experience of failure. The director, a well-intentioned Southern gentleman, said that his office had to be fair in giving equal opportunity to all the people.

Janet Bond was a nursing instructor at Duke University, and we had been classmates in the master's degree in public health class at UNC. I spoke with her about the possibilities of offering her students experience in public health nursing in the War on Poverty. Janet was enthusiastic to have her students provide some services to the community under her supervision. As a conduit, I discussed with the OEO staff, the community organizers, and several of the black leaders the idea of involving the Duke nursing students in Head Start and other programs. They, too, thought that it was a good idea and that it would benefit the community.

The packed auditorium at the North Carolina Central College was buzzing when Janet and I walked down the aisle. Jossie Block, solid, jovial, and handsome with her dark chocolate skin, was the OEO community organizer with whom I had spent many hours visiting the black community. Though she had invited us to the forum, she barely acknowledged us. Her gesture suggested to us that she would have preferred that we had not greeted her. Janet and I sat down in the front row for the meeting to begin, aware that we were the only nonblack persons in the packed auditorium.

"We ask our Heavenly Father for Thy blessing," the minister prayed in his high-pitched voice, thanking the Lord for the many new opportunities in their community that were the result of America's great war against poverty. The assembled responded with "Amen," and "Praise be the Lord," as hands clapped here and there.

The chairman of the forum banged his gavel to call the meeting to order. A man's voice rose from the rear of the auditorium: "Mr. Chairman, there are outside people here tonight who do not belong in the assembly. Those visitors should leave right now. We need to get on with our business and discuss the issues that concern us."

Stunned and confused, Janet and I got up and walked toward the exit while all eyes were on us. I had no idea what had just happened.

The next morning, when I saw Jossie Block in the OEO office, she avoided eye contact with me. I approached her and asked her why there had been such hostility toward us at the meeting last night.

Jossie, still avoiding eye contact, breathed deeply and said that people had heard on the radio that funding for the antipoverty program was in question for next year. They had heard about the nursing student project. A rumor had spread that Duke University was taking away the money that had belonged to them. Jossie herself had not been fully aware how volatile the situation was until she was inside the auditorium herself.

After what Jossie said, I went to the home of Mr. Brown, a retired black teacher whom I had met on two previous occasions, trying to get a sense of what he saw as the problem. Mr. Brown, balding and slightly bent, confirmed the rumor as he served me a cup of coffee and a piece of banana cream pie he had baked himself. He then spoke with emotion of the promise of freedom, justice, and equality dating back to the time of the Emancipation Declaration, and of black soldiers who had died fighting for their country in World War II. Yet the famed singer Marian Anderson was not given the right to appear at Constitution Hall because of the color of her skin. "Even today, my people are not allowed to sit down next to white people in many lunch counters. I hope you do not take what happened last night personally. Rather," Mr. Brown urged me, "take it as a learning experience to understand the fear, frustration and hope of my people."

My field experience in Durham made a deep impression on me, and the humiliation actually became a triumph. It led to a lifelong interest in community development. I saw poverty and racism as root causes of social dysfunction and ill health. I became cognizant that the poor and disenfranchised regard the professionals as the "hard to reach," because of color and social class, because of the categorical approach in treating problems and diseases, because of insensitivity.

On receiving my Doctor of Philosophy degree in 1968, I chose university teaching and research over other lines of work for the flexibility this would give me in arranging my hours. Douglas had already gotten a job with the Naval Research and Development Shipyard in Potomac and left the university, again due to unhappy circumstances concerning his salary. His move was good for me as well, since the District of Columbia and its surrounding communities in Virginia and Maryland offered many opportunities for me.

Looking around, I thought the best place to gain community development expertise would be the University of Maryland Cooperative Extension Service, which was an arm of the College of Agriculture, whose mission was to transfer knowledge and technology to rural America through agriculture, home economics, and youth work. I would tap into existing resources for health education for inner cities. I talked the extension service into creating a position for me as a health education specialist.

Until the children were in high school, half of my salary went to the live-in housekeeper. The amah from Hong Kong spoke only Cantonese, cooked only Chinese food, much to my children's dismay. Her presence gave the children, and me, too, the security of having an adult at home during the day. I encouraged the children to telephone me at work whenever they needed to talk with me. The boys seldom called, but Caroline often did.

Each morning, I saw my three children leave the house for school. Each would give me a kiss and ask: "What time will you be home?" I would say to each one, "Five o'clock." It was a ritual. My children kept reminding me that I was the only mother who was not home to greet her children when they came home from school. I had a sign-out book for them by the door. Besides telling the housekeeper when they left the house, they had to write down where they were going and the names of the friends they would be visiting and when they would return. That system worked very well. It gave the children the responsibility of letting me know how they could be reached, and I had the peace of mind of knowing where they were

When they were all still quite young, I had once explained to my children that the tension between their father and me was because we had problems. These problems were not because of them, but because parents are people, and people make mistakes. I told them that the problems between their father and me affected them only because we were a family and not because of anything they did. I tried to assure them that both their father and I loved them and told them that we made mistakes both with regard to each other and to them. I believed they understood what I said and were forgiving. Douglas played baseball, tennis, and Ping-Pong with the children. There was a genuine bonding between father and children. For that I have always been grateful.

My children mixed well with their classmates and friends in the neighborhood. They were involved in all types of sports, participated in school clubs and actrivities, and went on overnight sleepovers. But there were times when they were also teased in school or walking down the streets or in the malls, hearing things like, "Ching, Chang, Chong. An order of egg roll and spare ribs to go, please!" On one occasion, while driving my children around the nation's capital, we heard shouts, "Gooks, why don't you go home?" Facing these incidences of insults and prejudice, my children would come home angry and downcast. I tried to tell them that in spite of everything, this is still the most democratic and best country in the world, and that we must help it become better, so that there won't be prejudice.

But I myself felt the same deep hurt that my children did. I remembered shortly after my eldest son Mike entered kindergarten, he confronted me, "Momma, you lied to me." I asked him what I had said to make him think this. "You said I'm Chinese. I am not! I'm American. You and Daddy are Chinese. You were born in China, but I was born in the United States." His teacher had told the children in his class that the United States is a country of immigrants and all those born here are American citizens. Until then, I had always told my son he was Chinese, but I stopped after that. He had found his identity and I was glad of it. His identity as an American was so firm that, when he was six years old, he was very upset on hearing the nightly newscasters talking about the possibility of war between China and the United States. His face turned ashen. "I hope the United States and China will never fight each other," he told me. "It would be horrible if Daddy and I had to shoot at each other."

Early in my career I made the decision that my children and my work were my first priorities. That left me little time or energy for anything else. It was a conscious choice I made. Solitude was no stranger to me. My teen years as a displaced person, unfamiliar with the American culture and too shy to speak English, had taught me how to be at ease with myself. I was able to make the distinction between aloneness and loneliness. I was alone and self-directed. My evenings were always spent at home. On Saturdays or Sundays, I tried to do something together with the children—fishing, crabbing, baking, or visiting a museum. But they also had their friends and wanted their independence, and if the children chose to be on their own, I would work at my desk.

In 1974, the Johns Hopkins University School of Hygiene and Public Health recruited me with the offer of an associate professorship. Immediately, I organized a carpool from Bethesda to Big John in Baltimore. Two members of the nursing faculty, two doctoral students, and I commuted the 140 miles daily. We were all married to Feds who worked in the labyrinth of the Washington bureaucracy.

We never turned on the radio for the 140-mile round trip. Windows were closed for air conditioning in the summer and heating in the winter. There was a code of silence among all of us during our morning rides. We used this hour to get caught up with whatever each of us needed to do before stepping into the office or classroom. I reviewed lecture notes, or made comments on a draft manuscript or a new research proposal. This was the quietest hour of the day for me, away from my three noisy children, away from students and colleagues, and away from the distractions of household chores. At 5:00, however, it was a different story. Only then, on the drive back home, would we let our hair down, bantering about what had happened during the day, sharing bits of personal life here and there, and how women were making it in a man's world. It was comradely.

Caroline entered Duke University in 1980. She was the last of the three children to leave home. With that, Douglas immediately asked for a divorce and wanted me to file. I had no desire to contest this request and filed. The marriage was clearly not working for either of us.

I wanted to make a clean break and so I came West, when, in 1982, the School of Public Health, University of California at Los Angeles, was recruiting a faculty in health education and behavioral sciences. I applied for and was given a full professor's appointment.

A stranger to California where I had few friends, I joined the Sierra Club to get some outdoor exercise, never having been a hiker before. Hiking in the Santa Monica Mountains, I met a man with a headful of peppery hair wearing a T-shirt with the letters UCLA and it caught my eye. He saw the Chinese lady "huffing and puffing sitting on a rock by herself." A conversation opened up between us for the rest of the afternoon.

Leonardo Chait was a clinical professor at the UCLA Medical School and had immigrated from Argentina. From Russia, his grandfather had bought a boat ticket to America and landed in Buenos Aires, even though his intention was the United States, since he had not known that there was South America and North America. Leo had been trained in the Mayo Clinic and had had a flourishing practice in Buenos Aires, but in 1963 he chose to immigrate to the United States to get away from anti-Semitism and political instability. Being a foreign medical graduate, he had to start over with an internship in order to get a California medical license to practice.

Our meeting was serendipitous and fortuitous. We didn't lose much time and married shortly afterward, in 1985. The marriage, too, was a rebellion against the Catholic faith and Chinese tradition, which dictates that a good woman would not marry twice. At the time he proposed, Leo had me promise him not to be away from home any longer than six weeks at a time, as I often did consulting work internationally. He became a supportive partner and, eventually, changed his mind about the restriction he had placed on me saying, "I don't want to curtail your professional activities when you're in the prime of your career."

It was while we were dating that Leo discovered Chinese cuisine. Soon he gave up the overcooked rubbery chicken and red snapper that he cooked for "survival," in favor of Peking duck, tender and juicy sautéed chicken, pork, and beef, crispy vegetables, and even stewed sea cucumber. We still laugh and tease each other today that he had never tasted tender chicken until he met me.

Leo prefers the ocean and I the mountains. We moved from Westwood to our penthouse in the Edgewater Tower by the Pacific Coast Highway Pacific Palisades. Happily, we have both. My study faces the Palisades hills. Lights flicker at night from the houses hidden behind the trees. I admit there is something special about the ocean. The deep green water changes its hues by the rays of the sun or amount of light that hits it. At sunset we watch the blazing sun slipping down beyond the ocean. For an hour afterward, the clouds form a panorama of colors—red, yellow, blue, and gray—as if an artist's hand was painting the canvas. My eyes are dazed in marveling at this vision.

Leo has since developed his survival cooking skills into a culinary art, making his dishes with low salt, low fat, and low cholesterol, as well as low sugar. He would de-fat meats and sausages and use substitutes for cream and eggs in his desserts and breads. They actually taste quite good and we have no hesitation in serving them when entertaining guests, which we like to do at home.

For many years, Leo delighted in biking to work from the Palisades to Santa Monica along the beach bikeway, twelve miles each day. He used to say, "I am in heaven without dying."

One evening, standing there in his bike helmet, holding a frayed black belt with a tin buckle as I opened the door, "I feel like shit," Leo announced.

"You are not shit." I kissed his sweaty cheek.

"I didn't say I *am* shit," he corrected me. "I said I feel like shit."

"Where did you get a cheap belt like that?" I asked him.

"I am so ashamed," he told me.

"What have you done?"

Leo had been speeding on the bike path, enjoying the salty ocean air brushing his face. Secondly, the strap that held his briefcase broke, and his briefcase was flung onto the pavement, hitting it like a brick. He got off the bike to retrieve the briefcase, which, luckily, was locked. He put his briefcase on the bike seat but couldn't refasten it. As he was looking down and fidgeting with the strap, he felt someone hovering over him, a big hand grabbing his bike. Leo smelled alcohol on the man's breath and the foul odor of his shirt. He was scared. There were few people on the beach that early in the morning.

"That strap ain't doin' nothing for you," said the man. He looked around and took off the black belt around his waist. Leo told him he could manage by himself and to please go away. But the man wouldn't go away; instead, he used his belt to tie the briefcase onto the bike. "I took three dollars from my wallet to thank him for his belt. He sure looked like he could use it. I felt so small when the man said, 'Nope! Brother, I have two belts. You keep this one. No trouble at all.' He waved his hand and walked away."

Leo hung the belt on the wall of his study as a reminder that all mankind are friends and brothers.

Part III

TWO WORLDS ENTWINE

Chapter Thirteen

A Glimpse of the People's Republic

My first glimpse of socialist China came when President Nixon visited the People's Republic in 1971. I stayed awake until an early hour of the morning to watch Nixon's arrival in Shanghai on satellite television. The visit marked the beginning of normalization between the world's superpower and the world's most populous country—between my adoptive country and the country of my birth. It was a touching moment for me to see the president of the United States and the premier of the People's Republic shaking hands. In 1954, Zhou Enlai, who had helped design the Geneva Conference that temporarily halted the Korean War, extended his hand to the American secretary of state John Foster Dulles. Dulles publicly humiliated the premier, refusing to shake "the bloody Communist hand." My throat constricted on hearing the Chinese military band playing the national anthems of both the People's Republic of China and the United States of America, welcoming the American president at the airport ceremony.

In 1973, my brother Victor, who was a professor of international law at Stanford University, proposed that we organize a small group of public health professionals to study health care in the Chinese countryside. He thought that if we made a documentary film on the "barefoot doctors"—so-called because they worked barefoot in the fields as well—this would give us some insights into their political system as well. Victor had visited the People's Republic after Nixon's visit and was impressed with the barefoot doctors in the cooperative medical care system in the communes. Using these doctors, China "stretched" to provide health care to its vast rural population. Answering Chairman Mao's call—"In medical and public health work an emphasis must be given to rural areas"—doctors and medical students were sent out into the countryside in mobile health teams; young medics, many of whom came from peasant backgrounds, were trained to become doctors whose primary goal was disease prevention. Within the span of only two decades, life expectancy for the Chinese was extended from forty-five to sixty-five years.

My initial response to my brother's proposal was cautious. Although a window had been opened for exchanges between the United States and China, American attitudes toward China were still not really that friendly. After all, the saying "A good Communist is a dead Communist" reflected much of America's feeling toward Communism. During the McCarthy era of the late 1950s, the experts at the China desk in the State Department had been subjected to haunting persecution, as well as ruined lives and careers. Moreover, according to the doctrines of Chinese Communist ideology, either directly or indirectly I represented all of the "Four Black Elements" they were warning the population against: I was the offspring of a landlord, who was a member of the bourgeoisie and a Nationalist official, and I had become an American citizen with overseas connections. But with curiosity and the chance to do something positive at the time for U.S.-China relations, I overcame my initial misgivings and was soon involved in the planning of a study tour.

There were eight of us in our study group, all Chinese Americans so that it would be easier to mingle with the natives. Since China had no embassy in the United States as yet, we obtained our visas through the People's Republic's embassy in Canada. We were even given permission to bring camera equipment for our proposed film documentation.

I put together a simple wardrobe of white, black, and navy-blue blouses and pants, and stuffed my suitcase with toilet paper, Kleenex, and a few towels. I was warned of the need to bring one's own toilet paper to public facilities and that Kleenex was not readily available. I took a plane from Kennedy Airport to Hong Kong, where I met up with my group.

I was gripped with anxiety as our train left Kowloon for Shenzhen, crossing the border into China. I saw Red soldiers in mustard green uniforms standing guard with rifles. They reminded me of the sentinel soldiers who had guarded our home in Huanggong, except that they wore a Red star instead of the twelve pointed blue-and-white star of Guomindang—the Nationalist Party. The train rocked slowly, passing wide stretches of farmland and villages not all that different from what I remembered. Traditional agricultural technology dominated the landscape where men and women, all dressed in blue, tilled with a hoe, their backs bent to the sky.

We got off the train for customs inspection in Shenzhen and were met by three men in white shirts and gray baggy pants. Lao Chen, Lao Zhang, and Lao Kang were all party cadres in their forties. They were to serve as our guides for the duration of our five-week visit, courtesy of the United Front Bureau. The customs officers, dressed exactly the same as the guides, examined and eyed the contents in our suitcases as carefully as if they were threading needles. I wondered what they thought of the toilet paper and Kleenex that my companions and I had in our suitcases.

We ate lunch in a dining room for visitors in what appeared to be an office building adjacent to the station. Our party of eight sat around a round table covered with a white plastic cloth; our guides had their table next to ours. We were served hot soup and five tasty but simple dishes with eggs, some meat, and fresh vegetables. To avoid possible gastrointestinal problems from food and water, our group had decided to drink hot tea only, even in the ninety-five degree heat, or bottled drinks. We were served orange soda and beer without refrigeration along with hot tea.

Thirsty and sweating, I took a big gulp of the orange soda, which tasted bittersweet. I managed to swallow down what remained in the glass, as did my companions. Then I tried the beer, although in my entire life I had never drunk beer before. For the rest of the trip, I reached for the warm beer as soon as I sat down for lunch and dinner. It wasn't that I liked beer; it was simply that beer was more drinkable than the orange soda and I didn't have to wait for the steaming tea to cool.

Back on the train, we had a three-hour ride to Guangzhou, arriving in the late afternoon. Stepping outside the train station into the big square, my first impression of the city was that the buildings were badly in need of a coat of paint, but the square and the streets were remarkably clean. Painted on the walls were slogans in big black characters: "Long live our great leader chairman Mao," "Down with imperialism," "Down with Liu Shaoqi [an early victim of the Cultural Revolution, Liu was the head of state from 1959 to 1966] and the capitalist running dogs," and "Serve the people." The only bright colors were the five-star Red flags.

Riding in a van to the guest house, I saw streets filled with bicycles, and bicycle repair shops were as common as gasoline stations in the United States. Except for the Pearl River Bridge, after nearly three decades in the United States I had no recollection of the physical layout of the city. What I remembered were the haunting sights of beggars and the white ambulance picking up corpses. Now I looked around and did not see any beggars, let alone corpses in the streets. Everywhere I looked, I saw men and women dressed in unisex shirts and baggy pants, but there were no rags or patched shirts that had been so common in the days gone by. Gone, too, were the riverbank thatch and straw huts and under-the-bridge dwellings.

The new China was a stranger to me, as I was to her. My knowledge of her was basically what I had learned from the news media and an occasional book, plus tidbits from letters my parents received from Hong Kong. So it was a revelation finally to see China with my own eyes.

During our five days in Guangzhou, we visited neighborhood block organizations, schools, nurseries, a hospital, and a commune. Every time we stepped out of the van, we were warmly applauded by the cadres and by the men, women, and children standing around, a reception that was clearly orchestrated.

We quickly learned that every organizational unit, block, and commune had a revolutionary committee, a party secretary, a chairman, and deputy chairman. At every meeting, the party secretary was the spokesman giving the briefing, followed by the chairman and deputy chairman, each proudly explaining that every action they took was under the direction and guidance of the leadership of the Party. The chain of command ran from the state to the province, city/district, county, township, and communes/blocks, and the lower echelon received direction from the one immediately above. We were told that the revolutionary committee, along with the residents, would discuss the communal needs and then decide on priorities in the use of the communal welfare funds for nurseries, medical care, and schools, among others.

Throughout our trip, all the briefings had the same theme in tone and in words, acclaiming the political line of the Party and the thoughts of Chairman Mao. We repeatedly heard that attitudes were paramount. People were said to have "good attitudes" if they supported the Party, followed Mao's thoughts, were committed to the revolutionary causes, and were willing to sacrifice themselves for others and for the common good. The Cultural Revolution had begun in 1966, and, by the time of our visit in 1973, the fury and armed struggles had already subsided and rhetoric had taken over. It astounded us, in spite of our prior knowledge, that people were still being encouraged to observe each other and report on each other, and that regular meetings were held to criticize each other and for self-criticism.

We learned that employment could be broadly classified into two categories—cadres and the masses—and that where a person worked was assigned by the state. "Do you have a choice?" I asked. "We go wherever the state sends us, wherever the needs exist," came the proud and uniform answer.

The transformation was apparent in the children also. Kindergarten and little grade-school children, smiling and bouncy, greeted us with "*Ah Yi hao*—aunties, how are you?" and "*Susu hao*—uncles, how are you?" The children danced for us without a trace of shyness, singing, "The East is Red, the sun is rising. On the horizon of China appears Mao Zedong." They were eager to show their paper cuttings and drawings. The rather severe dictum that children should be seen but not heard—which was the norm when I was growing up in China—was gone. The little ones' happy faces and vivacity warmed my heart. But at the same time I couldn't help wondering if they would inform on their parents or point accusing fingers at their teachers.

Unsure what the new order had done with its old people, I felt good visiting the senior centers. There I saw elderly men and women come for adult education classes and recreation, where they painted, sang, studied, danced, and even did tai chi exercises. "There are senior centers in every city," we were informed. "Our block organizations and neighbors see to it that the elderly who have no family of their own are helped in their household chores."

Communist China had made it a legal responsibility for children to care of their aged parents. From all appearance, old people were well cared for.

Our guides, who were always in pairs when visiting us at the hotel, encouraged us to stroll along the streets after supper, assuring us that the streets were safe even at night. Many an evening we ventured out. To my eyes, accustomed to the high wattage and bright lights, the streetlamps were dim. People strolling often held hands. We always drew a crowd of people who looked at us with curiosity. Their faces were friendly and smiling, but they were silent. In spite of our best effort to disguise the fact that we were visitors, our cameras and the well-tailored pants we wore betrayed us.

My mind raced back and forth between what I saw now with my own eyes and what I had heard about present-day China and could not quite comprehend. In the back of my mind there were visions of the movements and the liquidations China periodically conducted, where landlords were beaten and hung by their thumbs, where rightists and "black elements" were put into "oxen pens," and where intellectuals became "stinking dung" and were banished to sweep corridors and clean toilets.

We left Guangzhou for Shanghai on a Russian-made aircraft. For a moment my companions and I were alarmed when we spotted the threadbare tires of the plane. Without air conditioning, the suffocation and heat inside the plane while waiting to take off was almost unbearable. Fortunately, the flight was uneventful. And when we arrived, we were taken to our rooms in the Peace Hotel, once famous for its cabarets and dance halls, on the boulevard known as the Bund along the Huangpu River. The elegant old buildings that flanked the Bund were once foreign banks and companies that symbolized international dominance.

Shanghai looked more familiar to me. My family had lived in the former French concession part of the city just before we came to America. Compared to Guangzhou, Shanghai had more consumer goods displayed in the shops, such as stylish swimming suits and fashionable women and children's clothes—items that were all manufactured for export. Once, Shanghai was the symbol of decadence and a national servility to foreign powers. Here brothels had been as numerous as street lamps, coolies lined the streets pulling rickshaws like beasts of burden, and beggars, to be found with outstretched hands in every street and corner, were desperately sick and hungry.

As we toured the city, our hosts pointed out to us the distinctive architectural designs in the various former concession territories—

those of the French, the English, and the Germans—residual imprints of foreign imperialism. We were shown a small bridge that connected the rest of Shanghai with the concession territories, which the natives dubbed Waibaidu Bridge, meaning "foreigners' free-crossing bridge." Under the concession rule, foreigners had the free right of way, but a toll was charged for any Chinese crossing it. Then the guides took us to the famed international club, which was now a cultural center. The club entrance had once displayed a sign, "Chinese and dogs are not allowed."

Xenophobia reached its peak in China with the creation of the People's Republic. With great emotion, our guides reminded us that the United States still refused to recognize the People's Republic as the lawful government of China, and that the United States led the blockade against giving the People's Republic a seat in the United Nations. They knew too well that this was in order to maintain the government of Chiang Kaishek in Taiwan to serve as a U.S. strategic position in the South China Sea.

China's xenophobia, as I saw it, was a reflection of fighting back to recoup the loss of national honor, territorial integrity, and of the injustices inflicted on the Chinese people by foreign powers for more than a century. In its hurt and pride, China roared about the wrongs that had been done, about the need for rallying her people to stand up in a collective new awakening to claim their rightful place in the world of nations. In the hate campaign against imperial powers, the one-time "Sick Man of Asia" was now crying out for dignity and self-respect, wanting to expunge the anguish and those enemies who had exploited and humiliated her.

One afternoon when I was in a shop on Nanjing Road, I bought a beautiful scented fan for a souvenir. A soldier saw the fan I was holding and wanted to purchase one for his wife. The shopkeeper told him that he couldn't have one because such items were for visitors only. I felt bad that he should be denied the pleasure of having something so small and just a little frivolous for his beloved one. In another store, where my companions and I purchased books and records, a crowd of people followed me as I moved from one end of the store to the other. Then I realized that I had on a pair of white pants and was wearing dark glasses, and these simple things had made me an attraction.

We traveled by car to the Four Seasons Commune in the outskirts of the city of Hangzhou, home of the famous West Lake, about one hundred kilometers from Shanghai. After the briefings, our group would often split up to pursue our own individual interests. While others were filming the barefoot doctors in the farms, I joined a study session on family planning, which the commune had just begun to promote.

I sat with fifteen women on short-legged wooden stools in a circle under a shady tree. The barefoot doctor her face smooth and pink, two long braids gracefully resting over her shoulders, wearing a light blue blouse and baggy blue pants, read from a booklet on the desirability of the pill for birth control. This was followed by a group discussion. One woman said she wanted a large family and was not ready for the pill. "Everyone should be ready," said another woman. "There are already too many people in the country; if we don't have birth control there will be no progress! The additional mouths will eat up all the resources and there will be nothing left for better schools and communal welfare." Someone else said fewer children are better for one's health. She cited her aunt who had given birth to nine children and had to work very hard in the field to support them in the old society— her back was bent by the time she was forty years old.

The first woman then said, "I worry what will happen to me in old age if I have only a few children—or only daughters who may well be married outside their area. I will have no one take care of me." Several women spoke all at once, telling her that she should have no fear as such mothers would be taken care of under the five guarantees that the government would provide: food, clothing, housing, medical care, and burial. The barefoot doctor explained the relationship between health and reproduction, saying the pill had no other effect than preventing conception, and that those who already had one child should use it to space births.

The discussions went on for several rounds with the pros and cons of small families. During the two-hour session, the barefoot doctor did not attempt to prevent any negative expressions from being expressed. Instead, she continued to give the "correct information" for family planning to encourage the women to learn more about the relationship between health and economic production. The discussions on the use of the pill did not come to a conclusion, but the women were clearly involved in thinking about family planning and their role in learning to become true socialist citizens. "We will have many more such sessions until the women are persuaded to adopt the pill for contraception and help others adopt it, as well," the barefoot doctor told the group.

When the session ended, I followed the barefoot doctor to deliver the contraceptive pill to a young woman with a two-year-old daughter in her home. The barefoot doctor introduced me to the woman and exchanged some small talk with her. Then she took the Thermos bottle of hot water from her bag and poured the water into a cup for the woman to take the pill, which she also took from her bag. "How do you feel about having your barefoot doctor bring you the pill?" I asked. The woman swallowed the pill and said, "This way I won't forget to take it. She brings the pill to me every day."

I thought about how we try to develop schemes to ensure patient compliance in medical regimens through behavior modification in the United States. One could interpret the Chinese way of delivering the contraceptive pill either as tender loving care or as coercion, depending on one's point of view.

From Shanghai we traveled by train to Beijing. Our party had two sleeping compartments, four booths to each. We were awakened by our guides in early dawn and informed that the train would be passing over the Nanjing Bridge in a few minutes. It was suggested we take a look. The bridge was a recent engineering triumph proclaimed as "Product of the Cultural Revolution," the longest bridge in China, stretching from Nanjing to Pukou, the caramel-brown Yangtze River rolling below. Actually, I was more taken with the muddy brown color of the river than the bridge.

Arriving in Beijing, we saw sentinel soldiers stationed in the streets, something we had not seen elsewhere. We stayed at the Friendship Hotel on the north side of the city, which was built on the Russian model with tall columns, high ceilings, marble floors, and spacious rooms. The hotel, a complex of several buildings, had once been the residence of Russian technicians before the Soviets pulled them out in 1958. I was flabbergasted to see exquisite, inch-thick hand-made woolen rugs caked with dirt, since apparently no one bothered to care for them.

We were the only guests in this huge compound. The Friendship Hotel in Beijing, as elsewhere, had air conditioning, which the management turned on especially for us. But as soon as we left the hotel in the morning, the air conditioning system was turned off. It was turned back on again when we returned for lunch and an hour's rest, and then off again until we came back before supper. We tried to convince the management that it was more energy saving if they just left the air conditioning on, but they didn't want to do that. We were served plenty of meat, but the best dish was always vegetables fresh from the field, picked that very morning. With few exceptions, we ate our meals in the hotel where we stayed, apart from the tour guides.

Between visits to various agencies, we had a chance to sightsee Beijing's historic sites. As I huffed and puffed on the steps of the Summer Palace, the sight of a little old woman at least twenty years my senior with bound feet climbing the steps of the Summer Palace put me to shame. The palace had been burned down by the Anglo-French allied forces in 1860 and rebuilt by the dowager empress Cixi with the funds that were allotted for building the Navy. I felt refreshed looking at the cuddly pandas in the zoo cozily chewing bamboo while children laughed and played. I marveled at the majesty of the Great Wall, which the Chinese call the "long wall of ten thousand kilometers." The wall, the first segment of which was built in the fifth century B.C.E., was completed in 221 B.C.E.; it had taken the labor of 300,000 men who worked for ten years under the reign of Emperor Qun Shi Huang, the ruler who unified China. The wall's interior stone road was wide enough to accommodate five horses galloping abreast.

From Beijing we flew to Shenyang, the capital of Liaoning Province in the Northeast, where we spent a day at the Liaoning School of Chinese Medicine. The school was known for integrating Chinese medicine with Western medicine and techniques.

We donned surgical gowns to go inside the operating room and observe a surgeon demonstrating a flexible splint on the fractured arm of a young worker. During the procedure, the surgeon inserted acupuncture needles into various parts of the young man's body to block pain. During the hour-long procedure, the young man was alert and without any sign of discomfort. After the surgeon finished, the young man got up from the operating table, shook hands with the surgeon and walked away. In another operation, we saw the removal of a fist-sized ovarian cyst on a thirty-six-year-old woman who was fully awake. Her sole anesthesia consisted of two acupuncture needles that were inserted into her legs and vibrated by means of an electronic device. Throughout the procedure a nurse spoke to her from time to time to inform her what the surgeon was doing, in order to ease her anxiety. From what I could see, the woman also showed no sign of pain.

The dean of the school told us that the present union between Chinese and Western medicine was one of techniques and not of theory, and that research was needed to take advantage of the two different ways of healing. Chinese medicine emphasized the care of the whole person. Its weakness lay in its lack of specificity in diagnoses and that treatment efficacy was largely garnered from practical experience rather than clinical trials. The strength of Western medicine lies in its scientific base and technology, but it treats an organ, or a disease, without the necessary concern for the whole person. But we also heard from this school, as well as other medical schools we visited, that they needed to return the medical curriculum to cover a full six years. During the Cultural Revolution, the entire program had been reduced to just two or three years.

That afternoon, I met with a group of medical students in a seminar. Of the students, half of them were women between the ages of twenty-one and twenty-four. They were all single and were required to remain single during the course of study. These students were middle school graduates who had had work experience on the farm or factory. Some of them had been medical corpsmen in the People's Liberation Army, and most had served as barefoot doctors for one to six years. They had been selected by their community for their medical study because of their "good attitudes."

I asked the students if they were "Red and expert." They laughed, saying that they were Red but would like to become experts. Once they graduated, they would go "where the state sent us," a phrase I was to hear over and over again.

The students wanted to know what my life was like in the United States. They were surprised when I told them that my education had been financed by American taxpayers through scholarships and traineeships, and that I had become a university professor. The Chinese people had been told that the United States was oppressive to all people of color and that people of color were at the bottom of the social stratum. I told them about the free enterprise system and people's right to dissent, such as against the Vietnam War. I confessed my love for the melting pot, telling them that America valued human resources. For this reason people all over the world wanted to come to the United States for a chance at the American dream.

The students brightened. They were surprised to hear what I had to say about the United States of America, though they made no comment other than wanting to hear more. I, too, was surprised to find China caring and altruistic for its citizenry.

The next day in the Eight One Commune, thirty kilometers outside of Shenyang, I saw one of our local hosts Lao Lung's eyes swell as he spoke of the bitter past. His poor parents had sold his two sisters, scrawny five- and six-year-olds, to a rich merchant in the city for next to nothing, so that they could have food in their stomachs. His mother gave birth to two more children, a boy and a girl, but didn't have enough milk to nourish them. For a while they survived on rice water, but both babies died within months after their births. When Lao Lung was eleven years old, his father died of a fever and his mother took him to his uncle's home, attaching themselves to his family of five who were just as poor as they were.

Then the Communist revolution came, and this was his *fenshen* — flipping the body—over for better days ahead. He learned how to read and write, followed what the chairman and the Communist Party taught him, worked for the communal good and served the people. "I was the first to line up in the morning to go out to the field and the last in line in the communal mess hall." Lao Lung glowed as he spoke. "Two years ago, I was elected captain of our production brigade. A thousand thanks to Chairman Mao and the Communist Party."

We joined the cadres and the barefoot doctors at lunch, hosted by the commune. The cadres and the barefoot doctors were laughing and telling jokes as they ate. So surprised was I at their lightheartedness and the fun they were having that I got up off my seat and said, "Communists know how to laugh!" Everybody roared. They thought it was the funniest thing they ever heard.

I had the image of Chinese Communists only as a stern and inhumane lot, incapable of any emotions of love and laughter, or any genuine concern for people. So it was somewhat of a shock for me to discover that they were people with a full range of emotions who cared deeply for one another. They happily acknowledged the progress made in education, health, welfare, and women's emancipation; they glowed with tender pride for the well-being of their children and the welfare for the aged. They were confident that whatever consumer goods they lacked today, they would have ten years from now—through hard work and sacrificing immediate gratification. For the present, everyone had food, shelter, work, and medical care. In the past, there were people who had to give their first crops to the landlords in return for the use of the land they tilled; people who sold their children to pay off their debts and to keep them from starving. For these people, life had never been so good.

Our hosts were eager for us to know more about them as fellow human beings and to be accepted as revolutionaries in their struggle for a voice in their own destiny. This may sound cynical for people looking in from the outside, but the desire to be understood and accepted must lie in the recognition of China's past, the conditions of that society and the degradation it had suffered as a nation both from powers from without and despots from within.

For me, the most unsettling thing about life in China was seeing the uniformity in people's conduct. I saw the same gestures and slogans taught to children from one end of the country to the other. Everybody quoted Mao just as the Mandarin scholars had quoted the classics in the old days, or American Southern Baptists quote the Bible even now. People were told what to think and how to act, and any deviance would soon be corrected by group pressure and brought to conformity.

On returning to the United States, I received a telephone call from an agent of the CIA, saying that he would like to interview me about my visit to China. Two men in dark suits and ties came to my office at the University of Maryland; they showed me their badges, sat down, and put a tape recorder on the desk. One agent reviewed with me the itinerary of our group and began to inquire about the members of my team and the experiences I had had during our five-week visit. After two hours, they were ready to leave. I told them that I had drafted three papers on family planning and rural health service delivery in China, and pulled copies from the bookshelf to give to them. The agent who did the interview took the papers and put them inside his briefcase. They thanked me, got up, and left. I never heard from any CIA agents again.

Chapter Fourteen

Last Journey of the Confucian General

In 1972, Zhou Enlai invited Father to visit the People's Republic. The message was relayed through my brother Victor during his first visit to China with a group of Chinese American academics that year. Premier Zhou met with them at the Great Hall of the People. "You are the son of Li Han Hun, are you not?" asked Zhou at the end of the meeting. Zhou asked Victor about Father's health, saying "Yes! We are all revolutionaries even though we have selected different paths. Please tell your father we welcome him to visit us." Zhou hurriedly walked toward the door, but then he turned around and came back to speak with Victor again: "Please do tell your mother that my wife Deng Yingchao sends her greetings." Mother and Deng Yingchao were both active in war relief efforts and had once worked together raising funds in Hong Kong in 1938.

My father declined Premier Zhou's invitation. "I have long since disengaged from politics," he told the family. "I shall remain a private citizen for as long as I live." Then, thoughtfully and with emotion, he added, "It is a pity that the Communists refuted the Confucian ethics that were the foundation of Chinese society for over two thousand years."

During our study tour the following year to document barefoot doctors in rural China, the United Front Bureau asked Victor and me to deliver another invitation to our father. "If the old general would travel to Hong Kong," a spokesman told us, "the government will send a plane to meet him there and fly him to Beijing. Certainly, the old general would be interested in seeing the progress in the Motherland during the past quarter century."

The People's Republic sought Father's visit because the government was trying to create a new image for the world, especially for the overseas Chinese abroad and the people in Taiwan. Father's visit would be emblematic of Communist China's redefining its position with regard to old adversaries. It would serve as a signal of letting bygones be bygones.

Once again, Father declined.

In 1980, when the family came together on the occasion of my father's eighty-fifth birthday, he finally had a change of heart. He told us that he would like to visit Nanhua Temple in Shaoguan, as well as the village where he was born and where his ancestors rested. His realization that his lifelong journey was nearing its end had kindled his desire to visit his ancestral homeland one last time. A devout Buddhist, my father was deeply attached to Nanhua Temple; in 1929, he had raised funds for its renovation. Built in the sixth century, Nanhua Temple was the largest Buddhist temple in South China. My father's pen name was Li Nanhua. He used this name in the hundreds of letters he wrote to Mother during their long engagement.

My father was consecrated to the lay monkhood in 1980. The simple private ceremony took place in the living room of my parents' Confucius Plaza apartment in New York. The person who received my father into the lay Buddhist monkhood was a lay monk himself. He acted as surrogate to the master monk in Hong Kong, who was a disciple of Xu Yun, the late abbot of Nanhua Temple. At the time Nanhua Temple was renovated, my father invited Xu Yun from Fujian to come to Shaoguan and revitalize Nanhua. A long friendship between Master Xu Yun and my father ensued. Only one friend served as witness at the home ceremony. My father, dressed in his traditional Chinese *maqua*, said a few prayers and was given a scripture on the ways of Buddha. In becoming a lay monk, my father sought his own liberation to disentangle the self by becoming non-egocentric and in harmony with all living things.

I discovered my father's lay monkhood only years later when I was going through his papers. "I take this step with deep feelings toward you," he wrote to Mother the night before his consecration. "You and I have a marriage of nearly fifty years and have shared so much. . . ." My mother confirmed Father's consecration to lay monkhood to me. She respected his desire and supported it. At home and in the bosom of his family, my father lived in much the same manner as before. He still read the daily newspapers and was cognizant of worldly events, even though he was detached from them.

I asked my siblings if they knew of our father's lay monkhood. Only Tina said she knew, that she had been told by our father himself. Like our mother, Tina respected his privacy and thus never mentioned it, although it was not a secret.

The government of the People's Republic welcomed the news of my father's intended visit. Within weeks, the United Front Bureau had planned an itinerary that included Beijing, Shanghai, and Guangzhou, as well as Shaoguan and Wuchuan, my father's home county. Our mother and Victor would accompany Papa for the trip.

But as soon as our father's intended visit to China became known, a bombardment of telegrams and letters came from friends and former colleagues in Taiwan, some in high positions in the Nationalist government. They urged him to abort his trip, admonishing him that a visit to Communist China would be tantamount to surrendering to the Communists—that it would be nothing less than a betrayal of old friends and comrades who had shared many life struggles with him. "Come to visit free China [Taiwan], instead" they advised. "You are welcome here."

Stunned and saddened by such reactions from friends and comrades whom he had known for more than half a century, my father canceled the trip two weeks before his scheduled departure. He could not bear the thought of being seen as betraying his friends. He was a Confucian scholar and a Confucian soldier, and loyalty was paramount.

When the news of my father's trip cancellation reached Taiwan, those who had urged him to give up the trip wrote again, congratulating him on his good judgment for the preservation of his good name. But our old father was sad; his heart longed for Nanhua Temple and his ancestral village. My mother was furious over such an infliction of cruelty on our father, and so were we his children. We understood that the journey was his last wish, in the evening of his life, and we felt he had the right to make this trip. Victor and I told our parents that we would accompany them to visit China and encouraged them to go ahead. They were hesitant to make the decision, concerned that there would be yet another furor.

In the summer of 1981, my parents attended Victor's inauguration as president of the East-West Center in Honolulu. They finally decided that they would go ahead with the visit to China, but first they would visit Taiwan. This would ward off the barrage of negative reactions from their Nationalist colleagues. Symbolically, it would be seen as an act of allegiance to the Nationalist government in Taiwan.

My father had his Chinese passport, having remained a Chinese citizen. My mother was a naturalized American citizen and needed a visa. Her application for a visa to the Chinese Coordinating Council in Honolulu was refused. She telephoned me to explain, "The government in Taiwan never forgot that Papa argued with Chiang Kaishek on his retreat to Taiwan and that he came to the United States with Li Zongren." Perturbed but not intimidated, my mother telephoned the council to say that as a loyal Nationalist she had the right to visit Chinese territory, even without official authorization—warning them that she would arrive without a visa. Three days later, the consul called to inform my mother that a telegram had come from President Chiang Chingkao, extending his welcome to my parents' visit.

My parents' arrival at the Chiang Kaishek Airport in Taipei was met by some fifteen friends, their former associates in Guangdong. Among them was Gao Xin, secretary general to the President's Office. While my father was governor of Guangdong Province, Gao was his secretary of state. More than anyone else, Gao had been most vocal in opposing Father's visit to China. He had written a seething letter to my father with the accusation that such a visit would be no less than treason. Immediately my parents were taken to the memorial tomb of Chiang Kaishek for three bows in traditional Chinese courtesy.

Chiang Chingkuo, who had succeeded his father, Chiang Kaishek, as president, made a limousine available to my parents during their stay. He received my parents at the presidential palace and presented them with two one-ounce Chiang Kaishek memorial gold coins. During the War of Resistance, Chiang Chingkuo had passed through Shaoguan many times and had been a frequent guest of my father's. He used to address my father as Li Lao Bo, Old Uncle Li. Thirty years later in Taiwan, their meeting was formal, and the whole gesture of my parents' visit and the gold coins signified a reconciliation and renewal of friendship. Following this act, a visit to the mainland took on a different meaning for the Nationalist government in Taiwan. While it was still considered a breach of conduct in Taiwan, it was no longer interpreted as favoring the Communist mainland over Nationalist Taiwan.

In June 1982, at the age of eighty-seven, my father made his last journey to China as a guest of the State, accompanied by our mother, Victor, and me. We flew on Air China from San Francisco to Beijing. The United Front Bureau in Beijing had planned a two-week itinerary for our father's homecoming and another week for our mother to sightsee. June and July were hot and humid in southern coastal Guangdong, Shanghai, as well as Beijing, and most places were without air conditioning. My brother Fred had advised limiting our father's visit to two weeks in light of his age and his health. He deferred to Fred's opinion as a physician; he and I would fly back to New York ahead of Mother.

In Beijing, we were lodged in the Beijing Hotel. My parents were assigned the grand suite, courtesy of the state, and Victor and I each had a smaller suite. The official host for my parents was Mr. Liao Chengzhi, chairman of the Overseas Commission, who was a former vice chairman of the People's Congress.

The story of Liao Chengzhi and my father was an intriguing one. During the War of Resistance, Liao was arrested by police security as he stepped off the train in Lochang County in Guangdong, which was under my father's jurisdiction. Until the time Hong Kong fell, Liao operated underground out of Hong Kong. My father told me the story as we were preparing to leave for Beijing:

"The central government had ordered me to liquidate Liao Chengzhi by whatever means possible. I had admired his father Liao Junghai, a much respected revolutionary who had been regarded as a potential successor to Sun Yatsen. Then the older Liao was assassinated in Nanjing shortly after Sun's death. Liao Chengzhi was an only son, and I couldn't possibly end the Liao family line. To save his life, I conspired with Zhou You, my deputy commander of the Police Security Force. The scheme we devised was to extradite Liao to Chungking and put him in the hands of Chiang Kaishek himself. Chiang would not want the world to see Liao Chengzhi's blood on his hands. In the unlikely event Chiang sentenced Liao Chengzhi to death, there would certainly be clemency appeals from the Nationalist elders who had been close associates of Liao Chengzhi's late father. Chiang Kaishek would be obligated to respect the plea of the elders and spare his life." The scheme worked. Liao Chengzhi was jailed until the end of the war, but his life was spared. The scheme remained a secret for many years.

Deng Xiaoping, now China's paramount leader, hosted a banquet for my parents, and Victor and I were invited to come along. Short in stature, Deng was charismatic and energetic, talking almost nonstop, enjoying the food and downing seven cups of maotai without blinking an eye and without even a sign of getting tipsy. In reminiscing over his travails during the Cultural Revolution, Deng said that on three separate occasions he had been paraded through the streets with a dunce's hat as a rightist counterrevolutionary. He pointed at Liao Chengzhi and said that Liao had been paraded twice. They both laughed as if the whole thing were comical.

I thought that in order to survive humiliation and pain of that nature, one needed to have a black sense of humor to be able to rise above the hurt and the injury.

My mother asked Deng if China would revert to the old policy of political movements like those of the Cultural Revolution. "No. We learned our lessons. That will not happen again." Deng was confident about China's future under his modernization plan that would reform the stagnating economy and move the country into democratic socialism. Throughout the banquet my father was quiet, and I could see his heart and mind were detached from the whole scene. He had come to his homeland for one purpose only—to visit the Nanhua Temple and his ancestral village.

Cigarette smoking was ubiquitous in China and any good host would offer cigarettes to his or her guests whether they smoked or not. Near the end of the banquet the dignitary who sat next to me was ready to light a cigarette for me. I seized the opportunity to tell everyone, but especially to Deng Xiaoping, about the harmful effects of cigarette smoking to health not only to the smoker, but because of passive smoking to the nonsmokers who inhaled the smoke. I was engaged in research in tobacco use and smoking prevention at the Johns Hopkins University at the time and got just a bit carried away. Deng listened. When I finished my little lecture, he looked me straight in the eyes and said, "You are absolutely right." Then he lighted his cigarette.

We visited Marshall Ye Jianying at his Xishan residence, thirty miles west of Beijing. As was the case for all the events, the United Front Bureau had made the arrangement for my parents, and Victor and I were invited to come along. Our limousine drove inside the walled compound, where guards lined the path every few yards.

This was my father and Ye's first meeting in fifty years. They had once been colleagues in the Fourth Army. They parted in 1927, when Ye took part in the Communist insurrection in Guangzhou. Ye was heavy now, his body movement slow and stiff. Two aides held him, one on each side, helping him to sit down and get up from the sofa chair.

"We were young men then, full of zeal and courage," reminisced Ye. "We fought the warlords together and we fought the Japanese."

"You scored quite a coup, giving China a new lease," my father complimented him. "We are old men now."

Ye Jianying was the key player, on October 6, 1976, in the arrest of Jiang Qing, the wife of Chairman Mao and head of the Gang of Four, the radical leadership that had instigated the Cultural Revolution. That courageous act brought the Cultural Revolution to a halt. Had he failed, history would have been far different for China.

I watched the two old men standing next to each other, moving around the room softly reading the calligraphy—poems of Mao Zedong and others—that was hung on the walls, and I wondered what they were thinking, how they were feeling about both then and now. How strange it was that my parents, Victor, and I were guests in Ye's home in Xishan.

When the visit ended, Ye Jianying insisted on seeing my parents out to the car himself. The two old men grabbed each other's hands tightly as they said good-bye.

"I am so glad you came."

"Take care of your health, I am happy I came."

Our car went slowly out the gate; when I turned my head around, I saw Ye waving. My father waved back to a friend lost and found for a last time. He then looked straight ahead, his mood contemplative, his eyes slightly wet.

We met Deng Yingchao in one of the exclusive government inner halls. She looked proletarian in the same gray pantsuit worn by the women of China. The widow of the late Zhou Enlai was affectionately called Deng Dajie—Big Sister Deng—by everyone in China. She and my mother had not seen each other since the early days of the Sino-Japanese War, when they worked together in Hong Kong for the war chest for medical supplies.

"What should be done to connect with the compatriots in Taiwan and abroad for a united China?" Deng asked, like an old friend would.

In one breath my mother answered without hesitation, "The Communist government must stop liquidating people. No more bloodshed, if the Communist government wants to gain the respect and confidence of those outside China. There are too many who feel anger and hatred toward the Communists because their families were persecuted and badly hurt in its many cleansing movements. It will be up to the Communist government to amend its policy and to heal."

I found a passage in my father's diaries that recorded this meeting. "My daughter Zhen told her mother that she thought her language was very blunt and could be offensive. Chu Fang said she had to speak out because few people would ever be in the position to speak so candidly. I thought she was right in making the point plainly and honestly." Reading this passage, I understood all the more why my parents succeeded on so many fronts and were able to do what they did.

From Beijing we flew to Guangzhou, where we were lodged at the Guangdong Guest House. Again, my parents were given a grand suite and Victor and I smaller suites. As soon as my father stepped outside the car onto the shaded ground of the garden, he said, "Aah! I remember this guesthouse well!" Years before, he had attended many meetings and banquets in the facility where many of the important government functions were held.

In Guangzhou as in Beijing, all the slogans I had seen in 1973 were gone. I looked for

"Serve the people," which had been everywhere during my last visit, and did not see it. China's enactment of a new economic policy and modernization plan has altered the country's outlook.

The cadres handed me a long list of several hundred names that included my parents' former associates and subordinates, friends, relatives, and a delegation from my father's home county who wished to see my parents. I was told that many had gotten in touch with the United Front Bureau to make contact with us; they had seen the news telecasts of my parents meeting with the many of top leaders from the time of our arrival in Beijing.

With few exceptions, I scheduled all the visitors in small groups, allowing half an hour each, starting at nine in the morning, ending at noon, and starting up again at two and ending at five. The evenings were reserved for special friends. I asked all the callers to try to make the reunion a joyful occasion for Father and to please not to bring up the strain and pains of the past, since many people had suffered so badly as "black elements."

For my cousin Youfei, I gave him a private hour alone with his uncle. Youfei, who had come from the village, was the son of my father's younger brother. Tearful, he started to tell his uncle what had happened back in 1949, when his father left for Hong Kong with his older children. Two-year-old Youfei, his elder brother and sister, and their mother, who was the second wife, were left behind in the village. Threatened with punishment for being a landlord's wife, Youfei's mother committed suicide.

For a while, he and his siblings lived with their maternal grandmother. Two years later, his destitute grandmother gave him up to a childless couple for adoption. During the famine, in 1959, his adoptive parents were no longer able to feed him and had to give him up to the orphanage. Because no one had bothered to check the background of the orphans and because Youfei was smart enough to keep quiet about his family background, he was well treated and learned the skills of a construction worker. He revealed his true identity only after the open-door policy was enacted in the late 1970s.

When Youfei finished his story, I saw tears glimmering in my father's eyes as he asked, "What happened to Ahnai's grave?" Youfei replied that our grandmother's tomb was dug up in the 1950s, when some villagers thought that treasures would be found inside. Her bones were simply dumped. I was hoping my father did not hear everything that he said. But I was upset with my cousin. I had asked him, as I had asked all the others, to make the reunion joyous for my father.

Several of the visitors whom I had known well as a child revealed that they were Communist party members during the War of Resistance in Huanggong and, unbeknown to my parents, had infiltrated the provincial government. Yang Hangfen was one such person. She had assisted my mother in promoting the women's movement and had come to our home often. In the 1950s, she became deputy head of the Bureau of Education in Guangzhou municipality. "When I received the orders from my Party to go North," Yang said, "I told your mother that I had to go home because my mother was very sick. Your mother gave me money for my trip up North." Yet, during the Cultural Revolution, Yang was badly persecuted, as were many of the cadres and party faithful.

Spring Grace was also at the Guangzhou Guest House to meet us. She looked healthy and was taller and darker than I had remembered her. I hugged her, as an American would; she just grabbed my hand and held it tight.

"Daxiaojie," she addressed me "Grand little miss," as she did years ago. "I remember how much you like peanuts. These twenty kilos are fresh from the field. When you go back to America, just boil them and eat them." She presented me with the peanuts in a big red duffel bag that was brand new.

My throat constricted. "Thank you. You still remember all that. But I cannot take the peanuts to the United States because Customs won't allow it."

"But these peanuts are very clean. Please, you must take them."

"I really would like to, but can't. It's forbidden for food and plants to be brought into America. The customs officers will give me a stiff penalty for the raw peanuts for sure. I accept your gift in my heart, but you take the bag home. When you eat the peanuts, you'll think of me."

Spring Grace was in tears. Then she turned somber as she began to tell her story.

At the time of the 1949 Communist revolution, she had just graduated from teacher training school. Hopeful of a bright future and proud to be a teacher, she returned to her village to teach grade school. She also volunteered to teach the illiterate peasants to read in adult literacy classes at night. There were many meetings for forming village cooperatives and propagandizing Chairman Mao's thoughts on building a Communist state—one in which everyone would share the labor as well as the benefits of the new society. She was accepted as a daughter of the village who had *fanshen*—having beaten the odds and made it. But soon a group of people accused her of being a spy for the Nationalists. The evidence presented against her was that she had been sent to the Girls Normal Middle School by the former governor and his wife. She was arrested and imprisoned.

During her trial, she was forced to wear a dunce hat and was paraded around the village square. The people's court sentenced her to three years' imprisonment and hard labor. She was given this "light" sentence only because she had been bartered into servitude on account of her parents' poverty and had been a victim of the old society. In the correction farm, the inmates labored, assembled for self-criticism, and studied Chairmen Mao's thoughts in order to arrive at correct thinking for self-renewal. Spring Grace wrote confession after confession as an act of critical consciousness and contrition. Pitying herself for being a victim of injustice for the second time, she thought of ending her own life. But she told herself that she must endure and not make her parents suffer any more than they already had.

The closest my father got to his home village was watching the videotape produced by the United Front Bureau of Guangdong. It showed the ancestral home built by my great grandfather and the surrounding grounds, the primary school my grandfather had built and that my father had enlarged and helped to maintain, and the house built by my father. All the structures appeared to have been well kept and painted with a fresh white coat; the graves were also well kept.

Victor and I had entered into a conspiracy, telling our father that it was not possible to visit our home village in Wuchuan because of poor road conditions—even though the United Front Bureau assured us that the roads were good and that the tombs had been reconstructed so that they were just as before. My mother, Victor, and I all feared his being confronted with the truth about the grave —about our grandmother's grave and her bones having been dug up and then just dumped—and about the relatives who died under persecution. We were sure that it would be emotionally too upsetting for our father and detrimental to his mental well-being as well as physical health.

When our father adamantly insisted that he must visit Jhanjiang, previously known as Guangzhou Bay, where his mother was buried, and his home village Lingtou to pay his respect to the ancestral graves, our mother told him that the original graves had been dug up, and that settled the matter for father. "Papa wept," my mother told me many years later.

After my father and I returned to New York, he told me he had known all along that we had not wanted him to go back to the village. "You don't think I know, but I do. You were protecting me." He said he forgave us for the pretext about the roads. We both let it go at that without further discussion.

Our final stop was Shaoguan, the wartime capital of Guangdong Province during my father's term as governor. The train that took us to Shaoguan was a special VIP car with red velvet lining the walls, provided to my father courtesy of the government. Our entourage included our local hosts, cadres, several journalists, and also a physician to look after Father in the event that he needed care. My mother came down with a high fever the day after we arrived in Guangzhou, which prevented her from traveling. She remained in the Guest House in Guangzhou.

The original layout of the Nanhua Temple had been a quadrangle. In the 1933 restoration, which took ten years to complete, the layout was changed into a central axle with many buildings.

We walked up the cobblestone-paved road leading to the tall arched entrance and then through the courtyards to the halls with painted red columns. During the Cultural Revolution, Zhou Enlai had declared Nanhua Temple to be a national treasure, and so it had been protected from destruction by the Red Guards.

My father and I walked through the halls that displayed the four huge statues of *jin-gon*—the guardian gods that had so frightened me when I was a child—as well as the smaller statues of the eighty-one monks, and the mummified body of the Sixth Patriarch, sitting in a lotus position. At the Patriach Hall there were the two painted blue columns inscribed with a couplet Father had composed in 1930, at the time of the temple's renovation: "Authentic heritage enlightens the human heart and nature through the robes and bowls; supreme wisdom sustains itself in leaves that descend to the roots of the sacred peepal tree." During the Cultural Revolution, the monks took these columns down and buried them under the ground with the other temple treasures, including the complete set of the Buddhist scripture—*Jishazang*—that my father had donated. That act was what saved these pieces from being destroyed by the Red Guard fever of that time. The monks proudly showed us the books and relics that had been preserved, as well as the robe granted to the Sixth Patriarch by Empress Wu Jetien in the Tang dynasty over a thousand years earlier. One of the monks had saved the robe by folding it and pretending that it was his head pillow in order to hide it from the Red Guards.

At noon my father rested in the little four-room house in the rear of the temple where he used to come for retreats while he was governor—a house he had built and still rightfully owned. Before we left the house for a walk on the temple grounds, my father told me, "I believe in Buddhism; I am not a superstitious person." By that he meant he was light to himself in all matters and that he would not rely on any rituals for salvation.

Walking the temple grounds under the tall trees, the abbot told Father that the groves of fruit trees and tea shrubs planted at the time of the renovation with funds my father raised had helped to sustain them in hard times over the past decades. "You are twice our benefactor," said the abbot. "The government painted and repaired this temple for your visit."

We looked for and did not see the little open pavilion under which my brother Shao was buried. My father inquired about the pavilion. The monks simply said, "Gone."

Quietly turning to me, his voice barely audible, my father said, "While I was governor, Old Master Xuyun said to me *fang xia chu le*—let go of everything. But I couldn't let them go. I have come to that junction in my life now, where I can finally let go of everything."

When we returned to Guangzhou, my mother tried to comfort our father. "Don't cry," she said. "So much has happened to everyone." But she, too, cried, thinking of Shao, his little pavilion, and his remains gone without a trace. She asked my father if he still wished to be buried at Nanhua Temple as he had stated in his will. "No," said my father. "My son's grave is gone, and so are the graves of my mother and ancestors. It matters not that I should be laid to rest in foreign soil."

In their retirement, my parents lived in an apartment on the thirty-sixth floor of the Confucius Plaza in New York City's Chinatown, to be near many of their friends. My mother hired a live-in couple to attend to my father and help with the household chores. The apartment was always a hub of activities. My parents were social beings, my mother in particular. Friends often brought food and they would go out together to dine or go to the theater. My parents also liked to invite their friends to dine at home. They were never short of company.

From the L-shaped living room and dining area, one could clearly see the majestic Empire State Building towering against the sky. At night the Chrysler Building glowed amidst the splendid colors of the Manhattan night.

With his lifelong habit of getting up at daybreak, my father would light some joss sticks in the incense burner on the dresser next to his bed. Sitting in a lotus position with his palms pressed together, legs folded, he would meditate for two hours before having his breakfast of Quaker Quick Oatmeal cooked with an egg. For a good part of the day, he would sit at his desk reading and writing. Letters from friends were precious to him and he replied to each of them painstakingly. The letters were his link with the ghosts of days long gone. He would struggle to recall the past, writing down his remembrances.

The desk in his bedroom was cluttered with carved marble chops, miniatures of the Golden Gate Bridge, the Statue of Liberty, and the Washington Monument. The miniatures were souvenirs given to him years earlier when we first came to this country as visitors. Months before Christmas my father became very excited about buying cards, reviewing the mailing list from the year before to address the envelopes. By the first week of December, the cards had already been taken to the post office and mailed. He did this himself until the last few years of his life when he could no longer handle some five hundred pieces of mail.

Two to three times a day my father would stand in the middle of the living room, knees slightly bent and parted, swinging his arms back and forth in slow motion to exercise his body as a mild form of *tai chi*, which he had adopted in his old age. Sometimes he stayed in the same position for an hour at a time. Except for his eyes that followed the movements in the room, his face would be expressionless. When we first arrived in New York City, my father did *kung fu* in the living room of the apartment, leaping so high that his head almost touched the ceiling. Then his feet would touch the floor without a sound and with the grace and dexterity of a jaguar. We children used to watch and marvel. Even into his eighties, his body was taut and solid.

Along with our children, my siblings and I tried to come back to our parents' home at Christmastime and on their birthdays, all three generations of us together. Sleeping bags would cover the living room and bedroom floors. The crowding and tripping over people only added to the intimacy. We would eat out in one group, cook or have food brought in from restaurants, and use paper plates and plastic cups to minimize dishwashing. When together, we often spoke English to each other and to our mother simply because it was easier for my younger siblings—and definitely the case for the third generation—as we all chatted away to catch up on the happenings in our lives. Usually our father just sat there smiling approvingly, pleased that we were all home in one big gathering. Now and then we would stop with what we were saying to one another and direct some remarks to him in Chinese, asking him how he felt or what he needed and telling little anecdotes. He would just say, "I am so pleased you are home, stay for a few more days. Stay longer." After that, we would resume our chatter. Only on one occasion, when we got carried away and left him sitting by himself, did he show displeasure at our insensitivity in speaking English. He got up from the sofa and said that he was retiring to his room because he could not understand what we were talking about. We realized that we had hurt him badly, and even more so, we had inadvertently contributed to his isolation. One by one we went into his room and spoke with him, trying to make up for our insensitivity.

Whenever I would visit, I would go into my father's room, sit by his side and hold his hand. He would stop reading or writing. I would listen to him.

"The ancients said the penalty for a defeated general is his head on the chopping block. I died a thousand times. The Communists would not have won except for the corruption of the Nationalists." My father said this slowly as if he were speaking to himself, his knotty arthritic hand limp and motionless in mine. He was loyal to his friends and comrades. He would not speak of the wrongdoings of Chiang Kaishek. Nor would he speak unkindly of Li Zongren. They were his former commanders in chief, and he was ever respectful of them.

Time and time again he would reminisce, reliving the world beyond. "To be neutral is to be out in the cold, pleasing no one. In my dreams, the muddy Yellow River churned, dogs barked, and the birds sang ever so mournfully. Water slapped against the rocks, the clear sky turned gray, and thunder pounded angrily like cannons. I heard thousands of voices speaking. So many dead in battles, in sickness, or simply disappeared. Never to be seen again. Grave mounds flattened. Liquidation, movement, another liquidation, another movement, by quota! Class struggle! Class hatred! Why kill and maim so many? My younger sister died of starvation. The poor woman, widowed with a child shortly after she was wed. Families dissolved by fiat, by children turning against their elders. Confucian teaching that had formed the basis of social morality for thousands of years was simply swept aside."

He bemoaned the fact that the Nationalist generals and officials were all said to be corrupt and that, in the eyes of many, he was guilty by association. He lamented the fate of China and said it was justice that the Communists had won the hearts and minds of the people. For all the deprivation the foot soldiers endured, it was no accident that they laid down their guns when facing the Communists. And the peasants? They simply exchanged hundreds of years of oppression for a chance to be masters of their own destiny.

He recalled the battlefields in which he fought during the War of Resistance. "To be a good soldier you must love your country and be willing to die for your country if need be. But to be a good commander you must be willing to sacrifice the soldiers you love. Many good men found it difficult to be good commanders." He was apologizing for old colleagues who opted for retreat to "preserve strength" in the face of enemy fire during the War of Resistance.

"A person's worth depended on the status of his country in the eyes of the world," my father told me. At the end of World War II, China was an acknowledged allied power. Father, as a general and a former governor, was cordially welcomed. When he visited Sacramento, he had met with Governor Earl Warren. But the fall of the Nationalist government changed the world's perception. The Chinese were now scorned and judged weak, to be pitied at best. Communist China's involvement in the Korean War further intensified America's aversion and hostility toward anything Chinese.

Letters and telephone calls that brought the news of someone who had died were ever a reminder to my father of his loneliness. He would cite a line from the Tang poet Du Pu: *fonzhui barnweiquei*—when visiting old friends, half were ghosts. He said that when he tried to visit his old friends they were all ghosts, for he had outlived them. He would shake his head slowly, lips tightly closed. He was homesick for his beloved China.

I listened and was moved by the sight and sound of my old father, who was now approaching his nineties. I shared his sadness, but there was no word of comfort I could think of except to say, "Let the past go!"

Yet, in all his sorrow, my father maintained a sense of optimism saying, "China is changing and the world is changing. If the right side would move a little toward the center, and the left side would also move a little toward the center, the difference between the right and the left would be reconciled. I believe the right and the left will go forward together some day."

In his last years, when my father and I spoke it was mostly about family. We talked about my four older brothers, who were my half brothers. My father had the softest spot in his heart for Brother Ban. He was Number One Son and had become motherless as an infant. Brother Ban was once wounded fighting in the Nationalist army in the last days of the Nationalists' retreat from Fujian, in 1949. After that, he had a hard time making a second career. Father never failed to send his eldest son money from the salary he received from the restaurants. When the restaurants were gone, he turned over the money from his social security checks to Brother Ban.

"The one regret I have in my life was that I wronged two good women," my father told me painfully, referring to his second wife. He had married her in the village when he was a young officer, and she was the mother of my other three half brothers and a sister.

"You were all victims of your time," I told him. "You were caught in the transition between the old era and the new. Your whole generation was caught in that bind." I tried to ease his self-recrimination. In his generation virtually all men had married village wives in arranged marriages while they were in their teens, as tradition dictated at the time. Later in life, if they became men of distinction, they would then marry modern and better-educated wives who could be of help to them in their careers.

"I don't blame your [half] siblings for being so distant. I wronged their mother. She was a good and gentle woman. In the course of my life and career, there was much over which I had no control. But this was something over which I did have control. I tried to do right by their mother. I provided for her. But this was no compensation for the suffering I caused her. I made life painful for her and caused anguish for your mother, too." My father was trembling.

"I believe you did what you had to do. We do not blame you." I held my father's hand, my heart grieving with him. Recalling what he had once said—that if he were to live his life all over again he would have lived it the same as he did—I saw human contradictions in life's journey and in the balance of things dear and close to one's heart.

"Your [half] siblings blame me. I don't blame them. There is no reason they should feel any affection for me."

I couldn't answer for my siblings. I hoped they did understand in spite of everything—and that they were forgiving.

When my father took inventory of his life, he said that of all the things he had done in his entire career, the one thing that he was absolutely certain had caused no harm, where only good had come of it, was building the Tsujiang Bridge in Shaoguan. Father had had this splendid structure built in Shaoguan while he was Pacification Commissioner of the Northwest District in 1932. Until the bridge was built, dozens of people died each year boating across the currents during storms. After the bridge was built, people crossed the river with ease and no more such tragedies occurred. My father was pleased with Victor's testimony on the normalization of the U.S.-China relationship and trade policy with Taiwan before the U.S. Congress, in February 1979. "This is a good thing," my father told me. "Victor succeeded in helping both mainland China and Taiwan more than I ever did."

He counted eleven doctorates among his progeny—his children and their spouses. On occasion he would ask, "Are my grandsons studying for their Ph.D.s?" I would tell him, "No, your grandsons do not necessarily feel a Ph.D. is as important to them as my generation did. They may not go on for one. They are not particularly attracted to university teaching the way we all were." I explained that in our time, becoming an academic was the avenue for us to make it in America. His grandchildren's generation was American-born. They had more opportunities open to them. Instead of teaching at universities, they might want to be in the mainstream of the free enterprise system. But I was not sure if my father heard what I had said.

"You should encourage your sons to study for their Ph.D.s. You all have yours. They should too." He paused and was pensive. "Ah, it's time for their generation to do something different. America is built on free enterprise. It's good to be an American businessman." He looked at the family photos that were hung around the walls, smiling as if to say, "All of you are doing fine." As it turned out, the MBA's have replaced the Ph.D.s in his grandchildren's generation; they opted for the private sector.

The last time I saw my father was in April 1987. I saw a hollowed death mask hovered over his face. I looked at him intently, as I did when I was a child and he was teaching me Tang poetry. Only now he was sitting in a wheelchair in a bare and sterile hospital room, his eyes staring straight ahead at the gray wintry sky, a life-sustaining tube hanging from his nose and a catheter dripping yellow urine into a large bottle. I held his cold hand, "Papa. How are you?" I said. He appeared to neither hear nor see me.

The news of my father's death reached me in Shanghai, while I was taking a group of health professionals on a study tour. He died on July 5, 1987, at the age of ninety-one. My brother Fred had taken care of our father during the last six months of his life after he suffered a stroke. Except for me, all his children and most of the grandchildren were at his funeral. Father was buried on a gentle sloping green hill in the Kensico Cemetery in Valhalla, New York.

I did not *banshaon*—rush to the funeral—as a filial Chinese son or daughter should. I changed my clothes to black; I wrote a commemorative article that was published in the *People's Daily*. I continued with the tour and then worked with the Shanghai-World Health Organization Health Education Collaborating Center with which I had been consulting. In the privacy of my heart, I mourned and honored him in my own way.

When I was a child, my father had said to me, "You must learn to serve like a foot soldier." What he meant was that I have duties, and that in the performance of those duties I should be humble, faithful, and willing to serve in tasks big or small. Later, when I was grown, he reminded me that the more I achieve and the more recognition I receive, the more I should be like a soldier.

Some ten years later, I met a ninety-three-year-old soldier who, decades earlier, had been a division commander under Father. This old soldier fondly recalled the time my parents entertained him at our home in Huanggong Hill, and how my mother served him the choicest morsels at the table. He told me about the memorial service in honor of Father in Hong Kong, where friends and former comrades who came to commemorate him were very upset that none of our father's children were there. The organizers had sent a telegram to the family in New York, urging that at least one of the children should represent the family in the memorial service. One individual who had served Father for decades was so upset and incensed that he wrote in the guest signature book, *I-tang marnborshee, I-jia wushiaozhi*—the hall filled with learned Ph.D.s, the family had no filial children.

I remember having spoken with my siblings from Shanghai about the telegram and the memorial service. I did not volunteer to go to Hong Kong, although I would have been the logical one since I could have easily gone from Shanghai. It did not occur to me then that I should go to Hong Kong and join my father's friends who had come to mourn and honor him, that my presence was important. I had always felt that filial piety should be expressed in the substance of how one lives one's life and not in form. I mourned him in private and in my own way. It saddens me now to realize, all too late, that I was not thoughtful enough of those who came to mourn, to show their love, and to pay their last respects for Father, and that I did not share this very special moment with them.

In all the years of my life, I only had one argument with my father. In Chinese culture, children simply did not argue with their parents, or, for that matter, with their elders. We bowed to our parents, to our elders, to our teachers, to each other, and we revered our ancestors. When I was a sophomore in college, I confronted Father about the wisdom of Confucius.

"Papa, I think Confucius was responsible for China's conservatism and under-development in industrialization. He was so disdainful of learned men working with their hands. It's a tragedy that Confucian teaching dominated Chinese thinking for thousands of years."

Surprised, my father straightened up from his seat and looked at me across the desk. "Confucius has given China a moral stability in human relations. He taught the Chinese people universal altruism, humility, and fortitude. These values have stood China well in the course of time."

"Confucius said 'Women without talent are virtuous.' He advocated the subjugation of women to men that resulted in the inequality of the sexes for centuries."

"You need to learn to see things in the context of the time. Confucius lived over 2,000 years ago. Beneath everything was the philosophical underpinning of the division of labor between men and women, and harmony in human relationships."

I retorted: "It is absurd what Confucius said about 'When the mat is not placed straight, do not sit on it. When the food is not cut right, do not eat it.' It is plain silly."

"Not as silly as you think. Confucius was suggesting that one should discipline one's mind and body and thus become a better person."

My father thought my understanding of Confucianism was immature and a product of incomplete learning. Then, in a clear and raised voice, he launched into an explanation of how Confucianism was a way of life and a way to be human, to harmonize with the universe:

"You should know that Confucius's teachings have given guidance to human society and social responsibility to its members. The ethical, legal, and ritual conventions of these teachings have provided Chinese society with both its system of communication and its rules of conduct. You must understand the five relationships that govern human conduct: affection, as between a father and a son; rightness, as between superiors and subordinates; a division of labor, as between a husband and a wife; a spirit of mutuality as between friends; and, a sequence of order, as between brothers.

"Central to Confucianism is *ren*—humanism. The Confucian emphasis on *ren* was on man seen first and foremost as a social being. In the social context, a person's well-being was seen as being entirely dependent on the harmony of the community. Confucian virtues value endurance and sensibility that support *ren* in all interactions. The Master taught that when a person is not certain whether or not he has done the right thing, he should simply ask himself if he would wish to receive the same treatment. This code was intended as being a formula for interpersonal relationships as much as for governance and statecraft."

I was standing there listening to my father, and I was not enjoying his exposition on Confucianism the way I had enjoyed his teaching of Tang poetry. Righteous in his convictions and annoyed at my ignorance, my father continued,

"The Master taught that through self-discipline one can become a *junzhi*—a morally superior man. A superior man seeks 'perfection' in one's self and tries to enable others to do likewise through setting an example. Confucius believed in the innate goodness in humans and in their educability. While the acquisition of knowledge is worthy in and of itself, the ultimate purpose of all learning is a virtuous life dominated by *ren*—humanism—as well as *li*—propriety and decorum—and *yi*—right conduct and duty to one's neighbor; all these are rules of conduct that manifest man's good will.

"For Confucians," my father continued, "and for the Chinese throughout the millennia, because the collective welfare is dependent upon the virtue of the individual, it follows that the education necessary for moral and virtuous living must be cultivated for the betterment of society and the betterment of mankind."

Here Father stopped for a moment, his face red and taut, sitting erect at his desk. Then his demeanor changed visibly, as if caught in a reflective moment. When he began speaking again, his tone was calmer and more even. He acknowledged that perhaps Confucianism had gone too far and become rigid over the centuries. Unfortunately, paternalistic government that emphasized communal well-being informed by a consensus had become bureaucratized to the point of rigidity; the concept of family that emphasized loyalty and cooperation had ended up supporting unrelenting nepotism. He was hopeful that someday there would be a fruitful interaction between Confucian humanism and democratic liberalism, perhaps in the next millennium. "Good!" I thought. At least he acknowledges that Confucianism has its flaws.

I have always remembered this encounter, mostly because my father was angry with me. That remembrance kept Confucianism alive in me, although I didn't think about it more seriously until I was more mature. I had seldom given thoughts to Confucianism because I had become a Catholic, and I had never formally studied Confucianism. Though even without formal study, every Chinese knows a good bit about Confucianism, much like the Christians about the Bible. My father was often referred to as the "Confucian General." I hadn't taken particular note of that, either, because I took for granted that he was who he was. Only in the course of reading and understanding his life and his era did I come to understand to what extent he was a Confucian man. The embodiment of *ren, li,* and *yi,* so

ingrained in his conduct, was cultural—cultivated in Chinese morality from childhood to maturity and highly valued in Chinese society.

My father, who founded the Lixing Middle School for the most talented of the war orphans and who was chairman of its board of directors, gave the school a name that was derived from the ancient axiom
"*lixing infuren*," roughly translated as "proceed with vigor in order to
approach benevolence." I can only surmise that he gave the school the
name *Lixing*—proceed with vigor, or enduring labor—for the meaning
it carries for *ren*, which was the aim of being human. He wrote the
mutual help-axioms for living, codified as the Lixing axioms, for Lixing
students, eight characters to a line and four lines in all:

Help yourself, heaven will help.
Help comes to those following the Way,
Turns back if disobeyed
Before one had been helped, I offer my help.
Help to one from all, and to all from one.

Tao, roughly translated as the "Way," is a moral philosophy
emphasized by the Chinese. To follow *tao* is to live in a simple and
honest manner, being true to one's self, turning away from the dis-
traction of power and material things. Tao prizes inner peace, accen-
tuating gentleness, serenity, and nonviolence. In Tao, the center of
the mind's activity or the person is not the ego, but rather the liberation of the ego to achieve *te*—virtue, or creative power in a person's
spontaneous and natural conduct and activity.

I attended my first year of junior high at the Lixing Middle
School, where responsibility to one another and to society was
heavily emphasized. I have always liked the Lixing axiom and had it
engraved in fine stone chops for my siblings, my children and grandchildren, my nieces and nephews.

A Confucian man at the core, within the constraints of loyalty
and order defined in the teachings of Confucius, my father rebelled
on numerous occasions when his conscience troubled him. The first
time was in a civil conflict in 1927, when his troops, without adequate supplies, were ordered into immediate combat after several
exhausting months of fighting and marching, where his superior
denied the troops a week's time to recuperate before resuming
combat. He resigned his post in protest. The second time he rebelled

was in the climactic act of *funginquoyin*, giving up his authority as the military commander in Shantou in 1936, when he could not support his superior's assertion of independence from the central government. Still later, he confronted Chiang Kaishek, in 1949, when Chiang was abandoning the mainland to the Communists without mounting a final defense of southern China.

My father stood steadfast behind my mother in her work with the war refugee orphans in the Guangdong Children's Homes and Schools and the women widowed in war in the Women's Brigade. Under conditions of hardship and scarce resources, he allocated funds and grain for their support. He never spoke of this. As I come to know more of his value system, I believe these were his deeds of redemption for having led his men—sons and brothers—into battles where, within six months, 50,000 men were killed, not counting any enemy casualties.

To better understand the life and times of my father during the war years, I sought out my father's former secretary, Mr. Lum Yum Po, who for many years had a Chinese press in Los Angeles. Lum's office had been next to my father's office in the annex in Huanggong Hill while my father was governor.

"I remember Papa's temper exploding from time to time. What was that about?" I asked.

"Your father was hard of hearing," Lum told me, "and he was quite sick from chronic dysentery. So at times he was impatient and very frustrated and lost control of his temper. But in all the years I served him, I never once heard him say a bad word about anyone, not even when he was maligned by gossips. He was *ren,* and he let *ren* guide his conduct."

My brother Victor summed up the life of our Papa well:

True to his hero Yue Fei, whose chronology he had written, in spite of his anguish Papa remained a staunch son of the Guomindang—Nationalist Party. He was loyal to his superiors and friends to the end. He was single-mindedly loyal toward the Guomingdang. As he often said, the fault was not in *Sanmin Juyi*—the Three Principles of the People—but rather in human failing. He kept the faith. Having done that, as was the case with Chinese cultural heroes, the rest did not matter. His role models were the traditional Chinese cultural heroes—single-minded, loyal, faithful and moral. He went down with the ship [at the fall of the mainland], and so be it.

Even before he fell down the stairs, I remember his spending hours at his desk writing at our red brick row house in uptown Manhattan. In a way, he had retired into a kind of a monastery, very much like the time he was at the Baiyun Monastery in his late twenties, after experiencing his first battles and seeing the slaughter. To him, writing was more than spiritual solace in times of trouble. It was spiritual and personal fulfillment—even as his material fortunes and hopes were shattered. Confucians valued fidelity to their emperors and superiors as the highest virtue, and the ancients celebrated this virtue and maintained their loyalty even when wronged. On the wall of his living room, Papa hung a photograph of Chiang Kaishek alongside that of Lin Shen (who was the chairman of the Nationalist central government during the War of Resistance whom he admired). It was not sentiment. It was not apology. Rather, it was a statement of personal values—Confucian values. It was a symbolic reminder that he was faithful to the Guomindang just as much as it was a reflection on how deeply he was ingrained in the Confucian tradition.

Whenever my siblings or I visited our father's grave, we would bring potted chrysanthemums, his favorite flowers. In our gardens in China, there were mums of all varieties and colors, big and small. It was his celebration of our mother, because her name was Chu Fang, meaning Vibrant Chrysanthemums.

We were four generations standing on the green lawn. There were my mother; my oldest son, Michael; his wife, Julie; their two little daughters, Michelle and Melinda; and myself. We formed a line beside my mother before the tombstone engraved with Li Han Hun, General of the Chinese Nationalist army 1894–1987, in both Chinese and English.

"Papa, we are here to visit you." My mother's voice was trembling.

"One bow," I gave the signal. "Two bows, three bows."

We were still until my mother broke the silence.

"Papa and I had a marriage of fifty-five years. Papa took care of me the first twenty years of our life together, and I took care of Papa the last thirty years of his life. We had good times and hard times, and we had the five of you children plus your brother Shao. In time to come, my name will be right there next to Papa's." Mother pointed to the tombstone.

My mother turned to leave, her eyes moist. I lingered for a moment. My hands touched the hard gray granite. I wished Papa peace before I turned to follow my mother to the car.

In gathering material for this memoir, I had several lengthy talks with my half brother Kam, who lives in Palos Verdes with his wife, Shirley. I told him that even though I had never known his mother, I knew that she was an extraordinary lady and I respected her. In my heart, I had a tender spot for her. I said that our father, his mother, and my mother were all victims of their time. I also told him that my one deep regret was that I had not gone to see her while she was living and ill in Los Angeles. I had thought about her but never acted to let her know that she was appreciated and respected.

Kam said that his mother had told him that she prized family harmony and that it was her wish that we should be one family, and he visited my mother when she spent her winters out on the West Coast, in Monterey Park, in a spirit of harmony.

When Brother Huon, now in his seventies and living in New Orleans, visited Los Angeles, I went with him to his mother's cemetery and placed a small pot of flowers before her grave. I held his hand and we bowed three times to pay our respect.

"Our mothers are two great women," Huon's voice quivered. "My mother never held a grudge. Your mother made it possible for us to be family. She was an educator."

"I know your mother had made a horrendous sacrifice," I told him. "I have thought of her time and time again. I know she was an extraordinary and noble woman. I'm just sorry that I never went to see her."

"You are here today," my brother told me, "and you've made up for it."

With tears in my eyes, I felt my brother's love—for our father, for our mothers. I too felt the love of the mother I had never met.

Returning to the hotel, we spoke more of things of the past. Brother Huon thoughtfully said, "Our father had striven to be a just, moral, and 'perfect' person all his life, but he was trapped in his time, in marriage and family. It pained him throughout his life."

"Did you know he became a lay monk?" I asked.

"I knew," he said. "In a manner of speaking, that was his reconciliation with life, with his family, and with himself."

Chapter Fifteen

Valleys and Countryside

Three or four times a year I went to China and traveled the highways and mountain roads of Yunnan. I was visiting village projects either with the consultant team or on my own—but always in the company of local cadres. Driving up the winding mountain roads, the driver blew the horn at every turn, warning vehicles speeding from the opposite direction. When it rained, or if it had rained the day before, roads became slippery and wheels spun in muddy puddles. Many a time we had to get out of our van, and the men would help push the van forward using rocks and branches to support the wheels. This could happen two or three times in any given trip during a monsoon.

Looking out the car window to the mountain hills and down the cliffs, I would see landscapes of deep valleys, trees, bamboo groves, a cascade of fields green as emeralds, and clusters of serene villages. As our van reached the destination, reality would then overwhelm me. I would see pigs, chickens, and ducks roaming about and children playing on unpaved narrow streets dotted with manure. The starkness inside the dark mud brick homes, the harsh terrain, the primitive and bare existence would then erase the idyllic scene that had so pleased the eye only moments earlier.

Yunnan, which means South of the Cloud, was best known to Westerners as the nesting place of the Flying Tigers during World War II—made famous in John Wayne's movie. Through the dynasties, the province on the remote southwest edge was long regarded as a semi-barbaric outpost of China. Economically, Yunnan is in the bottom quarter of China's provinces and home to the ethnic Yi, Bai, Miao, as well as dozens of aborigine tribes.

In 1991, the program officer in the Ford Foundation's Beijing office, Dr. Mary Ann Burris, invited me to work with Ford's newly initiated Women's Reproductive Health Program. Ford Foundation had selected Yunnan for its program site and already started numerous initiatives in poverty alleviation through agricultural improvement. I would be involved in designing a bottom-up approach to empower rural women to define their most critical and pressing health care needs. We were also to help bridge the bureaucratic divide that isolated one agency's program from another for the purpose of better coordination to serve the women's needs. Unlike one-shot and episodic consultations in most international programs, this program would allow me the opportunity to be innovative and possibly to follow it through to completion.

We enlisted the help of the provincial bureau of public health in selecting the county sites, asking them to pave our way to working with the villages. Our colleague from Beijing Medical University, who was my national counterpart, was no stranger to Yunnan. During the Cultural Revolution, Prof. Wang Shaoxian, an energetic woman of fortitude and foresight, had spent six years with a group of medical students in a mobile team, guiding them as they all traveled in the valleys and countryside by truck, on foot or riding donkeys. They trained health workers in the remote and far corners of Yunnan.

"The program sites should be within one day's travel time from Kunming," she urged. "Otherwise we will be spending days on mountainous roads just to get in and out. That won't work at all." Kunming is the provincial capital, so all the government bureaucracies resided there, as well as the Kunming Medical College with which we also collaborate. She also advised us that the existence of an infrastructure would be essential in the sites we select, since our goal was to strengthen services and local capacity. To the two suggestions Professor Wang made, as a third criterion for selecting the sites, we added that there should be a commitment on the part of the magistrate to match the funding.

Our visit to the potential sites was arranged through the courtesy of the vice governor's office. Mr. Tuan, the provincial representative who was our guide, met us at our hotel early in the morning. From

Kunming we were on the road on a four-lane highway, part of it under construction. We rode five hours before we reached the Chengjiang county seat, one hundred thirty kilometers, or about seventy-five miles, away. Children played along the side of the road, cows and goats roamed across the lanes, pedestrians carrying loaded barrels on shoulder poles walked along the two sides of the highway, and tractors raced with trucks, buses, and bicycles. I cringed every time a child wandered close to the center of the road, seemingly oblivious of any danger.

We arrived at the county guest house, a large building behind a gated courtyard. It was nearly noon; the county magistrate and the party secretary were waiting for us. Both men were in their forties. They dressed in white shirts and gray trousers looking like all other cadres. We immediately went into a conference room for a briefing on the economic conditions of the county, and continued our discussions during lunch in the guest house's dining room. Afterward, the magistrate and the provincial representative were to accompany us to Songyuen to visit a Yi village. A caravan of eight vehicles and a retinue of cadres were ready to go with us.

Mary Anne Burris, a brunette with delicate features and a big heart, was somewhat startled in seeing the caravan. "All these many VIPs will intimidate the village cadres," she told Professor Wang and me. "We really don't need the magistrate and the provincial administrator to go with us. Is there anything we can do?"

"We can ask them," said Professor Wang. She conferred with Mr. Tuan and came back to tell us it would be all right to make our wish known.

"I want to make a request." I directed my remark to the magistrate and the party secretary, apologetically explaining that their presence and the caravan would be intimidating to the locals. "We would prefer that you not go to the villages with us."

"All right! We respect your wish," the magistrate told me, surprised but without displeasure.

"We're accustomed to keeping company with visitors," the party secretary added. "But if that is your wish, we will accommodate."

I told them that I understood that to be the custom and are grateful for their support. "Is it all right to have the directors of health, poverty alleviation, and the Women's Federation to go with us?" I asked. "It would give us a chance to talk with them and learn more about their work."

"Sure, sure, no problem," said the magistrate. "They're all here." He gave some directions to the cadres and told the director of his administrative office to accompany us.

We left in four vehicles with the cadres and functionaries for a two-hour ride up the mountains. Straw huts spread out in the hillside like wild mushrooms. Lush green herbaceous plants and trees edged around them as the warm sun cast its golden rays. The village mayor led an assembled troupe to meet us as our cars entered the hill village. The women had donned their colorful embroidered costumes, usually reserved for holidays and special occasions. The minority Yi spoke a dialect that was totally unintelligible to me, and I depended on the cadres for translation and interpretation. But then I concentrated all the more on observing the manner in which the people interacted in garnering information.

In the village square, drums beat softly and rhythmically, villagers danced and sang in the open square honoring our visit. The mayor spoke, conveying the hope that Songyuan would become a site for the Ford-supported program.

Then the mayor led the way to show us several homes, starting with his own. Light came through the door and the small windows on the two sides of the hut. I saw the pigpen, which was separated by a knee-high partition in the one-room house. Chickens ran loose on the dirt floor like pets. At the far corner, covered with black soot, stood a clay stove built on the ground, with a large iron wok set on top. In the center of the room stood a rectangular wooden table and several straw hassocks. An electric bulb hung from the ceiling. Walls were black with the soot from burning firewood. The other side of the room had a loft. Beneath it was the storage area for grain, hoes, machetes, bamboo baskets, and other household treasures. The family of seven—the mayor and his wife, his mother, and the couple's four young children—slept in the loft, which had mosquito nets but no partitions.

We visited a second home about a hundred yards down the road. A strong rancid odor hit my nostrils as the door opened. Inside the dark hut were a horse, as well as a couple and their three children. The horse was kept inside the home for safety, but the horse's body heat warmed the unheated living quarters in winter.

For the next five days, we visited other villages of Han Chinese in two other counties. I managed to communicate with the villagers directly with my Mandarin while they spoke Yunnan dialects. The cadres were ever ready to translate, if needed.

I stopped at the house of an elderly woman standing by the door of her home. She was dressed in dark loose pants and a traditional high-collar jacket. Indistinguishable from other women in that area, her hair was held in a bun with a dark blue embroidered headband across her forehead. Her face was remarkably smooth and her back slightly bent.

"Nainai," I addressed the old woman with a kin traditional and respectful term. "How are you today? I hope you don't mind our intrusion."

"Welcome, my home is very simple," the woman said good-naturedly. "Do come in and look around."

I went inside the dark mud-brick house, where two small children were playing quietly in the corner. There was a big pile of cured tobacco leaves stacked in one side of the room. Yunnan, famous for its tobacco, derived its major share of revenue from tobacco growth and cigarette sales. Everywhere, villagers grew tobacco in little plots and strips of land surrounding their homes.

We sat down on a long bench chair for a brief interview. The woman, widowed, lived with her son, his wife, and their two children. While her son and his wife farmed, she took care of the two little children and helped with the cooking. Tobacco was an important source of the family income. "We have enough now, not like before," the old woman told me, her eyes brightened. "We slaughter our own pig for the Spring Festival."

I asked about her health. She made some reference to "the eggplant," the itch, and incontinence. I was puzzled. The cadre hastened to explain that "the eggplant" refers to uterus prolapse, which was a common ailment among elderly women who had given birth to many children, and who returned to hard labor in the fields within days after giving birth.

"How do you treat the problem? The itch?" I asked. The hanging "eggplant" boggled my mind and I hadn't recovered from the shocking revelation, unable to say, "How do you take care of your eggplant?"

"There's not much that I can do. The doctors can't do much either. It is lots of discomfort. Sometimes I stay in bed. I live with it."

These were the people and their spirit, toughened by hard living, was ever hopeful of the future and warm to visitors intruding from afar. The villagers welcomed me with generosity, allowing me to enter their homes, responding to my questions, and inviting me to come again. I felt humbled, inspired, and, at times, awed. I had a glimpse of their pain and needs. What these villagers lacked in material things was counterbalanced by the richness in human relations: because of neighbors reaching out to neighbors; because of the fullness and solidarity of family life, where three generations embraced one another; and because of the respect they tendered to the earth and the goods that came forth from the earth.

Nowhere in China had I seen so many elderly women with small bound feet as I did in Luliang. Some of the women, who looked as if they were in their fifties, were wielding a scythe and working in the fields, while others were walking in the street or standing in courtyards. "What happened?" I asked in dismay. "The prohibition against foot binding had been a law since Sun Yatsen's revolution in 1911." Mr. Tuan explained that the countryside was ultraconservative and that it wasn't until the Sino-Japanese War that the county had stopped the foot-binding practice.

Several months later, on a return trip, I held a focus group interview on health needs with five women who had bound feet, their ages ranging from fifty-three to sixty-seven. The women all said that their most urgent health concern was that no one would help them care for their feet when they grew old and became infirm. When they were four or five years old, their feet had been crippled with the arches broken, and, except for the big toe, the four little toes were bent under the arch. For centuries, a girl's marriageability depended on her "golden lotus," or tiny bound feet, which men found erotic. The long strips of cloth that bound the feet need changing and washing daily to protect the skin that had become tender like the skin of a newborn, and toenails had to be trimmed regularly with a pair of scissors. In the old days, this was the job of the daughters-in-law. But a modern daughter-in-law would do no such thing.

At the end of our visit to the three counties, we selected four impoverished townships for our community program: Songyuan and Haikou in Chengjiang County, and Chenming and Damougu in Luliang County. The four sites had a total of ninety-three villages. We were attracted to the counties because of the local leadership that represented health, education, poverty alleviation, and the All Women's Federation.

In our deliberations, we rejected a pure clinical approach in favor of a broader programmatic base that would also attend to the status and development of women. After all, reproductive health is intricately tied to women's education, their position in society, and the opportunities they would be able to pursue outside their homes. We conceived the Yunnan's Women' Reproductive Health and Development Program (WRHDP) as an experimental program involving multi-agency planning and coordination. It would emphasize learning by doing, in order to bring about a change in people's knowledge and practices, be they villagers, cadres, or bureaucrats. It would summon people's know-how as well as simple technology to modifying the environment, which, hopefully, would influence policy.

Immediately our colleague from the provincial Kunming Medical College organized a field workshop to train the fourth-year medical students to conduct a survey encompassing 8,500 households. For six weeks the students, most of whom had grown up in cities, lived in the homes of peasants. While one group of students interviewed the peasant women, a second group provided treatment to the peasants under the supervision of their teachers. We also trained young researchers and graduate students from the Yunnan Academy of Social Sciences and Yunnan University to conduct focus groups with villagers, cadres, and health workers.

I was on site during most of these activities. In one town, I saw a family mourning the death of a twenty-six-year-old daughter. On inquiry, I learned that the woman had quarreled with her husband, then taken a pesticide poison and killed herself. I wanted more information on the suicide, but was not able to obtain it. No one seemed to be as shocked as I was at such a wrenching death of a woman so young. Later, I learned that suicide of young women ages fifteen to thirty-four is the leading cause of death in rural areas of China. The details of these deaths are unknown. It saddened me to think that women in China today would resort to suicide, like their foremothers—indeed, like my own maternal grandmother—as a way out of their misery.

To get the villagers involved, we gave Instamatic cameras to sixty-three village women and taught them to take pictures so that they could record what they considered to be important in their activities of daily living. Some of the women were illiterate, and many of them had never had their picture taken before. The simple picture-taking instructions we gave them were to keep their fingers clear of the lens when shooting and to try to have the sun at their backs when possible. My daughter Caroline, who was then a doctoral student in public health at UC Berkeley, directed the photovoice project and conducted training for eight women cadre leaders. She then teamed up with a photojournalist, Yang Kelin of the World Women Magazine, a publication of Yunnan's Women's Federation, and trained the remaining participants by counties. They encouraged the women to select the pictures that were most meaningful to them and then talk with their family members, neighbors, and friends about what they saw in these pictures. The photovoice project aimed to create awareness and raise their consciousness about their needs and possible solutions.

But the innovation of the photovoice had also precipitated controversies. "Putting cameras in the hands of ignorant village women is wasteful," some argued. "Professional photographers will give you better pictures, faster and cheaper," said others. In the counties, bureaucrats surmised that having so many women taking photos all over and year round was a disguise for gathering intelligence. The deputy director of the Health Bureau intervened and photovoice went forth as planned.

The women looked at the pictures they took and showed them to their neighbors. Seeing babies lying by the fields while their mothers farmed, a customary practice that was passed on from generation to generation, women also began to ask questions: " Why do people in cities have nurseries and we don't?" "Why? Our babies are exposed to the sun and rain!"

They began to talk about the need for nurseries in their villages and to inquire about what it would take to make it a reality. Some of the pictures showed girls of nine or ten years of age taking care of their younger brothers and sisters at home instead of going to school. Others showed women hauling water from eight kilometers away because there was no potable water in the village itself. Children were photographed playing by the river unsupervised. One picture showed a happy eleven-year-old boy and his sister. One week after his mother took the photo—the only picture of him that was ever taken—the boy drowned while swimming in the river. These and thousands of other pictures each told a human interest story and provoked lengthy discussions among the women as well as the cadres and the bureaucrats.

To involve the village women in voicing the their needs and wants, we held a week-long program planning workshop, inviting the heads of the various bureaus, program administrators and managers, as well as village women representatives to review the data from the household survey and the focus groups. Village women presented the photos on a big screen; they spoke about the significance of the photos from their living experience and from their hearts. It surprised us that these photovoices became the most powerful tool in giving faces to the numbers from the household survey and to the themes garnered from the focus groups; they spoke to policymakers.

The women, the cadres and the program managers worked together to set priorities for program activities they desired, learned how to design the projects they identified and prepare proposals and budgets. Building into the proposals were contributions from agencies in terms of manpower or equipment and interagency coordination by sharing resources.

And we, too, learned.

When townships in Chengjiang County asked for funds for building a water reservoir, we told them this was beyond the scope of reproductive health, as well as being too costly. During one of my visits to township sites, the director of the health bureau then cornered me about the dire need for water in some of the villages. "May I have your permission to divert the funds for midwifery training for water work?" he asked. "Our problem is not that we, I mean the county, don't have the money; the problem is that the money is divided among several agencies and each does its own thing. If I can use the 240,000 yuan (U.S. $30,000) from the Ford funds, I can get them all working together in building water tanks to get water to the people."

"What about midwifery training?" I asked, with more than a bit of concern. "That's what the funds are earmarked for! You have proposed to conduct short courses to upgrade the skills of village doctors and midwives, and a residency at the county hospital." In these mountainous and remote villages, "modern delivery" meant using clean cloth and sterile blades, and thread to cut and tie the umbilical cord of the newborn in home birth. He said that as the health director, he could go to his district chief to ask for funds for training, but he was not in a position to ask for money for water work. He pledged that the midwifery training would get done just he had proposed.

I remembered my visit to the Caoge village site. It was a rainy day; pigs, chickens, and ducks roamed the unpaved streets, and our shoes were caked with mud mixed with animal urine and excrement. A dirty stream flowed through the village and the villagers used the water for washing their clothes and vegetables. I was told that the villagers walked two kilometers to hilly slopes to collect clean water for drinking and cooking. From the data of the household surveys, I knew that infant mortality in some of the areas was as high as 50–75 per 1,000 live births. Infants and children under five died of pneumonia, tetanus, as well as diarrhea and other preventable diseases. I was sympathetic to the hardships of the villagers for the lack of clean water, reminding myself of the importance of understanding local needs and respecting local opinions. "All right," I said to the director of health of Chengjiang. "You may divert the funds, but make certain that you're accountable for the midwifery training." I placed my trust in him, and he indeed did just what he promised. He got the agencies to get their acts together in giving money for the materials needed for water tank construction, use their technical know-how to help the villagers with the construction. The villagers contributed their labor as well as their money for the water work. This small initial investment stimulated collaboration among the agencies, and between the agencies and the people in the community. Consequently, the local contribution exceeded the Ford contribution by more than tenfold.

Working together, we took on new challenges through four two-year cycles. Over forty projects were generated from the umbrella program, defined by the village women in collaboration with cadres at the township and county levels, and supported by policy makers and program managers at the provincial level. Villagers built biogas tanks that generated methane gas from the fermentation of human and animal excrement, useful as fuel for cooking and lighting; they built solar baths and public toilets for hygiene, silage pits for pig feed to ease the necessity of chopping greens and cooking the feed with firewood daily; they built machine choppers that shredded turnips, obviating the endless hand motions women would otherwise have to perform in shredding seven hundreds of kilos a day on a wood bench built with a blade; and they built water tanks.

There were nurseries for preschool children, as well as cooking and nutrition classes. Girls in poverty families received a monthly subsidy of ten yuan—or U.S. $1.50—in order to keep young girls in school. Until the subsidy scholarship was initiated in Songyuan, girls had not been able to compete for entrance to the "central" schools. Five years after it was initiated, eighteen girls entered the "central" schools, which meant they would have a shot at gaining acceptance into a college or technical schools. The program also supported an information system at the provincial Maternal and Child Health Center.

As I looked back on our work in Yunnan, I feel gratified that the agencies, policymakers, town cadres, and village women have become partners in projects and activities important to the villagers' daily living. Together, they have claimed ownership and sustained the various projects and expanded many to other townships and villages even after the consultants were long gone and the program funds had been phased out.

Chapter Sixteen

Hong Kong's Return

A fter having made a stopover in Hong Kong in 1973, I refused to set foot in Hong Kong again except just to change
planes at the Kai Tek Airport. That rejection was from a deep feeling
inside that had stayed with me for many years, from my upbringing
and influences growing up in China. I simply refused to be perceived
and treated as a colonial subject.

Most visitors to Hong Kong were fascinated by its colorful landscape of turbaned Indians, men in Scottish kilts with bagpipes,
flotillas of rocking sampans and dragon boat restaurants along the
harbor, rickshaws racing cars along the streets, and bargain shopping. I saw Hong Kong differently. I saw the kilts and bagpipes as
residual symbols of the imperial British, who, pushing opium to the
Chinese people, had forced the defeated Manchu rulers to concede
Hong Kong. The turbans were reminders to me of the colonial
empire's importing Indian soldiers to keep law and order to hold the
Chinese in abeyance. For me the sampans and the rickshaws represented suffering humanity trying to eke out subsistence living.

During that short stopover in 1973, I reconnected with my grade
school classmate Yu Jinling. We had both left China as teens. When
I went to the United States, Jinling moved to Hong Kong with her
parents before the Communists defeated the Nationalists in 1949.
Her eyes were larger than I remembered, and crow's feet were
clearly visible on her thin delicate face. Jinling had taught Chinese
in middle school ever since she had become a teacher fifteen years

earlier. Happy in our reunion, Jinling was eager to take me to Hennesey Road to show off Hong Kong as a shopper's paradise.

Nighttime in Hong Kong was as bright and crowded as the day. Flashing neon signs for cameras, jewelry, and watches paraded before my eyes, as well as advertising slogans in large Chinese characters and English letters. Beaded slippers, fashionable sweaters and shirts, undergarments, leather purses, and household gadgets filled store windows; dried squid and sea cucumbers, smelly preserved turnips and orange peels in open urns, and knickknacks of all sorts were spread out on tables at reduced prices. Cars sped by. At the corner of the Lee Garden Hotel, which was later to be leveled and rebuilt, a fruit vendor sat in a semi-squatting position between two large baskets of luscious lichees the ruby color of pigeon blood. They were the first of the season. Men and women haggled with the vendor over the price. The bartering could be heard half a block away in crescendos resembling the falsetto voices of Chinese opera singers.

I bought a cashmere sweater in a little corner shop. When two Western women came into the shop, the sales girl turned away from me to wait on them. I had not minded this, as I had not decided between two colors, one blue and the other white. But later, I saw the sales clerk leave an elderly Chinese woman buying a gold chain in a jewelry store to attend to a white shopper who had just come into the store. I became aware that there was a pattern in how the Chinese and Westerners interacted. At every turn, the Chinese deferred to the Westerners as if it were the most natural thing in the world.

A white appliquéd tablecloth in a store window caught my fancy, and so we went inside the small boutique. Linen, embroidery, and crocheted goods packed the shelves. In a corner of the floor were piles of bundles wrapped in brown paper. Jinling signaled me to be quiet and let her do the bargaining with the shopkeeper.

Just as they agreed on the price and I took out my wallet, a large-bosomed woman with flaming red hair thrust herself between the shopkeeper and me. "I want to be served now," said the woman with a British accent, her eyes blinking behind long eyelashes and heavy mascara. An aqua-green floral polyester dress with a scooped neckline loosely fit her full body, and she held a shiny white patent-leather handbag under her arm. The shopkeeper, a young Chinese woman no more than five feet tall, with straight hair and no make-up, turned to attend to the woman, leaving me standing there holding my money. "Excuse me, I was here first," I said, addressing both the woman and the shopkeeper. The shopkeeper looked frozen. The redheaded woman took a step toward me, her chest heaved high, her head slightly tilted like a prima donna delivering an aria. "You need education," she thundered.

I told the woman that an educated person is courteous and thoughtful of others. "Where are you from?" I asked her. The woman looked surprised and took a step back. She hesitated for a moment, tilted her head back and left the shop. I looked at the shop-keeper, her eyes cast down at the floor. I looked at Jinling. She was staring up at the ceiling. I walked out of the shop without com-pleting the purchase. Jinling followed me and we walked several blocks in silence.

"You now have an accurate glimpse of Hong Kong." Jinling was the first to break the silence. She let out the frustration and the hurt she felt inside, acknowledging that the kind of rudeness I had just experienced was common, likening it to an everyday meal.

"The white people here," she told me, "always walk to the head of a line, and shopkeepers turn to them as soon as they enter the stores. Even now, if you were Chinese, banks such as Lloyd's or the Swiss would be interested only if you had lots of money. Chinese are advised to 'go to your own kind'—to banks like the Heng Seng, the Overseas Union, or the Hong Kong Bank. This happened to my hus-band and me when we tried to deposit our savings of 400,000 HK dollars, about fifty thousand U.S. dollars, into the Swiss Bank because it was safer. Our money was considered a pittance and the manager quickly ushered us out the door. I cannot imagine that the Westerners who come to trade and the tourists who come to shop would behave in their own countries the way they do here in Hong Kong. They would be too embarrassed to be seen acting with such pomposity." Jinling's eyes bulged conveying her anger as she spoke.

Jinling imitated the self-abasement some Chinese showed in Hong Kong, describing the knighted Chinese "sirs" and the hopeful "sirs" and their ladies who were so proud of their titles, showing how proud they were of being the Crown's subjects just in the way they walked. She took a step, mimicking the "sirs," the ones knighted by the Queen, by tilting her head slightly back, her eyes looking above head level, walking stiffly forward. She described the "yessirs," those Chinese who ran like the hounds in a game park for their masters. Then there were those who prided themselves on being Her Majesty's servants, and those who thought they were a cut above others just by mumbling "Crown this, and Crown that" every other sentence. "They have forgotten they are Chinese. They make you want to throw up."

The world knew Hong Kong mostly for its exotic sights and sounds and a free port full of bargain treasures. Hong Kong had been part of China for thousands of years. When Britain was the lord of the sea, reaching out to other continents for trade and to conquer, the British used Hong Kong's Pearl River Delta as an anchorage for their gunboats and opium-running ships, pushing the narcotic to the Chinese. Then China ceded Hong Kong to British rule after her defeat in the Opium War (1839–1842). The British further took over Kowloon after China's defeat in a second Opium War, and this in turn was followed by a ninety-nine-year lease of the New Territories.

For years, I called Jinling from Kai Tek Airport whenever I was in transit. Jinling would try to convince me that Hong Kong was changing for the better and was now different from what I had seen in 1973. Hong Kong had become one of Asia's "Four Little Dragons," and an economic power in the region and the Chinese had prospered. The social strata in Hong Kong had evolved. From the time Hong Kong was ceded to Britain until the turn of the twentieth century, the British and the white traders were at the top, followed by the Sikhs who were brought to Hong Kong to help police the Chinese. By the 1960s, with an influx of enterprising Chinese from the mainland, a rich class of Chinese merchants began to emerge. A decade later, a superrich class of Chinese businessmen had burgeoned forth and had somersaulted to the top stratum of society.

My airport calls always ended with Jinling saying, "Come visit me the next time you pass through. Come and see the changes for yourself." Jinling would remind me that, after all, the 1984 Sino-British Joint Declaration between Britain and China signed by Prime Minister Margaret Thatcher and Premier Zhao Ziyang had guaranteed that Hong Kong would be returned to China in 1997. My reply was always, "Someday, I will."

In 1985, I finally went through passport control to Hong Kong as a visitor. Near the airport exit, I looked for my friend amidst the multitude of people, some standing on tiptoe. I spotted Jinling, her head stretched to peer through the other faces, her hair short and smartly coiffured, waving her hand in the air to get my attention. Neither Jinling nor I was able to squeeze through the crowd to reach the other. She pointed to the transport area outside, signaling me to meet her by the taxi stand.

"You look the same—you haven't changed at all," said Jinling, once we were outside.

"We've both changed," I told her. I thought my friend looked older than her age, and her face was too thin. I knew I had changed, too. My size four pants had become a size eight.

We hugged, laughed, and held hands as we got into a cab. "Twelve years! It's been so long. Why are you staying only twenty-four hours?" asked my friend. I told her that I had no other business in Hong Kong than to see her. That brought a warm smile to my friend's face. Jinling had arranged for me to stay at the Omni Prince Hotel on the Kowloon side. She had selected a hotel conveniently attached to the Ocean Terminal shopping center, just a few blocks from the ferry, so it would be easy to cross to the Hong Kong side, but closer to the airport.

The next morning, Jinling knocked at the door promptly at 8:00 to take me out to breakfast and then hop around town. I told Jinling I preferred coffee and toast and suggested that we send for room service and stay in the room to chat for a while. Jinling put her handbag on the king-size bed, let herself sink into the sofa, and kicked off her shoes. She selected for herself the Chinese breakfast of congee and *char sui bao*—roast pork buns—and gave the orders on the phone.

"You are a stubborn one. I never thought you would stay away all these years!"

"I had to say 'Thank you, but, no, thank you.' There was no earthly reason for me to come to Hong Kong and allow myself to be treated like a colonial subject." Jinling was right. I could be quite stubborn.

"The British will be gone soon." Jinling remembered the incident with the big- bosomed red-haired woman in the linen boutique all too well.

"It's about time."

"You like international consultation?"

"I do. But international consultation is glamorous only from a distance."

"What do you mean?"

"It carries a certain prestige and offers the opportunity to see the exotic and different parts of the world. You get to travel and see the Third World countries as well as places like Geneva, London, Sidney, Rome, and Bangkok because international agencies like to convene their meetings in these places. But international consultation is hard work and can be very lonely. You work long hours, sometimes with no break on weekends and eat many meals alone. But then there is also the satisfaction and feeling of your work having an impact."

"You get paid well for that?"

"Not really. Some of the work is pro bono. It depends on the projects you choose and what you want to do."

Jinling took me off exploring Hong Kong, browsing through the antique and curio galleries. At a corner shop I spotted three wooden cabinets, the bottoms of which were built like cages. They were of solid wood, beautifully varnished, each with its own distinctive design. The saleswoman explained that in olden times these were chicken cages for the wealthy who raised their chickens as pets. I had particularly liked the one made of teak, and Jinling urged me to make the purchase. The saleswoman was eager to assure me that shipping was no problem at all, and the cabinet would arrive in Los Angeles in six to eight weeks; she could take care of all the necessary papers for customs. I was tempted. A chicken cage cabinet in the living room would make a great conversation piece. The saleswoman waited patiently for me to make up my mind.

Then I saw a gray-haired Western couple come into the store and begin browsing. The woman held up an antique jade horse, her husband nodded approvingly. I was waiting to see if the saleswoman would leave me, treating me as I had been treated in that linen boutique back in 1973. But the sales woman simply smiled at the newcomers and told them, "Do look around."

Jinling bartered with the saleswoman for a better price. The saleswoman called the proprietor on the phone, then informed us that the proprietor had reduced the price by 40 percent. The price was certainly a steal for a solid teak cabinet and I was excited at the prospect of having it in my living room. Jinling laughed, "I see that you haven't lost your Chineseness yet, turning a chicken-cage cabinet into a bookcase." The Western couple waited for their turn to be served, talking softly between themselves. I decided it was too much trouble to get the shipment from the Long Beach pier to my home. And now I've regretted not having bought the cage cabinet ever since.

We went into a café to sample my favorite chestnut cake, happy as children at the fairground. Rock and roll music in Cantonese assaulted my ears. "We are still the best of friends," said Jinling at the top of her voice. I felt it too and nodded.

I asked Jinling if the 1997 turn-over of Hong Kong to mainland China would affect her and whether she and her husband planned to leave Hong Kong. Jinling said that they were planning to emigrate to Canada. Since no one was certain what would happen in 1997, even though China had committed herself to "one country, two systems," a foreign passport could serve as a safety valve, if needed. The liquidation of the landlords and all the cleansing and sweeping that had gone on in the name of revolution had made them cautious. She and her husband would prefer to remain in Hong Kong, but they would simply have to wait and see. "We're not closing our business in Hong Kong. What we will do depends on whether China honors her word. I would be lying if I said that I have no worries."

Her husband's little herb store, which opened in 1950, had grown into an import and export business on three continents. She had looked forward to Hong Kong's return to China, and she saw it as a matter of rightful sovereignty as much as a matter of her own dignity. I understood the strategy of having a safety valve and thought they did the right thing.

"You know," she told me, "I don't speak English. I will have to depend on my husband to speak for me when we live in Canada. His English is fluent." Jinling looked sad as she refilled the chrysanthemum tea in my cup.

"What? Didn't you study English in school? You've lived in Hong Kong for over thirty years." What she was telling me sounded incredible.

"I did learn some in school. But I let it go and didn't use it, so I forgot." Jinling took a big gulp of the tea, holding the cup with both hands. "It was passive resistance, my meager form of protest against British colonialism."

I wanted to say that as a teacher she should know better, that language was a tool and that she could use the tool to serve her purpose. I stopped before the words left my mouth, wondering if I would have done the same had I faced the predicament of living in the Crown Colony. I felt the same pity for my friend that I did when I watched her in the linen boutique years ago, but without the rage I had felt then. A new tune came over the music system. A vocalist sang "We will no longer be second-class citizens." I heard the lyric repeated clearly and melodiously two more times before the song faded away. It pleased my heart.

I stopped in Hong Kong for short visits many more times after that. Meeting Jinling again in 1996, I asked her what she thought of the proposal by Christopher Patten, the last colonial governor of Hong Kong, to give a pension to every Hong Konger and implement the scheme before the British left. Jinling said that the idea was good, but the way the British government was going about it was treacherous. It meant China would have to pay the bills after the British left, and that would drain China and create discontent among the mainlanders.

"The British haven't done any of these things—democratic elections and all that—for over ninety years of their occupation there," Jingling fumed. "They waited until their exit to make a scene. Did you know that for decades, terms such as representation and democracy were not allowed to appear in any school textbook? Democracy was an alien concept that was neither pursued nor discussed."

Jinling was indignant. "Until 1992, when China was about to reclaim Hong Kong, every one of the British governors behaved like a rajah surrounded by his court. It was only after Pattan's arrival that reforms were instigated, including elections. To most Hong Kong people, these late reforms were the ultimate in hypocrisy, designed to create trouble and dissent for China. Months before the Joint Declaration, the Colonial government began to raise the salaries and compensations of the civil servants, with the British at the front of the columns. The salaries of civil servants have increased five-fold between 1985 and now. Today, British servants who served in Her Majesty's Crown Colony of Hong Kong fare far better in their retirement than those who served in Great Britain."

When the Joint Declaration was announced, many rich Hong Kongers sold their homes and businesses and emigrated, like a hemorrhage from a punctured vessel, mostly to Canada and Australia, where British subjects could buy their residencies in the commonwealths with money and make investments. But even before the end of the decade, many had already returned, because few of them had found gainful employment or were able to start anew in unfamiliar territory.

As the 1997 reunification was approaching, I followed all the news on the return of Hong Kong to its motherland. I saw quite a difference on how the return of Hong Kong was perceived and reported on the national networks in China and the Chinese-language channels and newspapers in Los Angeles in contrast to major national channels and newspapers in the United States. Western journalists highlighted the concerns for democracy in the future governance of Hong Kong under China. On the other hand, Chinese reporters—Hong Kong and Taiwan included—emphasized the history of the Opium War, the subjugation of China by foreign powers, and rejoiced at clearing away the last vestige of colonialism. Chinese people saw any problem of China as a Chinese problem that should be addressed by Chinese people, whereas American politicians, TV anchormen, and talked show hosts unabashed declared, "We will watch and monitor China's handling of Hong Kong very carefully" in cynical paternalism.

My telephone rang early in the morning on July 1, 1997. "We missed you at our celebration party," Jinling told me at the other end. "It was like a New Year's celebration, only so much grander and more joyous."

"I'm celebrating with you in spirit." I told Jinling that I had seen the ceremonies on television, switching between CNN, the major networks, and the Chinese-language channel, and I had noticed the pouring rain. "Some six thousand journalists descended on Hong Kong and saw the turn-over take place without a hitch. They were waiting for riots and explosions, and seeing the Red Army surrounding Hong Kong," Jinling told me, bubbling. "It's been raining for days here. The biggest downpour came at the moment when the British flag came down and Prince Charles took the platform and delivered the farewell address. We say here that the rain washed away the shame of one hundred years of British rule. It washed away all the dirt."

Chapter Seventeen

Mama

During my mother's 1992 visit to Guangzhou, her former refugee children—over a thousand strong—gathered at the Memorial Hall of the Sun Yatsen Medical University for a reunion with their mama. They affectionately called her "President Mama," or simply "Mama." These children, now gray-haired men and women in their sixties and seventies, had come from far corners of the province and beyond. Splendid in a pale yellow suit and full of emotion, Mother spoke from the stage, "My dear children. I am crying not because I am sad, but because I am happy." They, too, cried. "I will be back to see you again," Mama told them.

This occasion was the third and last time my mother was to see the children she had rescued from the war zones. When all the speeches were done, applause followed her to the exit door. She stationed herself at the exit and hugged each one as they came through. They embraced her, not wanting to let go, saying: "Mama, come see us again." "Mama. Without you, I would not have survived. . . . I would not be alive today." "Mama, take care of yourself." Among them were teachers, journalists, engineers and managers, a director of the bureau of light industry, and a chief justice of the Supreme Court of Guangdong Province.

After the banquet and for two hours, the gray-haired men and women performed on stage—dancing and singing old songs they had sung when they were children, and songs and operettas with lyrics they had written themselves. Someone read a poem he wrote, "Our adoptive mother is dearer and closer than our birth mother." Amid joy, tears flowed freely and unabashed.

I had accompanied my mother on all of her three trips to China. On this trip, her final stop was Nanhua Temple in Shaoguan. I walked the grounds with her in the company of the head monk and city dignitaries. We came to the spot where my brother Shao was buried, but there was not a trace or mark of the little pavilion under which he lay. "Shao would be fifty-eight this year had he lived," my mother said, directing her remark to me. I took her hand and gave it a squeeze.

That evening, some two hundred of her children in Shaoguan hosted a dinner in her honor in a restaurant. For this very special family occasion, and having heard that their Mama liked the delicate flavor of turtle, the organizers had stewed gold-coin turtles—so called for the coinlike pattern on their shell—for every table. After the formal toasting, a frosty-haired man presented Mama with the couplet my father had written for the temple, engraved in solid brass that he had crafted. Someone else presented her a large brush painting of peonies on behalf of the Shaoguan's Alumni Association of Guangdong's Homes and Schools that he himself had painted. When the formalities were done, chairs shifted, people got up and swarmed around our table to toast their beloved Mama, wishing her good health and a long life. They toasted me, too, saying they remembered me as a girl of eight, nine, or ten, visiting the refugee Children's Homes and Schools with Mama.

Afterward, we visited the home of the president of the Shaoguan alumni association, Wang Chiaoyun, and met his family. "I feel good seeing your three generations living together in such a nice modern apartment," my mother said to Wang, whose wife had died in the 1960s and who had remained a widower, devoting himself to bringing up the children. She was happy that life had turned out so much better for so many people since the economic reform Deng Xiaoping initiated in 1978. I saw her fixing her eyes on Wang's little grandson and her tears gleamed. I knew she was thinking of my brother Shao who died at aged five.

The next morning her children came to see their Mama off at the train station, bringing their children and grandchildren with them.

Seven red banners with white characters, each of them three meters long, were held up with stretched hands representing the seven Homes and Schools that had flourished during the war years. They applauded as Mama made her way toward the platform. I followed behind. We shook hands along the way and Mother stopped to hug many. Then came the singing, "Our mother, we say good-bye now. . . ." The singing started from the back and was picked up by everyone assembled. This was the song the refugee-children used to sing more than half a century earlier. The words came back to me immediately, and I joined in, along with the others. There were more tearful hugs and handshakes, and the gray-haired men and women clung to their Mama like kindergartners on the first day of school.

Aboard the train Mother and I stood at the very end platform of the last car, waving to the tens and hundreds who had lined both sides of the rail waving. As the train whistled and moved away from the platform, a man broke from the crowd and ran out onto the track after the train, arms outstretched, shouting and crying, his words completely drowned out by the droning of the moving train. We waved back until his figure blurred and the people lining the platform disappeared into the horizon.

Through the years my mother had kept the letters of her refugee-children—dating as far back as 1941—in half a dozen large manila envelopes in a file drawer. The letters, written in ink, were now fading on the thin paper. Some of the paper had turned sandy brown. Many of the letters had come from the eighty children transferred from the Experimental School to Zhirui Middle School, the young cadets in the air academy, officer schools, and volunteers in different branches of the armed service. "Many a night, when I feel lonely, I read these letters," my mother told me. "When Zhang Fakui founded Zhirui to commemorate his division commander who perished, he asked that I give him the best and brightest of the refugee children. I felt so sad to give them up. But Zhirui had more resources and it was to their advantage to transfer."

I have read many of the letters she kept. "Mama, we cried when we left the Homes and Schools," wrote the children from Zhirui Middle School. "Mama, you so surprised us when you came to see us in Chungking," wrote an air cadet. "Mama, thank you for the money you sent. I am well now," wrote another. "When Guangzhou fell, I was among the youth group retreated to Shaoguan. After Hong

Kong fell, my siblings left our parents and fled to the interior, They were rescued. . . . It was in the Guangdong Children's Homes and Schools that my eight siblings and I passed our childhood into youth." wrote one in 1992.

My mother did not return to China to visit her children again. Her health was failing and the long hours of flight were not advised. I represented my mother at the sixtieth anniversary celebration of the founding of the Guangdong Children's Homes and Schools in Guangzhou, on August 14, 1999.

I arrived at the movie theater that had been rented for the gala celebration at 8:30 in the morning. Already, men and women were milling on the square outside the theater. Some of them had come holding onto canes and in wheelchairs. Meeting old friends, they slapped shoulders, gleefully exchanging greetings. At 9:00, six hundred people filled the theater. A red banner with gold characters reading *Guangdong Ertung Ziaoyoungyuan*—Guangdong Children's Homes and Schools—60th Gala Celebration, hung from the center stage. A commemorative couplet on two sides read, "Eight years of separation and hardship on the hills and rivers of Guangdong," and, "A thousand years of meritorious humanitarian work begun in Lianton Shayuan." The couplet referred to the years of the war of resistance against Japan and the thousands of children who, upon rescue, had been brought to Lianton in Shayuan. Seated on stage were the officers of the alumni association, speakers, and special guests.

I read Mother's message and conveyed her greetings and good wishes to the assembled. The Guangdong Children's Homes and Schools alumni association had printed a photo of Mama with her greeting for all. I received gifts of plaques, banners, and paintings from each of the Homes and Schools on my mother's behalf. The spontaneous expression of emotion and heartfelt love of the men and women, all of them old and some of them infirm, was without a trace of pretense. I wanted to hug each person as my mother would have. At the exit door, my reserve had me shake hands instead, when several men who were first to come through extended their hands for mine. Hugging is not in the Chinese tradition, not even between parents and their adult children, nor is kissing.

At the luncheon banquet, I met some forty octogenarian teachers. Half a century ago, I had met many of them in my visits to the Homes and Schools. Once young, they were brave souls steeped in altruism and were fearless when duty called. They were the role models for the refugee children with whom they shared their lives. They were teachers, helpers, and friends as well as big sisters and big brothers, loved and remembered by the children who have also grown old. I saluted these men and women on my mother's behalf.

When I got back to the hotel, I telephoned my mother in New York to tell her about the celebration. "Did you hug them?" was the first thing she asked. When I told her that I had shaken hands, she was disappointed and told me, "You should have hugged them. I would have."

Each year, the entire family would get together for a family reunion, usually during the New Year holidays. My sisters and brothers and I would take turns making the annual arrangements. The one responsible for the year's event would act as "dictator" in selecting the site and booking the hotel facilities. In 1999, because of the concern for Y2K air safety, we chose a weekend in late August before the children returned to school to celebrate our mother's birthday and hold the family reunion.

At this gathering the only missing members were my daughter Caroline and her family. Caroline presented her grandmother with a great-grandson while we were at the Darrowwood Resort reunion in Rye. She named him Michael after his uncle, her brother.

Mother always gave a little speech at the reunion banquets. She began slowly but zestfully: "I am very happy and I am thankful to all of you for coming here to celebrate my birthday. My biggest success and happiness has been my family. My children have distinguished themselves in their respective fields and we have remained a close family. We were transplanted to America when the Communists took over China. As displaced persons we had no money, no connections, we lost our social position and were faced with a language barrier. The fact that we had no money and had to struggle had its positive effect. Out of necessity, my children all learned to be self-reliant."

She then directed her remarks to the grandchildren and great-grandchildren, reminding them of their heritage. "All of you have done well. My children have wonderful spouses and lovely families. I have eleven grandchildren and four great-grandchildren who are healthy and good. I wish that my grandchildren and great-grandchildren will also be successful. I am a happy and fulfilled person. Now I want to hear from you. What did you do last year that made you feel proudest? Thank you all very much."

One by one, the children, the spouses and the grandchildren would got, telling anecdotes and describing their accomplishments to the matriarch. Then it was the great-grandchildren's turn. Our matriarch laughed, making a remark here and there. She was happy and so were we.

My mother grew old gracefully; but old age was merciless. Once she called me up early on Valentine's Day full of sadness. "Another one gone yesterday. Do you know that I have already sent out eight wreaths since the first of the year?" Hearing her sigh on the other end of the line, I searched my mind to say something, but words failed me. In her last years her hearing was almost gone and her sight blurred with macular degeneration. Her skin was discolored, her hair thin and white under a wig. Because of the annoying surrounding noises, she loathed wearing her hearing aid and often refused to do so. Because the cane made her looked like an old lady, she wouldn't use it for support. "I used to be so angry with Papa when he wouldn't use his hearing aid and his cane. And now I am becoming like him."

Mother had learned to swim when she was in her seventies and gave it up a decade later only because the chlorine in the water made her skin itch. She danced at the senior centers once or twice a week. She didn't like being a wallflower, not for a moment, and she hired her dance instructor as her partner. To our embarrassment, she bragged about her children. When I reminded her that other people's children are successful, too, she countered, "I am proud of you; they can brag about theirs."

Independent to the end, she had a live-in housekeeper, who also wrote letters for her while she dictated. Even in her eighth decade, she cared about her appearance and was well groomed, touching up her prominent cheeks and her nose with just the right color of Elizabeth Arden cosmetics and carrying herself with style and elegance. Her hip replacement in the last year of her life had not diminished her zest for life and she recovered her mobility, exercising daily without fail.

I visited my mother in New York the first week of October, just before the millennium. For several years, she had spent her winters in California. As cross-country flight had become harder for her, she had given up her apartment in Monterey Park in the spring of 1999. In spite of a hip replacement ten months earlier, her physical condition and spirit were so good that she broached the subject of visiting her former refugee-children in Guangzhou the next spring. I told her that I would not be against it, but the trans-Pacific flight would be very hard on her body. If she really wanted to make the trip, I would accompany her. My brother Victor and his wife Arlene also offered to make the trip with her.

During my five-day visit, she canceled all her engagements with her friends so that we would have more time together. We walked ten blocks from her apartment to the South Ferry to have lunch, and we saw the Broadway show *Ragtime*.

Each night, my mother and I would stand by the window in the apartment looking at the moon beaming so bright above Manhattan Bridge. Afterward, she would sit in her armchair in her bedroom, insisting that I recline on her bed while she talked. For an hour or more, she would reminisce about her deprived childhood, her partnership with Papa, her "opportunities and challenges" in caring for the refugee children and war widows, and how Papa's head injury changed that partnership, making her the breadwinner.

She told me her philosophy of child rearing as if she were speaking to an old friend: "I believe that in education, children should be guided, encouraged, and disciplined with parental caring. Intelligence itself is insufficient if a child is to succeed and become a productive and well-adjusted member of society. I did not subscribe to the old Chinese way of education by rote. In China and Taiwan children still spend long hours on homework after school and on weekends. Nor do I subscribe to the way of modern American education that learning has to be playlike. American children are left to their own devices with so much free time. Early childhood and the teen years are the most precious time for learning; the young mind is curious, and it absorbs new information like a sponge.

"When we were in China," she went on, "I hired tutors for you all year round. In America, I put a restriction on you children watching television. Papa taught you Chinese after school. We sent you to summer camps even when times were hard. Papa always supported what I did, and you children understood that. Because of my own deprivation as a child, I became very aware of the importance of maternal love in a child's life. I never felt I had given enough love to my children. I loved my children without indulging. I expected you to respect others and to respect yourselves, to be frugal and to work hard.

"To teach and to discipline," she continued, "is not the same as applying pressure or controlling. I enjoy talking with all of you and respect you children. I've always treated you as confidantes and friends. Unless a loving and honest relationship exists between parents and children, the children will drift away when they get older and leave home. I never scolded, but rather talked with you when you had concerns and problems, to help you come to some resolution. Do you agree?"

"Sure I do," I told her. Indeed, I don't remember ever being shouted at by my mother.

I listened to her words, her faculties were completely intact and her speech was perfectly clear. I hope that I will have as clear a mind when I reach her age. My mother was beautiful, vivacious, elegant with a special presence—even in a soldier's uniform. All her life, she mixed well with the humble, the young, the old, as well as the powerful. Her friends loved and pampered her. When she visited Chungking during the Sino-Japanese War, some of the elders who held the highest offices of the land would give her their time generously. She sought their advice for the Children's Homes and Schools, and she would ask questions about their life experiences. They would tell her stories, so that a half-hour appointment often extended to an hour or longer. "I learned so much listening to the wisdom they accumulated in a lifetime," my mother told me. "They taught me how to look at problems, how to deal with situations, how to be a human person."

When I left to return to California, she called for a limousine to take me to the Newark Airport and saw me off at the curb. I embraced my mother saying, "I might just surprise you and see you at Y2K here in New York." I lingered and looked at my mother intently. Her hair was all white, but her skin was still smooth without a wrinkle; now she was elderly, so strong and yet fragile. She embraced me. I wanted to cry but didn't. I thought of my father who was a Confucian to the very end and proud that "I am a soldier." We kissed and gave each other more hugs. I got inside the limousine. She stood close to the window waving good-bye.

My mother's death came quickly two weeks before Christmas, on the early morning of December 10. It started with a cough, which turned into pneumonia.

Tina made all the arrangements for the funeral at the Frank Campbell Funeral Home on Eighty-first Street at Madison Avenue, as she had done for our father. We laid her to rest in a formal embroidered black jacket and a traditional red skirt, also embroidered; her casket was opened for only the family to view. She had often said that she would want her friends to remember her as in life, not in death. On December 14, her family and her friends said a final good-bye to her and accompanied her to the Kensico Cemetery. We buried her next to our father.

In his eulogy, Fred summed up our mother's life and her legacy:

"Our mother gave us life and her unconditional love for nearly seven decades. She was born into a place and time of war, famine, and pestilence. She shielded us from these dangers, even as she pursued humanitarian efforts to save the orphans and widows of my father's soldiers and others who died in the defense of China. . . . By example, she taught us moral values, ethical behavior, a love of learning and the willingness to persevere in the face of adversity.

"In recent days, I have pondered what Mom would say if she were to speak through me. I think she would focus on her most treasured possession, her family. She would focus on the grandchildren and the great-grandchildren. She would say that you are fortunate to live in a place and time of peace and plenty. However, you have a duty to make the world an even better place for future generations. She would say, 'Do not be afraid of daunting obstacles. You have inherited from me great strengths to be used for the good of others. Do so, and you will find true joy and happiness in your heart.'

"That is the way Mom lived her life, and she rests in peace. Lastly, Mom would remind her offspring that we need to maintain the tradition of family reunions and holiday gatherings. Although we are geographically scattered and engaged in diverse pursuits, Family is the bedrock of our existence and identity, so don't sweat any of the small stuff. As the consummate modern woman, Mom's last words would be, 'May the Force be with you.'"

Chapter Eighteen
Going Forward

The first time I ever sat across from a Japanese American colleague, in 1968, I wanted to throw up. The rape of Nanjing, the ruthless Japanese mentality of "kill everyone, burn everything, loot everything," the toll of the bells and the aftermath of the air raids, and the memory of the multitudes of refugees fleeing from Japanese aggression had left deep marks on my psyche. Years later, my daughter told me that she wanted to make a documentary on the injustice of the Japanese American internment in the United States for her honor's thesis project at Duke University. "Why do you have to select the Japanese?" I asked, thinking that she could have selected almost any topic.

"The Japanese American internment was unjust. It was illegal and against the principles on which our country was founded," my daughter told me. She was wise beyond her years. Let no rancor pass from one generation to the ones that follow.

One month after the terrorists' attack on the World Trade Center, I left Los Angeles for a four-week visit to China with anxiety and some fear. The image of the Twin Towers tumbling had changed the New York skyline as much as the sense of security that Americans feel. I had not wanted to cancel my trip, but after several friends expressed concerns about my safety, I did think of switching to a non-U.S. carrier. Then I thought of all the times my mother had flown on the small military planes from Guilin to Chungking to plead for funds for the wartime refugee children. The planes flew low on misty days for "safety," so that they would less likely be chased by Japanese fighters. Certainly, I could fly the friendly skies of United.

I had put several consultations together in this trip. Entering from Hong Kong, my first stop was a training workshop on AIDS prevention in Fuzhou. Fuzhou has become a flourishing garden city with money and investment from Taiwan businessmen whose forebears were from Fujian Province. When I first visited Fuzhou in 1985, the city was dilapidated and all the buildings appeared to be in need of repair and a coat of paint. For decades, the people of Fuzhou had steeled themselves for anticipated shelling from Quemoy and Matsu, Nationalist Taiwan's military bases, in the event of armed conflict. The government of the People's Republic had opted not to invest in Fuzhou, even as other cities in China were benefiting from the country's economic reforms. But the enterprising people of Taiwan saw it differently and, with the abundance of cheap labor and ease of transportation, they brought money and technology to Fuzhou and turned it into a modern and prosperous city.

From Fuzhou I visited the Shantou University Medical College and the Guangdong Medical College in Jhanjiang. The invitations from the medical colleges for me to lecture were offers for friendship to connect, to learn about their needs, their aspirations and achievements, and to see more of China as she evolves in the twenty-first century. I met determined faculty committed to building new curricula to reflect the advances of science and technology. I listened to students asking questions about new research findings and speaking of their hopes for more exchange in information, in technology, in research undertaking.

Both Shantou and Jhanjiang have special meaning to me: Shantou, with its splendid harbors, was where my father confronted the Japanese admirals and their warships, and Jhanjiang was the port where, at age sixteen, he took flight on a boat to Guangzhou to escape from a greedy uncle who was out to harm him.

My father's village, Lingtou, was only forty kilometers from Jhanjiang, which is the second largest city in Guangdong Province. The west side of the city including its harbor, ceded to the French at the end of the Second Opium War, was returned to China in 1945. Today few vintage colonial buildings with French architecture remain, instead new high-rises, both commercial and residential, dominate the landscape. The foreign warships that once patrolled the harbor have been replaced by transport carriers exporting Chinese goods to Southeast Asia and to the Western Hemisphere. Jhanjiang and its adjacent counties have opted to stay agricultural and use their harbors for shipping rather than developing an industry.

My visit to Lingtou village was the homecoming of a daughter who was born far away and married in a foreign land, now returning to her ancestral roots for the first time. My second son, Lawrence, flew down from Beijing, where he is based, to meet me and to visit our ancestral home and attend the opening of the Shayuan school building honoring his grandmother. Our hosts from the medical college, representatives from the Office of Overseas Chinese Affairs and Federation of Returned Overseas Chinese, relatives, and village cadres all graciously met me at the airport. The next morning they came back to escort me for my visit to Lingtou.

Along the two sides of the highway were farmlands cultivating rice, sugar cane, yams, taros, and vegetables. When our caravan of eight cars stopped at the village entrance, the Yuying elementary school band was playing. I shook hands with the young captain and received a bouquet of gladiolas from a girl and a boy about twelve years of age. Students in light blue uniforms lined the two sides of the road leading to an unpaved open square; behind them stood hundreds of villagers clapping and smiling. The square was filled with old and young. Many people held infants in their arms. I shook hand with many, especially the older folks, greeting them and exchanging a few words. An old man, his eyebrows were as white as his mop of hair, missing teeth and back still straight, he told me that he had served my father as a young soldier seven decades earlier. I saw tears in his eyes when I gripped his hand.

Yuying was the school my grandfather had founded and named, which my father had maintained. Now my siblings and I were trying to extend a helping hand to the school through a scholarship fund. An impressive large four-story modern structure, designed to house both the elementary school and a new middle school, had replaced the old village school of cement and bricks, built by the local government. But the middle school had still not materialized and students from Lingtou must walk several miles in order to attend middle school.

In rural China, if a school child is unable to advance to the better-equipped and scholastically superior county middle school, whether for financial or scholastic reasons, his chance for successful competition for university entrance is virtually nil. Lingtou had not shared in the economic boom of the country's modernization, and many children had not gone beyond elementary school.

The principal invited me to speak to the assembled students in the school patio. "You are lucky to be citizens of the new China in the twenty-first century, and I hope you will become her young vanguards," I said, looking at the neatly-dressed children in blue, whose eyes fixed on me. But my throat constricted on seeing these children so small for their age, some appearing to be malnourished. I encouraged them to learn not only in school, but also at home and in society, and to strive to attend middle school and university, if possible, and to become contributing members of society. Afterward, I met with the thirteen students who had been given scholarships. Except for several first graders, the children had not attended school the past year, and some for an even longer period of time, in spite of compulsory education. Their parents had been unable to pay the school fees, which, in Lingtou, came to about sixty-five U.S. dollars a year.

Among the students receiving scholarships was a thirteen-year-old boy in the third grade who looked more like an eight-year-old. I asked him if he liked school. "It's hard," he replied in a voice barely audible. "But I will try."

The dignitaries of the city of Wuchuan, formerly a county, were on hand to serve as my hosts and to accompany me to my ancestral homestead that had been built by my grandfather and my father. Since the ancestral home had become confiscated as property of the government at the time of the Communist revolution in 1949, I visited the compound inside the alley as an interested tourist. Except for the broken glass in the windows, the exterior of the solid three-story brick building, known as Jianyuan, had remained intact.

Inside the house was a small open courtyard badly in need of repair, although it still had the original glass panels on the doors. The ground floor now served as sleeping quarters for the troupe of village actors; the second floor, unoccupied, was full of debris. The terrace, which had near shoulder-high walls with gun holes, was a miniature of the archers' holes in medieval European castles. The holes were built into the wall for shooting out. The four corners of the terrace floor also had numerous holes through which guards could watch the movements inside the courtyard down below, looking for intruders or bandits, and shoot. In front of the house were barracks for soldiers when my father was in residence. Two turrets still stood in front of the barracks. The holes on the terrace wall and floor and the turrets told of a very troubled time.

I did not go inside Chinyuan, the house my grandmother had lived in. I was told that it had been converted to apartments and families lived there and we should not disturb them. About fifty yards away was Shoumouting, a small open octagonal pavilion that my father erected for my grandmother. The Chinese take to these little open pavilions in summertime as Americans take to the swimming pools. I understand this was the place where my grandmother would sit for many hours enjoying the garden and relishing the lichee and fruits from the trees planted in the garden. Next to Shoumouting stood a beautiful tall curved Cunninghamian pine looking like a dragon reaching toward the sky. My father had planted two of them, but only one remains today. Paoyuan, the house my grandfather built on the other side of the alley, no longer exists. I was told that homes had been built on the land where Paoyuan once stood.

My final stop in Lingtou was the ancestral tomb, a flat white plaster structure that resembled a seashell in a wooded area outside the village. Standing before the tomb next to me were Spring Grace and my cousin Youfei, who is the youngest son of my father's brother. Two years ago, Youfei oversaw the excavation and transport for reburial in the ancestral tomb what was left of the remains of our grandmother Ahnai, who had been buried in Jhanjiang during the War of Resistance. This excavation happened when the local government informed my mother that it would reclaim the land area where Ahnai was buried for development. Only one long bone and a few small bones along with a single earring were left in the grave, since it had been dug up once before. Spring Grace was on site for the re-entombment with the offering of a "golden pig." "I have always felt that I am a member of the Li family. I came into your grandmother's household when I was four years old," Spring Grace wrote to me. For all the suffering and anguish she bore, she is now a fulfilled and happy woman. Her daughter has become a physician, one son a mechanical engineer, and another son operating a small business. Her grandchildren are entering universities.

I first met Youfei at the Guangzhou Guest House in 1982, when he came from the village to visit my father. I had forgotten about him until after my father's death almost ten years later. I found a greeting card with his name in my father's desk drawer at the Confucius Plaza apartment where my mother was still living. Then guilt beset me. After he told the story of his orphaned childhood and how our grand-mother's grave was vandalized, I gave him some money and sent him away, instead of asking him to spend some time with the family at the guest house in Guangzhou. I had not given my cousin the warmth of support that he undoubtedly needed even more than money.

I thought of Youfei's visit with my father and of the many people who had come to see my father. They came to touch his hands, to remember the old days and the struggles they had gone through together in good times and bad. Perhaps they had come to tell him how things really had been since they parted. For all the others, I felt that I had handled the situation correctly out of concern for my father's well being. After all, my father was eighty-seven years old at the time, and I wanted him to have as good a time as possible. For Youfei, I bore a deep sense of remorse for having rejected him so unkindly.

When I located him in Hong Kong and spoke with him by phone, I told him that I owed him an apology, recalling the time of his visit with my father. He came to my hotel room the next day, looking solid, fit, and strong, his complexion darkly tanned. He was no longer the thin and nervous young man I remembered. I apologized to him again, telling him that I had done him wrong. "Sister, I under-stand what you did," my cousin told me. "You must not feel bad about it. I am just so happy to hear from you." We spent the morning getting to know each other. He made his livelihood as a construction worker specializing in steel beams. Youfei was a big man not in physical size but in generosity and good will. "My wife and two chil-dren live in a small apartment we own in Kowloon. Someday, I'll have a larger one, and you can stay with us when you come to Hong Kong," Youfei told me. "We are family."

On our way back to the medical college, I was shown a new vil-lage twenty kilometers from Lingtou, built with money the villagers earned themselves. The large, modern, villa-like compound, com-plete with gardens, schools, and a community center, was built with funds contributed by local villagers who had made good, but every household gave a share, too.

Seeing the new village, I held great hope for China's peasants, 70 percent of China's population. This prosperity could happen elsewhere, if people would share their wealth, if the officials would act in the best interest of the people on health, education, and welfare, if the unemployed could find work, if the population remains stable, and if peace prevails.

On my flight from Jhanjiang to Guangzhou, a group of Americans holding infants in their arms were among the last passengers to board the plane, bubbling with excitement. The infants, one- and two-year-olds, quietly clung to their adopted parents. Some slept soundly. I got up from my aisle seat to let a couple, a Caucasian man with his Asian-American wife holding a Chinese infant, get into theirs. The woman, who was by the window seat, held the child on her lap; the man cooed, broke a cookie to put into her mouth, and dangled a rattler before his new daughter to keep her content and quiet as the plane lifted off the ground.

"We're from San Jose," said the father sitting next to me. "My wife and I came to pick up our daughter."

"Your child has probably never had as much attention in her life as she has had in the last twenty-four hours," I observed.

I had visited an orphanage the day before. Orphanages in China had only girls abandoned by parents who wanted boys. In the large airy room I saw some sixty infants in their cribs, attended by eight caretakers. The infants were wrapped in thick blankets; the younger ones, about six to eight months old, wore woolen caps. They looked healthy, well-fed and clean, but there was not a whimper or sound in the room, no human voice or music. On the second floor, I was shown a group of three-year-old girls behind a barred door. The girls wore no underpants. They sat on the floor or just stood around, silent and expressionless. When I told the director, a woman in her forties, that children need stimulation and that music can help their mental development, she explained that the equipment was out of order. I had the impression she was quite satisfied that the children were bodily well cared-for, far more concerned with having a safe environment than with the children's mental growth.

"Last night was the first night we had her," said the man sitting next to me, still dangling the rattler and playing with his daughter. "We were really scared. For about three hours, every time my wife and I touched her, she fussed and screamed. That went on until 3:00

this morning. Then she began to calm down. This happened to several other couples. Today, the babies have all calmed down and seem to like the attention we give them."

"The babies aren't used to getting picked up and fondled," I suggested. "That must be a little scary for them."

"I think you're right," he agreed.

"Did you pick out the child yourself?" I thought his child looked somewhat undernourished, compared to the other babies on board. But he did not appear to be disappointed in the least.

"We didn't pick her out, but the adoption agencies did try to take into account what we wrote down on the form we submitted." He went on to explain that the caregivers in the orphanage feed all the babies the same amount of food without taking individual differences into consideration. His daughter never refuses any food he and his wife offer.

"How many babies are there in your group?"

"Twenty-two babies, with two sets of twins."

"They are very lucky children." I was still thinking of the infants in the orphanage I had seen the day before. It warmed my heart to see that the children on board were wanted and loved by their adoptive parents

"We are very lucky to have them," he replied, and his voice rang with joy.

I felt tears in my eyes. Love had bridged the distance, ethnicity, nationality, and ideology.

I took time out for my journey to Shayuan, in the company of nearly four hundred septuagenarians, once refugee children. We started off from Guangzhou on train. The occasion was the unveiling of the "Chu Fang Building" at Shayuan Elementary School, which the former refugee children had named it after their Mama. They had come from all corners of Guangdong Province, Hong Kong, Taiwan, and beyond. I went through several cars to connect with them, greeting the white- and gray-haired men and women who were my extended family. They grabbed my hands warmly, shedding a few tears, recalling Mama.

When I first learned of the building project the alumni association proposed, I asked: "Why Shayuan? It's such an isolated village. Why not Shaoguan?" After all, it was the provincial capital during the War of Resistance. Then I understood that Shayuan was the place where they, the refugee children, had been brought after they had been rescued from the occupied territories. It was the place where they found love and a new family after they had been orphaned and their homes burned; where they had received the first glimmer of hope amidst the devastation of war. They wanted to create a permanent exhibition room in commemoration of Guangdong Children's Homes and Schools and its affiliated schools and to remember their Mama.

On the morning the building was unveiled, the Shayuan school children were at the entrance to the village, vivacious and smiling, chanting *"Huanying, huanying, rilie huanying*—welcome, welcome, we heartily welcome you." In front of the new building, the spirited school band, in white uniforms with red sashes, played with the intensity and energy of a symphony orchestra. The three-story white building stood proudly and majestic among the humble village flats. Firecrackers exploded all around. Alumni, guests, and students, numbering about a thousand, sat on benches that had been temporarily set up on the school ground. They clapped while the deputy mayor of Shaoguan and I pulled the string to unveil the characters Chu Fang Building, etched above the main entrance.

Following the speeches, the septuagenarians performed dances, recited poems and songs they wrote for this occasion. From a brass horn blew the melodies of the old routines of the Guangdong Children's Homes and Schools—the morning wake-up call, the melody for the flag raising and mealtimes, and the call to retire at the end of the day. He played the Song of the Brave, a favorite of my childhood and now China's national anthem. I requested that he play the song once more and asked the audience to stand up and sing. I've always liked the strong rhythm of the melody accompanying the words: "Rise, people who refuse to be enslaved. Let our flesh and blood build a new Great Wall."

After the formal ceremony, we elbowed our way into the exhibition room on the top floor. The walls held the display of historical pictures of the refugee children, their teachers, and the alumni. In the center was a large photo of my parents in soldiers' uniforms edged in gold-toned metal, a gift from an alumnus. A model of the

Shayuan center as it existed back then was on display, along with uniforms, utensils, sandals, and other paraphernalia. We concluded the ceremony by walking along a narrow dirt path to Yueyueting by the riverbank. The rectangular-shaped small open pavilion had been erected by the alumni in remembrance of the children who had died. We planted a banyan tree next to Yueyueting. Across the river was a cemetery where some three hundred children were buried. One of the most merciless killers had been an outbreak of diphtheria. Each spring, alumni would come to burn incense in the cemetery to the young dead.

We ended the day with a banquet in the hotel in Shaoguan where we were staying for the night. Milling around and chatting with the alumni in the hotel lobby, I was introduced to the person who had hand-crafted the model of the Shayuan center displayed in the exhibition room. He looked pale in his brown sport jacket and walked with a slight limp. "They told me you had a recent operation that caused you lots of physical pain while you were working on that beautiful model. You have done so much to make this day," I thanked him.

"I can never do enough for Mama." He put his hand over his contorted face and began to weep. "You must excuse me for crying. I can't help it."

"But you have done so much for her," I assured him and gave his hand a squeeze. "You, all those who are here today, all those who were children at the centers made her life rich and full."

The unveiling of the Chu Fang Building also brought old "foes" together. Among the six sitting at the table in the dining room of the Tungfeng Hotel in Guangzhou was Au Jiahe, a retired air force colonel from Taiwan. He was one of the fifty-some children from the Guangdong Children's Homes and Schools who entered the air force academy in Chungking at the height of the Sino-Japanese War. Eventually, Au and those who joined the Nationalists went to Taiwan and became fighter pilots.

"In the early fifties, our mission was to shoot down Communist China's planes raiding Quemoy" said Au. "Your planes bombed Quemoy right after midnight on even-numbered days; our planes gave chase. We had radar and accurate intelligence. We always knew the names of the pilots." With his thick waist and arthritic knees, Au looked more like a businessman than a retired air force colonel.

"We also knew who the pilots were, flying on your side," said Long Hongquan, a child of Number One Home and School and also a graduate of the air cadet academy. He had remained in the mainland on the Communist side. His back was straight as a young fir, which he attributed to the military drills in his youth.

"Why bombing only on even-numbered days?" I asked. "Why midnight raids?"

"That was a tacit agreement between the two sides to give the local people a respite so that they could go about their lives," Long explained. "At one minute after midnight on raid days, our planes would be right above Quemoy, dropping bombs along the seaboard to avoid killing the population." He told the story of a reunion of an air cadet academy alumnus from Taiwan visiting his former classmates in Guangzhou. During dinner, the wife of the visiting pilot came before a China mainland pilot and bowed to him three times in a show of gratitude. She had thought this was the pilot who had chased and damaged her husband's plane, but then turned around without shooting it down. In her mind, it was a deliberate act of mercy to spare her husband's life. But Long said what really happened was that the plane had run out of fuel and had to return to its base.

Everyone around the table told stories of schoolmates fighting opposite one another as guerrillas in 1948 and 1949 when the Nationalists and Communists were at each others throat, and over Quemoy and Matsu. But reminiscing about the past dug deep into memories, reviving feelings that had been buried. As children, the men had lived together, eaten together, played together, studied together, laughed and cried together. Tonight they were cherishing the old bond that still held them.

"Civil war is cruel. Brothers shooting and bombing each other," Au said thoughtfully, his voice trailing off. "We meant to kill you all."

"We, too, wanted to kill you. To shoot you down meant we would survive," said another alumnus, who is also a former air cadet, his hand in a tight grip around his wine glass.

"We have no reason to fight like we did," said Xu Fung, who had brought us together at the dinner. "Look, Taiwan businessmen are heavily invested in China. It's the best thing that happened. Let there be no more war."

"Let there be no more war," everyone around echoed.

For years, I had distanced myself from Taiwan because I detested

Chiang Kaishek's dictatorship and capriciousness and because Taiwan was Chiang's domain. My feeling toward Taiwan today is one of warmth. It has grown from my contact with my former students who returned to Taiwan. Over time, Taiwan changed from a repressive society to a democracy. My former students invited me to Taiwan, and, with each visit, I have come to admire its industrious people who have propelled this small island into a global economic power. I prayed that peace reign among brothers and all humankind.

Our family reunion at the Lawrence Welk Resort in San Diego, California in August 2002, brought together the largest gathering of siblings and children and grandchildren—more than sixty strong- -since our father's death. It marked the first time that the two branches of the Li family got together in such a manner. Lingtou's Li family is now international. Adding to the Lis, the spousal surnames include: Pong, Chen, Tang, Wen, Wang, Chait, Scholz, Greany, Lum, Shiang, Mak, Lin, Chu, Law, Tsao, Sassur, Repac, Ayres, Sevilla, Brient, Shimamoto, Igawa, and Kreiser. Seeing their bright faces, gentle and full of vigor, it was one of the happiest occasions in my life.

We remembered our father as a soldier and a Confucian man. We cherished our mothers whose love and sacrifices have made us whole.

Almost every year, I cross the Pacific Rim to consult and teach, often making several trips a year. I know that next month, next year, I will go back to the villages, towns, and cities of that other side of the world that I have come to know. Workshops, projects, fact-finding tours, as well as the occasional pleasure trips—the bulk of which are in my beloved China—have made the teacher the learner. I look at life's inequities, the often painful and surreal struggle for survival and, if possible, a piece of the good life.

Do my privileges stem from fate, providence, or an accident of birth? I wonder. I am someone who comes to China from afar, bringing bits of new knowledge, new technology, offering a hand, at times some funding. What little I can bring is swallowed and absorbed the way thirsty men gulp down cupfuls of water on a hot day. I see eyes darting about, faces red and taut with anguish and frustration. I am wanted for my fresh insights and know-how, for being a channel to the outside world. I am resented for being so like them and yet so unlike them. I am bilingual, Western-educated, and a university professor who left for the United States in my teens.

In my privileged position, I am housed in hotels that cater to visitors from abroad, hotels that have flush toilets, air conditioning and heating, telephones for international calls, television that can access CNN and the BBC, and fresh linen and towels daily. My hosts and associates are gracious, seeing to it that my accommodations are comfortable. They have never told me directly that I was extravagant in spending almost the equivalent of half their month's salary for one night of lodging. They would only say that a room in a domestic hotel could be had for a fraction of the cost, but it would mean no international calls, direct or operator assisted. Understandably, they do let their anger slip through. After the departure of a project officer from an international agency—someone with whom they have had a long association with and apparently liked very much—I heard the hosts comment on what they perceived as "imperial style visits," of bringing along one or two, sometimes even three, secretaries; of one secretary occupying a suite for meeting purposes and everyone having a room of her own. They perceived her successor as self-serving, because she buttressed those who would be in positions to advance her aspiration to become a university professor when she returns to the United States, and because she calculatingly ingratiated herself, designing a consultancy that would give her return visits to China after her tenure.

The developing world needs money and technology. The international agencies often demand civility and deference in exchange for support offered. Swallowing one's pride to obtain what is desired or needed simply intensifies anger that is hidden.

I have the good fortune to have been nurtured in a land of equality and liberty that encourages the pursuit of happiness and have flourished with these values. In my search for the new century, for the divine, for humanism, for peace, I have come to understand that things are not all black or all white, but often shaded in gray. Because of our humanness, perhaps nothing is absolute. The religious leader who professes to hold the only truth and speak with the voice of God can be oblivious to human sufferings and, with the cruelty of a demented zealot, can damn all who would dare to be different. The revolutionary who burns for justice and puts his life on the line for his beliefs can just as easily end up a bloody tyrant corrupted by the excesses of power. So too can the freedom fighter's zeal for human rights turn into arrogance if she comes to believe in only one way, her way, and in only one view, her view.

Coming from blind faith to humanism, I try to keep my sights on the Fatherhood of God and the brotherhood of humankind. As I mentioned earlier, while I was a student at the Sacred Heart Academy, I saw in the newspaper a picture of an emaciated Chinese mother cradling her dying child with the caption "Madonna and Child." That wretched image of hunger and despair has stayed in my memory to this day. Working in the field of disease prevention and health promotion in the United States and abroad, I have encountered countless such madonnas and children. They gazed out at me in all shapes, sizes, and colors. Gingerly, I have gazed back, timidly trying to extend my hand to touch theirs but not quite able to, for fear of losing my bearings. But I tried.

My view of humanity was passed on to me, like DNA in our genes, from my father and mother. My learning of it was encultured in me by osmosis, and it has become visceral, running deep in my being. I pursued a line of work consistent with the values my parents held, desiring to give something back to the community of which we are members. What my parents did and what I do now was not personal salvation, but rather something larger than ourselves from which salvation would come.

This humanism that is cultural and visceral was manifested in the lives I saw and the stories I heard from the septuagenarians of the Guangdong Children's Homes and Schools. They all came back to one theme. We learned self-reliance, how to use our heads and hands, how to share and care for one another and for the commonweal. Like the classic hymn "Ode to Joy," from Beethoven's Ninth Symphony, they bonded in heart and spirit, "All mankind are brothers." This driving force had stood them well in spite of the hard times and persecutions so many had gone through in the many extreme "anti" movements of the right and left and during the Cultural Revolution. They were like so many others I met throughout China, the powerful and the ordinary, who rebounded from the fire and brimstone of the anti movements and branding of the Red Guards. In their transcendence, they forgave everyone and steeped themselves in helping each other and in building a commonweal.

The folks who made good and helped turn the old shacks into garden villas with schools, a clinic, and community centers for the old and the young were *ren,* grounded in the desire to make their village a better living place for their neighbors. This humanism is often unacknowledged and sometimes unconscious, but in the enduring Confucian tradition it is so ingrained in Chinese culture and manifest at every level of life station, attitude, belief, and behavior.

Remembering the time when my father taught me Tang poetry, I bought audio tapes of Tang poems for my bilingual grandchildren so they could share my father's gift to me. At our family reunion, I watched my five-year-old granddaughter, Michaela, and my three-year-old grandson, Michael, sing, "You Are My Sunshine," in Mandarin Chinese, and my seven-year-old grandniece, Theresa, demonstrate karate with grace and confidence. Seeing these children gives me hope that their generation will integrate their cultures of heritage, birth, and adoption, so that our many worlds might some day become one.

Index